CROSS COUNTRY

CROSS COUNTRY

30 VFR Flights for Microsoft Flight Simulator 5.1

by Alfred Poor

Published by

Desktop Wings, Inc.
161 North Main Street
Dublin, PA 18917
800-848-6198
215-453-1405
FAX: 215-453-0286

Copyright © 1996 by Alfred Poor

All rights reserved. No part of the contents of this work may be reproduced or transmitted in any form without the permission of the publisher.

ISBN 0-9651975-0-6

Printed and bound in the United States of America

Flight Simulator is a registered trademark of Bruce Artwick.
Microsoft is a registered trademark of the Microsoft Corporation.

Many of the designations used by manufacturers and sellers to distinguish their products are claimed as trademarks. Where those designations appear in this work, and the author or publisher was aware of a trademark claim, the designations have been printed in initial capital letters or all capital letters.

The author and publisher have taken care in preparation of this work, but make no expressed or implied warranty of any kind and assume no responsibility for errors or omissions. No liability is assumed for incidental or consequential damages in connection with or arising out of the use of this information or the programs described in this work.

NOTE: This information is *NOT* intended for use in actual flight situations. While every effort has been made to make the charts, logs, and other information as accurate and realistic as possible, *this information <u>must not be used</u> for actual flying or flight instruction.*

Contents

Dedication xi

Acknowledgments xiii

Introduction xv

Part I: Default Scenery Areas

    Section A: **Chicago**

        CH1. *To Buy a Burger* 3
             Meigs to Morris

        CH2. *NORDO to Gibson City* 12
             Morris to Gibson City

        CH3. *Cheapskate GPS* 19
             Gibson City to Joliet

Section B: **Los Angeles**

- LA1. *Island Adventure* 27
  McLellan-Palomar to Avalon

- LA2. *Wedding Cake Blues* 35
  Avalon to El Monte

- LA3. *What You Can't See...* 43
  El Monte to Riverside

Section C: **New York**

- NY1. *Hudson River Tour* 52
  Westchester local flight

- NY2. *Buzz Over to Block Island* 60
  Westchester to Block Island

- NY3. *Confronting a Fog* 67
  Block Island to Southbridge

Section D: **San Francisco**

- SF1. *Gold Rush!* 76
  Reid-Hillview to Columbia

- SF2. *Lake in the Mountains* 85
  Columbia to Lake Tahoe

- SF3. *Big Mountains, Little Mountains* 93
  Lake Tahoe to Yuba County

Section E: **Seattle**

    SE1. *Airport Hopscotch* 101
        Olympia local flight

    SE2. *A Sound Plan* 108
        Olympia to Harvey Field

    SE3. *Head for the Mountains* 115
        Harvey to Pierce County

Part II: Optional Add-On Scenery Areas

Section A: **Hawaii**

    HA1. *A Spin Around Niihau* 123
        Princeville to Port Allen

    HA2. *Triple Play* 130
        Kapalua to Kalaupapa

    HA3. *Vulcan Visit* 136
        Hana to Upolu

Section B: **Las Vegas**

    LV1. *Lake Cruise* 143
        Perkins to Temple Bar

    LV2. *Making a Pass* 148
        Temple Bar to Henderson Sky Harbor

    LV3. *Leaving Las Vegas* 153
        Henderson Sky Harbor to Tahoe

Section C: **New York Add-on**

    NYA1. *On the Beach*.................................160
        Republic to Linden

    NYA2. *I Follow Roads* 165
        Linden to Lincoln Park

    NYA3. *Dawn Patrol*..................................171
        Lincoln Park to Westchester

Section D: **Caribbean**

    CA1. *Keys to the Bahamas* 177
        Marathon to South Bimini

    CA2. *From Paradise to the Stars*...............184
        Paradise to Stella Maris

    CA3. *Flight to Visit the King*....................190
        Ponce Mercedita to Cyril E. King

Section E: **Japan**

    JA1. *Mt. Fuji Fly-By*................................196
        Oshima to Matsumoto

    JA2. *Peace Pilgrimage*............................201
        Okayama to Hiroshimanishi

    JA3. *Concrete Compass*..........................206
        Nyutabaru to Kanoya

Appendix A: Situation Files and the Disk 211

Appendix B: As Real As It Gets 213

Appendix C: Flight Simulator 5.1 Techniques 226

Comments and Orders 231

Dedication

To Bebe...

...my partner in this project, and in so many others as well: I hope that the hours of work and struggle bringing this to life will prove to be worth the effort. I have so many reasons to count myself among the most fortunate, but you are the first reason on the list.

With all my love, always,

Alfred

Acknowledgments

I appreciate the many people and companies who provided materials and support for this project.

The photographs of New York Harbor (used on the cover), Kennedy Airport (the NYA1 flight), and Newark Airport (NYA2 flight) were provided by the Port Authority of New York and New Jersey.

The aerial photo of Block Island airport (NY2 flight) was provided by the Rhode Island Airport Corporation.

The Columbia Airport photograph (SF1 flight) was provided by Frank Robinson of Aerial View Productions in Columbia, California.

All four photographs used in the Chicago area flights were provided by Airpix of Romeo, Illinois.

The opening photograph for the Seattle area and the Puget Sound photo (SE2 flight) came from a Vintage CD-ROM from Seattle Support Group, Pacific, Washington.

All the other photographs were taken from Corel Professional Photos CD-ROMs, from Corel Corporation, Ottawa, Ontario.

I also want to thank Sean Tracy for teaching me how to fly, and to blame Dan Goodman for getting me hooked on it in the first place! I want to thank all the folks who have given me rides in their airplanes, especially Steve Gawrylewski and his beautiful Saratoga.

Thanks also go to the folks at Microsoft, BAO, MicroScene, and other companies for creating the products that made this book possible in the first place, and for providing support to me in this and other projects over the years. Special thanks go to Bruce Artwick, for having the vision, the skills, and the persistence to make this world of simulated flight a reality.

I also am grateful to Tim Boone and Gregory Harris and the rest of the people at the Cobb Group for giving me the opportunity to share my love of simulated and real flight.

And finally, thanks to my family—Bebe, Anna, and Alex—for their support in this project. It wouldn't have gotten off the ground without all their help and hard work.

Introduction

Welcome to *Cross Country*, a book filled with flights designed to make Microsoft's Flight Simulator 5.1 more fun for you than ever.

Many Microsoft Flight Simulator fans find themselves sitting in their planes on the ground at the end of the runway at Meigs field wondering, "where will I fly today?" Sure, it's fun to poke around, but there are times when you want a reason to go from here to there. *Cross Country* gives you the places to fly, and the reasons to go there.

In each of the 30 flights in this book, I'll provide you with a completely planned cross country flight for Flight Simulator 5.1—including a reason to make the trip. Along the way, you'll also learn about real world flying. I'll show you how to read aviation sectional charts, navigate through different classes of airspace, use radio navigation aids, as well as fundamental, seat-of-the-pants pilotage.

These flights are easy enough for novice pilots to enjoy; in many cases, the hardest part is the landing at the end of the trip. There are enough challenges and tricks involved to keep more experienced sim pilots busy. And in case you want to increase the pucker factor, I offer suggestions on some flights for changes that can make it even more challenging.

WHY I WROTE THIS BOOK

I've been a fan of Bruce Artwick's flight simulator programs since the early days on the Apple][with subLogic's A2-FS1, which came on a single floppy disk with a thin manual (that had a bright yellow cover), all packed in a plastic bag. I can't claim that I am a total fanatic; I've never bothered logging my flight time, and I have never undertaken any flights of more than a few hundred miles (well, at least not without using time acceleration). And I don't think that I've ever missed a meal in favor of finishing a Flight Simulator session.

On the other hand, I do have copies of just about every PC and Apple version of the program, and I have copies of almost all the commercial add-on products that have ever been sold for it. I've also had the good fortune to be able to write about flight simulation in the computer press, first with reviews for *PC Magazine*, followed by my "Aerodrome" column that ran for two years in *Computer Shopper* and that now appears on America Online and the World Wide Web as part of *Computer Life Online*. (You can find the AOL version by using the keyword LIFE, and the Web version can be found by going to:

```
http://www.zdnet.com/~complife/filters/aero.html
```

which will take you to the latest issue of the column.)

But this book really started nearly three years ago when I got a call from Tim Boone at the Cobb Group. He told me that they were thinking about starting a new magazine, just for the Microsoft Flight Simulator market, and what did I think of the idea? What did I think should be in such a magazine? I gave him a few ideas, and we talked for a while about them, and that was about the last I thought of it... until a couple of months later when he called back. They had decided to go ahead with the project, and asked if I would be interested in writing for it. I was. He asked if I had a preference for any of the suggestions I had made in our original discussion. I did.

I wanted to write the column about places to fly and how to get there. And thus the "Cross Country" column in *Full Throttle* was born. Editor-in-Chief Gregory Harris soon came onboard the project, and his continued support and encouragement (plus the positive

feedback from the readers) has made this column even more fun to write.

But there were limitations in a magazine column format. First, you only get one flight per issue, and I know that there are fans out there who want more. Also, since we can't count on the readers of the magazine to have anything aside from the Flight Simulator program itself, I only write the magazine flights for the default scenery that comes with the program. And finally, if you haven't been a charter subscriber to *Full Throttle*, there are flights from the early issues that you may have missed.

So this book is my attempt to resolve all those problems. It includes all 15 of the first flights that have appeared in *Full Throttle*, so you get a complete collection of default scenery flights in one handy bundle. It also includes three flights for each of the most popular add-on scenery collections: Hawaii, Las Vegas, New York, the Caribbean, and Japan. If you have one or more of these add-on packages, you'll find new ways to enjoy them with these Cross Country flights.

AS REAL AS I CAN MAKE IT

When I earned my Private Pilot's License in 1992, I used Flight Simulator to practice many aspects of my training, including cross country navigation. I used FS4 back then, and it was a huge help. Now, we have FS5.1 which is even better than FS4, in terms of providing visual landmarks, realistic weather conditions (such as the reduced visibility feature), and all VOR navigation beacons.

All Cross Country flights are designed to make the experience as realistic as possible. The flights are carefully planned so that you will comply with all the FAA rules and regulations (as much as possible). Each flight uses real navigation charts, and relies on the same navigation techniques that you might use if you were to make the flight in a real airplane.

For example, many airports are surrounded by special use airspace (SUA). Some classes of SUA require that you make radio contact with a specific Air Traffic Control facility before entering the airspace. Since FS5.1 doesn't yet have interactive voice recognition, we can't talk to these controllers. As a result, I have planned the flights to avoid such airspace as if your airplane has no

communications radio (which is a situation faced by hearing-impaired private pilots on every flight in the real world).

I have planned each flight for the Cessna 182RG aircraft that is included with the standard FS5.1 program. To make it easier for novice pilots, I recommend setting the engine control to Fixed Pitch, which makes it more like a Cessna 172RG. If you prefer to have a variable pitch prop, then don't choose the Fixed Pitch option. You may also want to fly the flights with a different aircraft—either slower or faster—but remember that you'll have to adjust the speeds and estimated times in the flight log accordingly.

For each flight, you get a scanned image of the appropriate navigation chart, plus a flight log that lists all your checkpoints, headings, information about your destination and arrival airports, and other details that you will need to complete your flight. The text for each flight describes how the flight plan was developed, and why certain choices were made.

Your next step will be to set up your aircraft for the flight. The steps are detailed for each flight, but you'll also find Situation files for each flight on the disk that is included in the back of this book. See Appendix A: *Situation Files and the Cross Country Disk* for the details on how to use these files so you can take off right away. Each flight has its own situation file, and I include its name at the end of each flight. For example, at the end of the first flight in the Chicago area, you'll find this note:

    🖫 Situation file: XC-CH1

SO WHAT'S IN THE BOOK?

The book is divided into two main parts. Part I has the flights for the default scenery areas, and Part II has the flights for the add-on areas. Each area has three flights, and the second and third flights start where the first and second ended, so you can fly them in sequence if you want. There is no particular order to the scenery area sections so you can pick your favorite and fly that first—there's no need to go through the book in sequence.

Appendix B has information on how you can set up your flight simulation environment to enhance its realism. Some of the ideas are nearly free, while others can cost you a bundle. All of them can help make flying FS5.1 more fun.

Finally, Appendix C has some information on how to use FS5.1 and its many features. This section is not intended to be a tutorial for the program or teach you how to fly; I assume that you already know how to get the plane off the ground and back down again. (If you don't, the manual that comes with FS5.1 is pretty good, but "Adventures in Flight Simulator" by Timothy Trimble, published by Microsoft Press, is the best book about the program for beginners that I have seen.) This appendix will explain some of the features such as the mixture control or how to set the navigation radios.

HEY KIDS: TRY THIS *ONLY* AT HOME!

Please note that the information in this book is only intended for your entertainment, and for use with Microsoft Flight Simulator 5.1 and its various add-on programs.

If you want to learn how to fly a real plane, take lessons from a trained and licensed instructor. Just because you're able to get from here to there on your computer is not sufficient to make you a skilled or safe pilot in the air. (I do believe, however, that skills learned with FS5.1 do translate into the cockpit, and can make it much easier and faster to learn how to fly.)

Also, note that the charts used in this book are out of date and not legal for use in real flying. Do not rely on the charts or flight plans provided here for use in the real world. They are realistic as I can make them, but they're not real enough for use a mile up in the air.

I admit to feeling a little silly even having to *write* this here, but I figure it's better to be absolutely clear about this so that nobody is tempted to do something foolish.

SO LET'S GO FLYING!

I have just one last request before you taxi to the active runway; remember to file any PIREPS (Pilot Reports) that may occur to you. If you find any problems with a flight, or have suggestions about new flights or improvements that you'd like to see (maybe you'd like a collection of "heavy iron" flights, designed for airliners), please take the time to let me know. I want this to be as much fun for you as it is for me. There's a form in the back of the book that you can use to

send in a message (or order more copies of this book if you need them; they make great gifts!) to make it even easier.

Okay. Pick your favorite scenery area, grab your RayBans, strap on your David Clark headset, and let's get ready to rock and roll. You're cleared for take-off!

PART I:
Default Scenery Areas

The first half of this book contains 15 flights, designed for use with the default scenery that comes with Microsoft Flight Simulator 5.1—nothing else is required. In fact, the flights are designed for the floppy-disk version of the program; the CD-ROM version includes some additional scenery features, such as mountains and other physical features, but you will not need those extras in order to complete the trips.

These 15 flights are the same ones that appeared (in slightly different form) in the first two-and-a-half years of *Full Throttle* magazine. If you like the flights in this book and want more, there is an offer for a free copy of the magazine at the end of this book.

Section A: Chicago

The "Windy City"—Chicago! Home of the Cubs and the Bears and the best deep-dish pizza anywhere in the country... if not in the world! And Chicago is home to Meigs Field, made famous to millions through the most popular computer game of all time: Microsoft Flight Simulator.

Chicago Flight 1

To Buy a Burger

Meigs Field in Chicago is the most famous airport in all of flight simulation because it is the place where Microsoft Flight Simulator has put users by default, going all the way back to the Apple][days.

It is only fitting that the first flight in this book begin at Meigs, using the familiar starting point. Your destination is Morris Municipal in Morris, Illinois, about 45 nm (nautical miles) away. We'll keep this flight fairly simple—or at least as simple as general aviation flying can be in a crowded urban airspace. The flight should take just over a half an hour to complete.

Why would you want to go to Morris? In real-world flying, the $100 hamburger is a pilot's favorite treat. ($5 for the burger, $95 for the plane rental, fuel, etc.) Morris Municipal happens to have a great airport restaurant right on the field, named *Runway 47*. (It gets its name from Highway 47 which runs next to the airport.) Come for lunch, and you can enjoy homemade soups and pies along with your burger. (There's a breakfast buffet on the weekends.) And it's a convenient distance from Meigs.

PLANNING OUT A ROUTE

Though the straight line distance is only 45 nm from Meigs, you can't fly that route in the real world. The FAA has regulations governing airspace use, and the sectional marks a variety of airspace restrictions that you would have to deal with in the real world, so we'll follow the regs here as well.

There's the O'Hare Class B airspace (formerly a TCA, or Terminal Control Area) where you need to get Air Traffic Control permission to enter. Midway has a Class C airspace (formerly an ARSA, or Airport Radar Service Area) where you also need to establish radio contact before entering. Combined, the two effectively block your travel to the southwest from Meigs. If you go too far down the south shore of Lake Michigan, however, you run into the Gary Regional Class D airspace (formerly an ATA, or Airport Traffic Area) which also requires radio contact before entering.

(Meigs Field has a control tower which you have to contact in order to depart from the field, but it only operates from 6:00 am to 10:00 pm. You can either make the required calls and assume that you've been cleared to take off, or you can plan a dawn patrol flight that gets you off the ground before the tower opens for business.)

We'll chart a route that takes you down the shore to a point where you can clear the Midway airspace, but before you encounter the Gary airspace, all the while staying below the floor of the O'Hare airspace. To find your way, you'll use a combination of radio navigation (using a VOR) and old-fashioned pilotage. For this trip, IFR stands for "I Follow Roads."

The first step in planning out a trip like this is to draw out the route on a sectional. From this, you can determine the magnetic headings for each leg. You can also identify convenient checkpoints that you can spot along your route. Airports and large roads are the most reliable landmarks in FS5.1, though you will often find lakes and rivers that you can use.

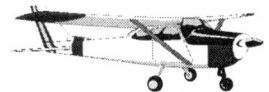

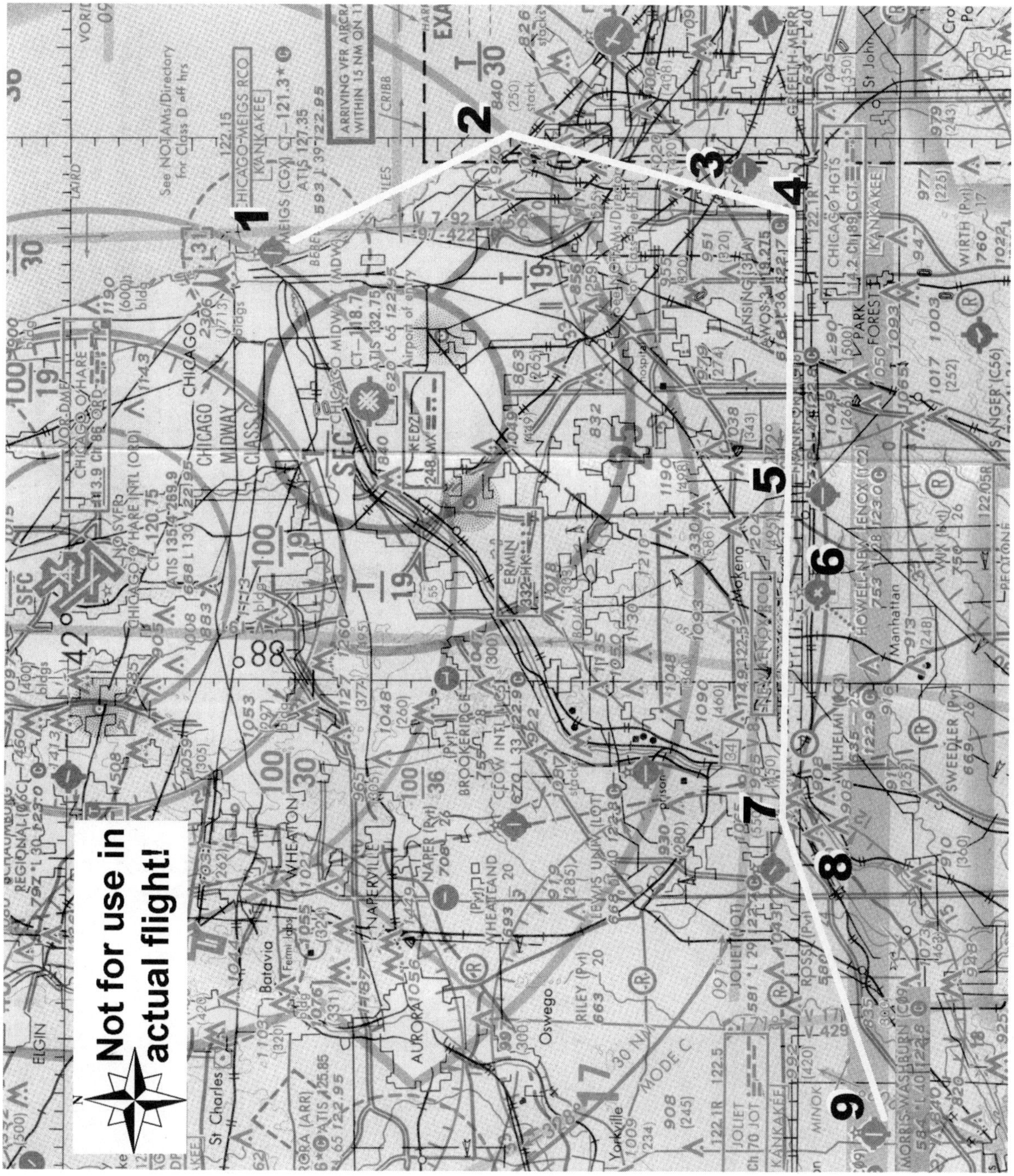

Not for use in actual flight!
1
2
3
4
5
6
7
8
9

One problem with pilotage is that you may see more than one landmark that could be your checkpoint. You can increase your chances of a correct identification by knowing your current position. To do this, you need to know the distance from one checkpoint to the next, as well as your planned cruising speed, so you can estimate how long it will take to get from one checkpoint to another.

A LOOK AT THE LOG

I've already prepared a flight log for you that you can use for your flight. The Fixes column lists the departure and destination points, as well as turning points and visual checkpoints along the route. The Route columns list the magnetic course for the leg, and the cumulative distance (in nautical miles) between points in the log.

The Estimated columns include the Ground Speed and Total Time entries. Since we're planning this flight for calm wind conditions, the ground speed will equal the airspeed, so there's only one entry in that column. (You can dial in some wind to make the navigation a bit trickier if you want, but I recommend that you just use the default weather settings for this first flight.) I have also assumed that you're not in any particular hurry to get your burger today, so I've planned on a fairly sedate 130 knot speed for the Cessna 182.

You can use an E6 circular slide rule—a *whiz wheel* in flying lingo—or your favorite spreadsheet program to figure out the estimated cumulative elapsed times for each point in the log. I've already done the math for you. I've also factored in three minutes at the start for your take-off roll, climb-out, and turn. At a 500 foot per minute climb, you should be nearly at the right altitude for the first leg, and ready to level out and trim for your cruise speed of 130 knots.

The Actual column is for you to use. Use a stopwatch or the clock on the airplane's panel to keep track of the elapsed time, and enter the time at each point of the trip. You'll know when you should be coming up on the next checkpoint or turn, which helps you stay "ahead of the airplane" by anticipating the next step before its time comes. Keep in mind that the estimated times are based on when you *pass* the point in question; you'll have to look to the side or down (press the Slash key on the numeric keypad, followed by 4 for left, 6 for right, or 5 for straight down) to get an accurate timing. If you pass

close to your checkpoint, either pan your side view downward (Shift+Enter) or use the Map window to see when you pass it.

You can also use the flight log to "keep score" on your flight, by seeing how closely your actual times come to the predicted numbers. If you can arrive in the pattern at Morris within two minutes of the predicted time, you are doing well. (Firewalling the throttle to make up time or executing 1-mile S-turns to lose time are cheating!)

HOW HIGH TO FLY?

There's one detail that is not shown on the log: the altitude for the flight. In the real world, there are lots of factors that govern a choice of altitude.

First, you have the FARs (Federal Aviation Regulations) which have rules for VFR flights. From 3,000 feet above ground level and below 18,000 feet above sea level, and on a magnetic *course* of 0 to 179 degrees (heading east of north or south), you should travel at odd thousands of feet plus 500 feet above sea level: 3,500, 5,500, 7,500 feet and so forth. On a magnetic course west of north or south, fly even thousands plus 500: 4,500, 6,500, 8,500 feet and so on. Since this is based on dividing the compass rose into two halves, it is frequently referred to as the "hemispheric rule."

Note that we have emphasized the word *course* in the rule. This is because you may be flying a different *heading* due to wind corrections. So pick your altitude based on your planned ground track, not where you point the nose of your plane.

For most efficient fuel burn (assuming a properly leaned engine), you want to travel as high as you can. On the other hand, you don't want to waste all that fuel gaining altitude just so you can finish with a brick-like descent at the other end.

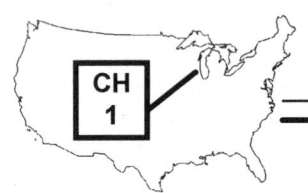

VFR Flight Log

Departure: Meigs (CGX)
Destination: Morris (C09)

Fixes	Route Mag Course	Naut. Miles	Estimated Ground Speed (Kt)	Total Time	Actual Time
1. Depart Meigs southeast along coastline	160°		130 knots	3 *	
2. Intercept CGT 190 radial	190°	11		8.1	
3. Lansing airport		20		12.2	
4. CGT: turn to west	270°	22		13.2	
5. Frankfort airport		34		18.7	
6. New Lennox airport		38		20.5	
7. Joliet: follow I-80	245°	45		23.8	
8. Joliet airport		49		25.6	
9. Arrive Morris airport		61		31.2	

* take-off, climb-out, and turn

Merril C. Meigs
Coordinates: 41-51.33; 087-36.47
Location: 15.4 nm from O'Hare VOR (ORD) 113.9, 118°
Elevation: 593 feet MSL
Pattern altitude: 1392 MSL
Runways: 18-36 3,904x150
Tower: 121.8 (6am to 10pm); UNICOM/CTAF: 121.3

Morris Municipal (James R. Washburn Field)
Coordinates: 41-25.88; 088-25.29
Location: 8.3 nm from Joliet VOR (JOT) 112.3, 210°
Elevation: 588 feet MSL
Pattern altitude: 1388 MSL
Runways: 18-36 2,897x60
UNICOM/CTAF: 122.8

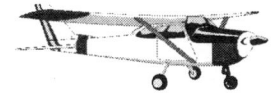

And finally, there are the airspace restrictions to consider. The Chicago sectional indicates that the outer ring of the O'Hare Class B airspace has a floor of 3,600 feet (as shown by the "100/36" notation.) The Midway Class C airspace has an outer region with a floor of 1,900 feet, and extends all the way up to the Class B airspace (as indicated by the "T/19" notation.) And the Gary Class D airspace extends up to 3,100 feet (the "[31]" notation.)

Put all these together, and we'll settle on an altitude of 3,500 feet for the first leg of the flight (which takes you to the edge of the Class B airspace), then a climb to 4,500 feet for the remainder of the flight. Be extremely careful not to overshoot the altitude on the first leg, however, because an incursion in the Class B airspace frequently is followed by a visit by the FAA. (You could also complete the entire flight at 3,000 feet and be okay, but it's easier to see your checkpoints from higher altitudes, and the extra distance between you and the ground gives you more time to find a safe place to set down in the unlikely event that your engine should quit.)

CHECKING THE CHECKPOINTS

Take a moment to look at the sectional and find the checkpoints we have picked for the route. There's no good visual reference for the turn at the end of the first leg, so you'll have to rely on VOR navigation to find that turn. You will pick up and follow the 190 radial of the Chicago Heights VOR (CGT, frequency 114.2); this leg takes you close to Lansing airport, which should pass on your left. Chicago Heights VOR is a key approach point for both O'Hare and Midway jet traffic, so keep your landing lights on for visibility and your head on a swivel watching for traffic.

When you reach the Chicago Heights VOR, you turn west toward Joliet. This route follows US Route 30, but in the real world it can be difficult to see the road, and it's not there at all in FS5.1. So use the airports on the route as checkpoints, which should pass by just to the south of your route, on your left. First you'll come to Frankfort (with US Route 45 running north and south about a mile beyond it.) Next comes New Lennox.

Next, you'll come upon the city of Joliet. Avoid flying too far north of the town, because the guards at the state prison there don't like it when small planes fly too close. Before you reach Joliet airport

(which should be on your right,) turn and follow Interstate 80, which will be the second highway that heads southwest out of Joliet. Your heading will be about 245 or 250 degrees magnetic, depending on where you make your turn. Since you'll need to lose a bit more than 3,000 feet at this point to get down to Morris's pattern altitude of 1,388 feet, now would be a good time to start a controlled descent of about 500 feet per minute, since you should be about six minutes from the airport at this point.

When you arrive at Morris, you can plan on entering the pattern with a 45-degree entry on a left downwind for Runway 18, and take it on in for a landing.

PREPARING TO FLY

Now that you've reviewed your flight plan, you're ready to make the flight. Before you take off from Meigs, however, there are a few steps to add to your preflight checklist.

First, you'll want to set your NAV 1 radio for the Chicago Heights VOR. It's easier to do this on the ground before you blast off, so set the frequency to 114.2, and set the OBS to 190 degrees. As you fly down the lake shore from Meigs, the OBS needle will slowly move to the center of the dial. When it reaches the center, turn to a magnetic heading of 190 degrees, and keep the needle centered (don't forget to also start your climb to 4,500 feet!) and you will fly straight to the Chicago Heights VOR.

You can also use your other navigation radio to help provide a backup for your pilotage in finding the Morris airport. The field is located along the 210 degree radial of the Joliet VOR (JOT.) By setting your NAV 2 radio to the Joliet frequency—112.3—and the OBS to 210, the needle will center when you cross that radial. Think of this as an invisible fence in the sky; if you cross it, you've gone too far. If the field isn't under you at that point, you can fly toward the Joliet VOR (heading 30 degrees) or away from it (heading 210 degrees) to find the field. This backup may come in handy, since there are a number of highways coming out of Joliet, and it can be easy to follow the wrong one.

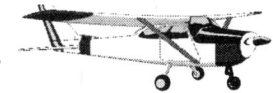

TAKE OFF

Now you're all set to take off from Meigs on your cross country adventure. Remember that the Meigs traffic pattern calls for right-hand turns for Runway 36 (keeps the noisy planes over the lake, instead of over the downtown buildings.)

If you want to vary the flight, change the time of day to dawn, and enjoy the rosy sky at sunrise. Or take off at dusk, and try your hand at the challenge of nighttime pilotage and landings at small fields in the dark.

No matter what time you fly, however, remember to keep a close watch on altitude and airspeed, and time your progress past each checkpoint. By the time you reach Morris, you're sure to have worked up an appetite for that $100 burger that is waiting for you.

▣ Situation file: XC-CH1

Chicago Flight 2

NORDO to Gibson City

Gibson City, Illinois, has a wonderful German restaurant, "Bayern Stube", where you can enjoy all sorts of authentic German dishes. And if you're a bit tired out after your flight, you might even consider staying the night in their new bed and breakfast.

On this flight, you can leave your fancy electronic navigation radios behind. You'll be taking off and landing at fields that do not have control towers, and you will not be flying through any special airspace, so you will not need to use your communication radios at all. (It's still a good idea to self-announce your position in the pattern during take-off and landing, however.) You'll also remain outside the 30 nm limit of the Chicago Class B airspace, so you won't need to use your transponder (regulations do require that if it is installed and working, you must use it, so set it to "1200" for VFR flight and forget it). And even though there are VOR and NDB beacons available for your flight, we're going to ignore them entirely.

LOOK MA, NO RADIO!

You have now become an old-fashioned "IFR" pilot; in this case, the acronym stands for "I Follow Roads"! You can pretend that your

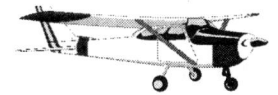

aircraft doesn't have any radios—this is known as "NORDO" (for "no radios").

If you were to use VORs (or GPS or Loran if you had it), you could fly direct from Morris to Gibson City over a distance of about 57 nm. In the real world, you could come close to this distance by following the river from Morris to Kankakee, but unfortunately the river was not included in the FS5.1 default scenery, so you'll have to take the long way around.

There are a lot of highways included in this part of the FS5.1 world, so your pilotage skills will get a workout. You will need to keep close tabs on your flight log and elapsed time so that you can be certain of the various checkpoints. (Don't be surprised if there are a few times when you struggle with disorientation over which town along the highway is which....)

Finally, this flight will test your landing skills. The landing phase of any flight is one of the trickiest parts, but after a long cross-country where you have to pay close attention to your navigation, you may find that you're not quite as sharp on final as you might be when you're just practicing bump and goes in the pattern. To complicate matters a bit, I picked Gibson City as your destination on purpose. There's no shortage of runway length to land on, with 3,400 feet of tarmac to aim for, but you may find the strip a bit narrower than what you are used to; it's only 30 feet wide. This has some implications for your landing, which we'll cover a bit later.

A LOOK AT THE LOG

I've marked your route and major checkpoints along the way on a portion of the WAC (World Aeronautical Chart) for this part of the country. I also have prepared the flight log for this trip, with the fixes corresponding to the numbered points on the chart.

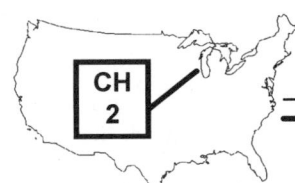

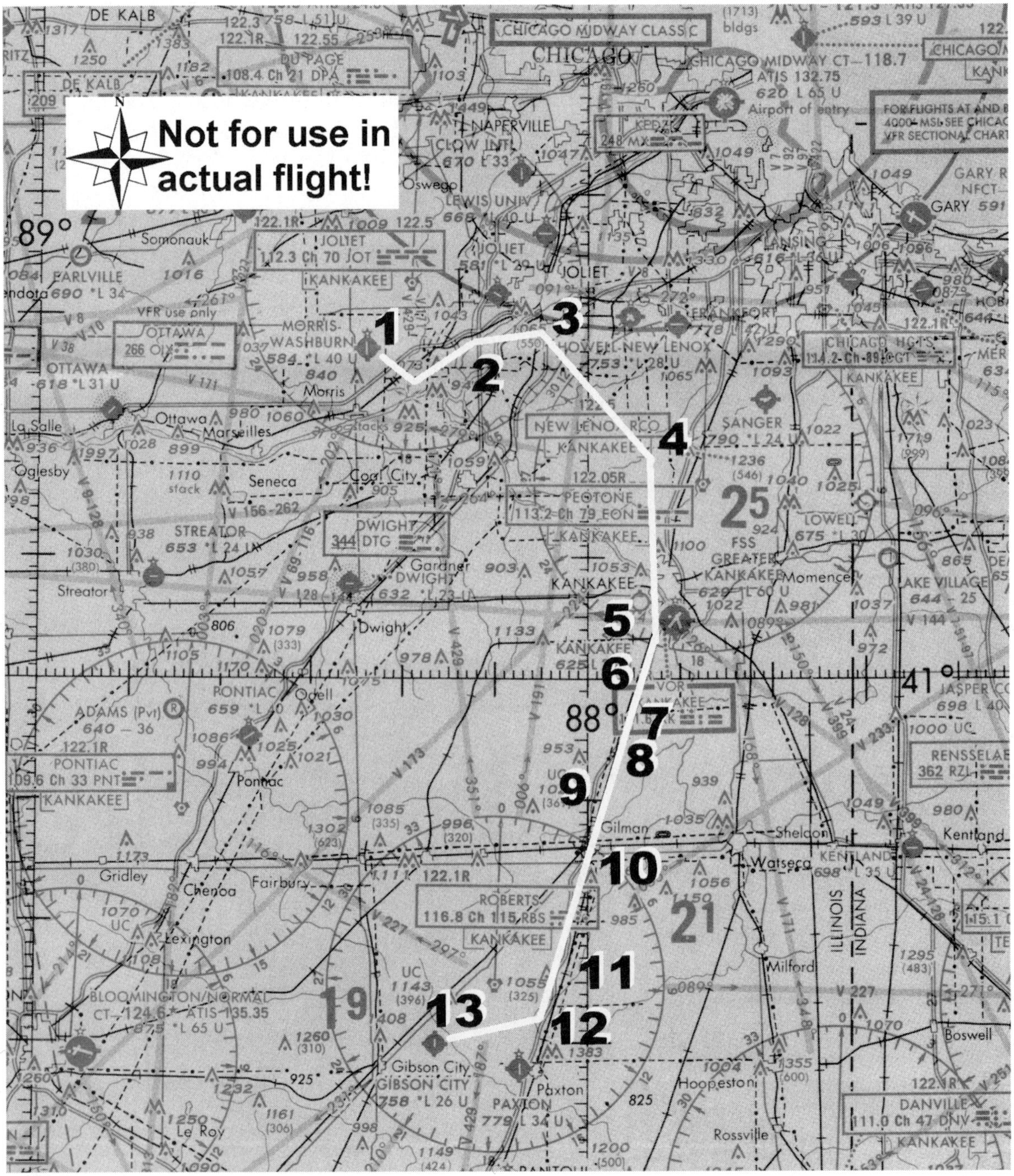
Not for use in actual flight!
1
2
3
4
5
6
7
8
9
10
11
12
13
DE KALB
CHICAGO MIDWAY CLASS C
CHICAGO
CHICAGO MIDWAY CT-118.7
ATIS 132.75
620 L 65 U
Airport of entry
FOR FLIGHTS AT AND B
4000' MSL SEE CHICAG
VFR SECTIONAL CHART
DU PAGE
108.4 Ch 21 DPA
NAPERVILLE
CLOW INTL
Oswego
LEWIS UNIV
GARY
89°
Somonauk
JOLIET
112.3 Ch 70 JOT
KANKAKEE
EARLVILLE
VFR use only
OTTAWA
266 OIX
MORRIS-WASHBURN
584 *L 40 U
Morris
HOWELL-NEW LENOX
FRANKFORT
LANSING
CHICAGO HGTS
La Salle
Ottawa
Marseilles
NEW LENOX RCO
SANGER
Oglesby
Seneca
Coal City
PEOTONE
113.2 Ch 79 EON
DWIGHT
344 DTG
STREATOR
653 *L 24 U
Streator
Gardner
DWIGHT
632 *L 23 U
Dwight
KANKAKEE
GREATER KANKAKEE
629 L 60 U
Momence
LOWELL
675 *L 30
LAKE VILLAGE
644 - 25
FSS
25
PONTIAC
659 *L 40 U
Odell
ADAMS (Pvt)
640 - 36
41°
JASPER CO
698 L 40
88°
VOR
RENSSELAER
362 RZL
PONTIAC
109.6 Ch 33 PNT
Pontiac
Gilman
Sheldon
Kentland
Watseka
KENTLAND
698 *L 35 U
Gridley
Chenoa
Fairbury
ROBERTS
116.8 Ch 115 RBS
21
ILLINOIS
INDIANA
Lexington
Milford
BLOOMINGTON/NORMAL
CT-124.6 ATIS-135.35
875 *L 65 U
19
Gibson City
GIBSON CITY
758 *L 26 U
Paxton
PAXTON
779 L 34 U
Hoopeston
Boswell
DANVILLE
111.0 Ch 47 DNV
Le Roy
Rossville

You will depart from Morris on Runway 36, then turn to the southeast. About four miles away (all references to miles are nautical miles) you will see two roads, and you'll follow the southernmost of the two; this is Route 6. It will lead you northeast to the intersection of Interstate 55 southwest of Joliet.

There is a break in the road about two miles east of this intersection, and a new road, US-52, starts at Preston Heights and leads you southeast. The road jogs to the left where it joins Route 20, but you can continue on straight to pick up US-45/52 about six miles north of Kankakee.

South of Kankakee, Interstate 57 crosses US-45/52 near the Kankakee airport. Turn and follow I-57, and keep track of the towns as they pass by. There are five towns, each about 4 miles apart, which means that you should pass one every two minutes or so. Right after Gilman, there is the town of Ornaga (which shows as two parts on US-45 in the scenery) but it's too close to Gilman to use as a checkpoint.

Buckley is 10 miles from Gilman; next you'll come to Loda about file miles after Buckley. At this point, you should be able to see Gibson City off to the southwest, about 10 miles away. If you can see the airport, go ahead and turn toward it.

If you continue to follow I-57, you'll come to Paxton about four miles after Loda. It has an airport of its own, on the west side of the highway. Turn west and you should be able to see Gibson City.

Use the flight log to track your progress and to keep track of your position. You won't have any of those new-fangled radios to help you find your way, so pay close attention to the roads and towns as you pass them.

GETTING READY TO FLY

Start by using the World Airports menu to position yourself. Choose "Morris - Runway 36" from the "USA - Chicago" area. Set your transponder to the VFR code: 1200. You can ignore all the other radio settings.

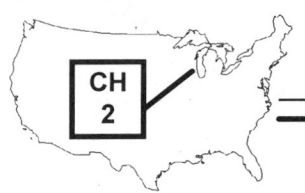

VFR Flight Log

Departure: Morris (C09)
Destination: Gibson City (C34)

FIXES	ROUTE MAG COURSE (1)	NAUT. MILES	ESTIMATED GROUND SPEED (KT)	TOTAL TIME	ACTUAL TIME
1. Depart Morris southeast	130°		70	7 (2)	
2. Follow Route 6 to I-55 intersection	70°	12	135	10.7	
3. Fly past break in roads to Preston Heights	130°	14		11.6	
4. Follow US 52, then US 45	145°	29		18.5	
5. Take US 45 to Kanakakee	180°	41		24.1	
6. Take I-57 past Chebanse	195°	45		25.9	
7. Pass Clifton		49.5		28	
8. Pass Askum		53		29.6	
9. Pass Danforth		56.5		31.2	
10. Pass Gilman		60		32.8	
11. Pass Buckley		70		37.5	
12. Pass Loda, turn southwest		75		37.8	
13. Arrive Gibson City		85		44.4	

(1) All courses are only approximate
(2) Includes time for take-off, climb-out, and turn to course

Morris Municipal (James R. Washburn Field)
Coordinates: 41-25.88; 088-25.29
Runways: 18-36 2,897x60

Gibson City
Coordinates: 40-29.15; 088-16.04
Elevation: 758 MSL; Pattern altitude: 1,500 MSL
Runways 18-36 3,400x30 asphalt; 9-27 2,400x100 turf

Even though you'll be flying by the seat of your pants, there are still some requirements and suggestions to keep in mind. First, climb to pattern altitude at Morris (1,400 feet) before turning to the southeast. Since your course will be to the east of north, you should fly at an odd thousand plus 500 foot altitude, so continue your climb up to 3,500 feet. You could climb up to 5,500 feet, but this might make it more difficult to keep track of the roads and towns.

Once you reach your cruising altitude, adjust your pitch and throttle back for a cruising speed of about 135 knots. This is what we have used to come up with the times in the flight log, though you can change them if you pick a different cruising speed.

There's no Class D airspace at Kankakee, even though it has a control tower, so you won't need to talk to anyone on the radio as you go by. Out of courtesy, however, you might give the tower a call to let them know where you are and where you're going.

After you turn to follow I-57, your course will be west of north, so you should climb to an even thousands plus 500 foot altitude for VFR flight. Go to 4,500 feet.

What goes up must come down, and the pattern altitude at Gibson City is 1,500 feet. This means that you will need to lose 3,000 feet before entering the pattern. Since you will be approaching from the east, and you will use Runway 36 for your landing, the best approach is to cross over the runway at midfield, above pattern altitude. Then make a 270-degree descending turn to the right which will put you on the proper 45-degree entry into the pattern. Assuming that you want to cross the field at about 2,000 feet and will make an en route descent at 500 feet per minute, you will need to start your descent about five minutes from the field, or about 10 miles. This means that you should start your descent just before you arrive at Loda.

As mentioned at the top of this article, Gibson City is a long and narrow runway. If you're only used to landing at big fields like Meigs where the runways are 100 to 150 feet wide, you will need to be prepared to make a number of adjustments when landing at Gibson City. The narrower runway means that it is harder to get lined up on final; plan on extending your downwind leg just a bit more than usual, so that you have plenty of time to get established on a controlled final leg. Also, the visual cues will be very different as you cross the threshold, which can wreak havoc with your flare and touchdown. Don't be dismayed if you bounce the first time or two when landing at a narrow field, since you will feel as if you are higher off the runway than you are. Finally, Gibson City is so narrow that FS5.1 doesn't show a center stripe for the runway; be careful to keep it on the straight and narrow after you touchdown.

If you want to add some challenge to the flight, consider setting up the weather so that you have 10 or 15 knots of wind out of the north. If you make it directly out of the north, you won't have to worry about cross-wind landings (which are difficult without rudder pedals) but will still have to cope with crabbing your course to stay over the roads. If you have rudder pedals, veering the wind around to the northwest by 20 to 30 degrees will keep you busy on your final approach and landing.

Whether you choose to fly with wind or in the calm, clear skies of the FS5.1 world, you'll have the satisfaction of knowing that you can find your way around without relying on radio navigation aids. And when you get to Gibson City, don't forget to try the sauerbraten.

💾 Situation file: XC-CH2

Chicago Flight 3

Cheapskate GPS

New technology touches our lives in dozens of ways every day, from faster computers to cellular phones. Global Positioning System (GPS) satellite navigation has revolutionized the art of finding your way from one place to another, for everyone from hikers and boaters to pilots. But in the real world of general aviation, yesterday's technology still rules—the average pilot flies an airplane that is at least 20 years old, and is outfitted with navigation equipment of similar vintage.

The same is true for FS5.1 pilots; the Cessna 182RG comes equipped with a pair of VOR receivers (one of which can be swapped for an ADF—automatic direction finder—for use with NDB—non-directional beacons). A real-world pilot can spend $1,000 and get a handheld GPS receiver complete with a moving map display, but you don't have that option for FS5.1 (at least, not yet).

With this flight, you'll learn a handy navigation technique that will let you fly direct to your destination under most conditions, even without a GPS.

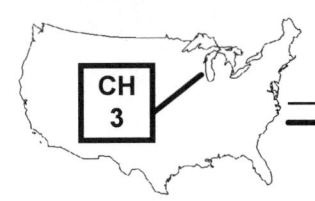

VOR DIRECT

FS5.1 pilots (as well as most real world single-engine aircraft pilots) must rely on VOR beacons as their guideposts in the sky. And a typical flight route goes from one to another to another until you reach your destination.

This routing is fine as long as your VOR targets are more or less in a straight line from your departure to your destination, but this is rarely the case. Instead, you may have to fly a considerable distance out of your way to reach the nearest VOR, and then go out of your way again to reach the next one. If your route zig-zags across the straight-line path between your departure and destination, you can waste a lot of time and avgas in the process.

Safety is another issue. Flying directly over a VOR does make navigation easy, since you always know exactly where to turn and what heading to use. The problem is that other pilots are using the exact same strategy, so as you get closer to the VOR, the chances of your path converging with another aircraft's increases. Two planes trying to occupy the same airspace at the same moment generally does not result in a desirable outcome.

There is a way that you can simply launch directly from your departure point and head straight to your destination, just as you could with a GPS device. In fact, if you have a VOR with DME (Distance Measuring Equipment) readout—as the FS5.1 Cessna panel does—and you spend a little extra effort planning your route, you can fly direct using just VOR beacons.

I learned this technique from "The Proficient Pilot", by Barry Schiff, which is a book that I strongly recommend for all pilots who want to become more skilled and knowledgeable.

Not for use in actual flight!

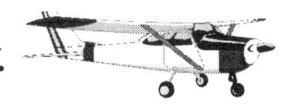

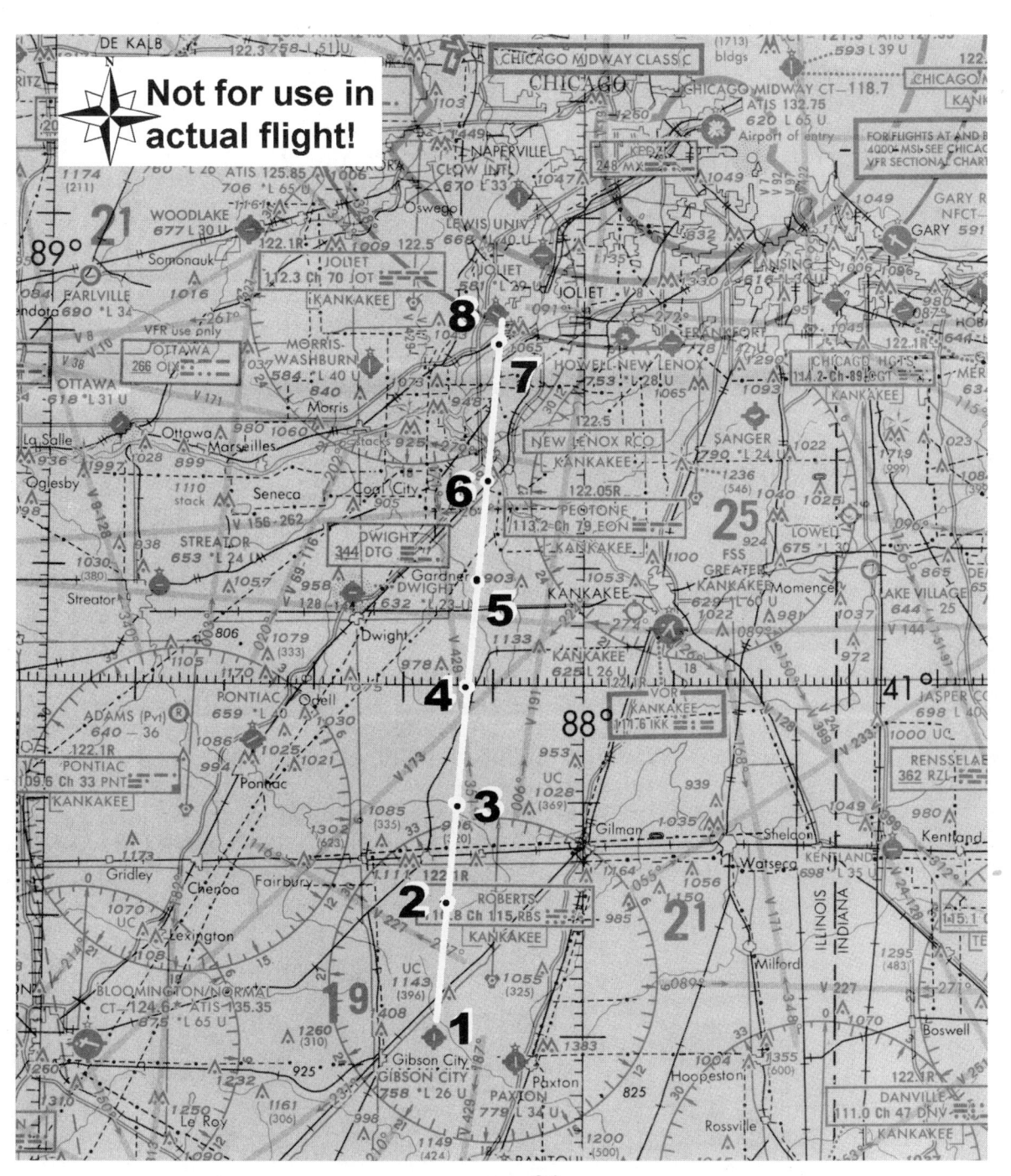

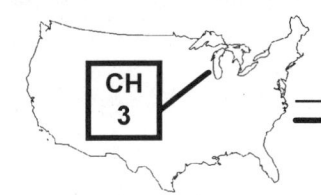

GIBSON CITY TO JOLIET

Since your last flight in this region ended in Gibson City, you'll start there and fly directly to Joliet. Your planned route is highlighted on a section of a World Aeronautical Chart (WAC). (For a more detailed view of the route, you should use a sectional chart.) As you can see, a direct route between the two airports is almost due north—actually, I make it out to be 1° magnetic. The distance for this route is 62 nautical miles.

If you were to plan the flight going to VORs, you would probably choose Roberts (RBS) and Peotone (EON) as your waypoints, which would add 12 more miles to the route. This means 20% more fuel burn and 20% more flying time compared with the shorter, direct route.

But what can you use as checkpoints along the direct route? As the chart shows, there seem to be few notable features in the real world, and FS5.1 will show even less than that.

The answer is that you can use the VORs that are to either side of your route. The first step is to draw your line of flight on the chart, and then make tick marks at regular intervals along the line. You'll want to pick a distance that will make the navigation easier; in this case, I have planned the flight at a sedate speed of 120 knots, so you should travel each 10 mile segment in five minutes. I have made the tick marks for your check points 10 nautical miles apart.

The next step is to choose your VORs. The ideal candidates are fairly close to your route of flight, so that you get a large bearing change as you proceed along your path. For the first half of your route, the Pontiac VOR (PNT 108.2) will do nicely. About halfway to Joliet, the Pontiac VOR will be fairly far behind you, so the bearing angles will change more slowly, so it will not be as useful, but fortunately, the Peotone VOR (EON 113.2) is in a perfect position to do the job.

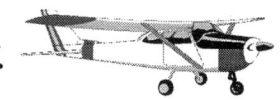

VFR Flight Log

Departure: Gibson City (C34)
Destination: Joliette (JOT)

Fixes	Route Mag Course	Naut. Miles	Estimated Ground Speed (Kt)	Total Time	PNT VOR OBS DME	EON VOR OBS DME
1. Depart Gibson City	1°		70			
2. Checkpoint A		10	120	9	289° 23	
3. Checkpoint B		20		14	264° 22	
4. Checkpoint C		30		19	241° 25	
5. Checkpoint D		40		24		70° 19
6. Checkpoint E		50		29		100° 18
7. Checkpoint F		60		34		127° 21
8. Arrive Joliet airport		62		35		

Gibson City
Coordinates: 40-29.15; 088-16.04
Runways: 18-36 3,400x30 asphalt; 9-27 2,400x100 turf

Joiliet
Coordinates: 41-31.08; 088-10.52
Location: 6.7 nm from Joliet VOR (JOT) 112.3, 103°
Elevation: 581 feet MSL
Pattern altitude: 1382 MSL
Runways: 12-30 2,940x100 asphalt; 4-22 3,432x125 turf
UNICOM/CTAF: 122.7

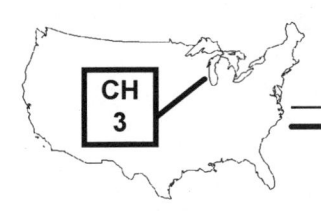

Now, draw lines from the VORs to each checkpoint along your route. Then record the bearing *to* the VOR from the checkpoint, and measure the distance. For each checkpoint, you should have a bearing and distance to a VOR.

Your flight log is already filled in for your flight. The mileage and time between checkpoints are at even intervals. The time to the first checkpoint is longer than the others to account for take-off and climb to cruising altitude (assuming about a 500 fpm rate of climb).

As you fly, you'll watch your OBS and DME readouts for your NAV radios. As you reach each checkpoint, change the OBS setting for the planned bearing at the next checkpoint.

You can use the DME and OBS information to tell whether you are to the left or right of your planned course, and ahead or behind schedule. For the first half of the flight, a DME distance from PNT smaller than shown in the flight plan means that you are to the left of your course, and a greater distance means that you are off to the right. If the OBS needle is to the right, then you are ahead of schedule, and to the left means that you are behind.

For the second half of the flight, the indications are reversed, because the VOR is located on the opposite side of your course. A distance from EON smaller than planned means that you are off to the right, and the OBS needle to the right means that you are behind schedule.

The only other planning detail is the question of how high to fly. The hemispheric rule indicates that you should fly at odd thousands plus 500 feet, and given the relatively short flight, you might consider either 3,500 or 5,500. Since there are no airspace restrictions to worry about and the tallest obstructions en route are only a bit higher than 1,000 feet MSL, you might as well go with the 3,500 altitude and enjoy the sights.

Remember that you have to get down to Joliet's 1,382 foot pattern altitude before you enter the pattern—plan on making a 45-degree entry onto a left-downwind leg for Runway 30. At a 500 foot-per-minute descent rate, this means you'll have to start down about four minutes out, or soon after Checkpoint E.

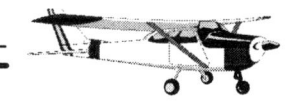

GETTING READY TO FLY

The first step is to position yourself at Gibson City field. Use the World Set Exact Location command and enter the following values to place your plane in position at the end of Runway 36.

    North/South Lat.:   N 40 28 38
    East/West Lon.:   W 088 16 03
    Altitude (ft):   761
    Heading (deg magnetic): 1

Next, tune your NAV radios for the two VOR beacons you will use. Tune NAV1 to 109.6 for PNT, and set its OBS to the first checkpoint's bearing: 289°. Tune NAV2 to 113.2 for EON, and set its OBS to 70°. Both OBS dials should read "TO", with the NAV1 needle deflected to the right, and the NAV2 needle deflected to the left. The DME readouts should be about 29.6 miles for DME1, and 52.2 for DME2. (You can also use the Nav/Com Navigation Radios menu choice to verify that you are receiving the signals from the correct VORs.) And make certain that your transponder is squawking 1200, the VFR code.

All that's left is to take off, and watch the clock. Adjust your speed and course so that you hit each checkpoint right on time. With a little practice, you'll find that this method is almost as easy as using a GPS, and a whole lot cheaper.

    🖫 Situation file: XC-CH3

Section B: Los Angeles

Lights! Camera! Action! Los Angeles is home to Hollywood and Disneyland, but it is also home to one of the largest concentrations of general aviation aircraft in the country. The desert climate provides good flying weather throughout most of the year, and there are lots of great sites to visit by plane. Besides, flying is a whole lot faster than trying to travel on those multi-lane parking lots that Southern Californians call "freeways".

Los Angeles Flight 1

Island Adventure

(Imagine the gentle strumming of an acoustic guitar as four young voices break into close-harmony singing) "26 miles across the sea, Santa Catalina is a-waitin' for me. Santa Catalina, the island of romance, romance, romance, romance...."

The Four Preps helped the country fall in love with Santa Catalina Island back in the early 60s, and this California get-away is still a favorite destination for sight-seeing, recreation, or just soaking up the rays while stretched out on the beautiful beaches.

The good news for pilots is that the town of Avalon is home of the Catalina airport, with a 3,200-foot asphalt runway. Even better news for FS5.1 pilots is that Microsoft included the island and the runway in the default scenery for the Los Angeles area.

This Cross Country flight takes you for a day on the beach, and since you'll want plenty of time to enjoy that famous Southern California sunshine, I've planned the flight so you'll get an early start on the day.

There's a lot more to plan with this flight than just the time of day, however. The Los Angeles basin has some of the most complex and restrictive airspace of any metropolitan area in the country, so you can't just fire up the fan and go boring holes in the sky. And there's another aspect of this flight that is different from most of the Cross Country flights in this book; you'll be crossing a large expanse of open water in a single-engine plane, and this requires some special planning of its own.

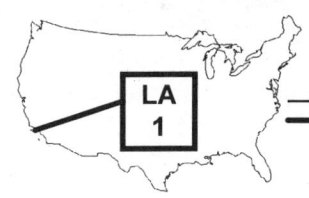

PLANNING THE FLIGHT

You'll be departing from Runway 24 at McClellan-Palomar Airport in Carlsbad, California, about 75 nm. southeast of Los Angeles. You could simply launch and head out over the Gulf of Santa Catalina on a bee-line for the island, but this would mean flying over the water for more than 50 nm. Engine or other mechanical problems are extremely rare in the real world, but why take an avoidable chance? I'll plan the flight to minimize your over-water flight as much as possible, even if that means flying a bit more distance than the direct routing.

You'll start with a straight-out departure, then head northwest up the coast toward the Oceanside VOR. This VOR is located near the beach, south of Camp Pendleton, as shown by the highlighted route on the section of the WAC (World Aeronautical Chart) for that area. (Under real world circumstances, you would use a sectional or the Los Angeles VFR Terminal Area Chart, but we have chosen this chart for its larger scale.)

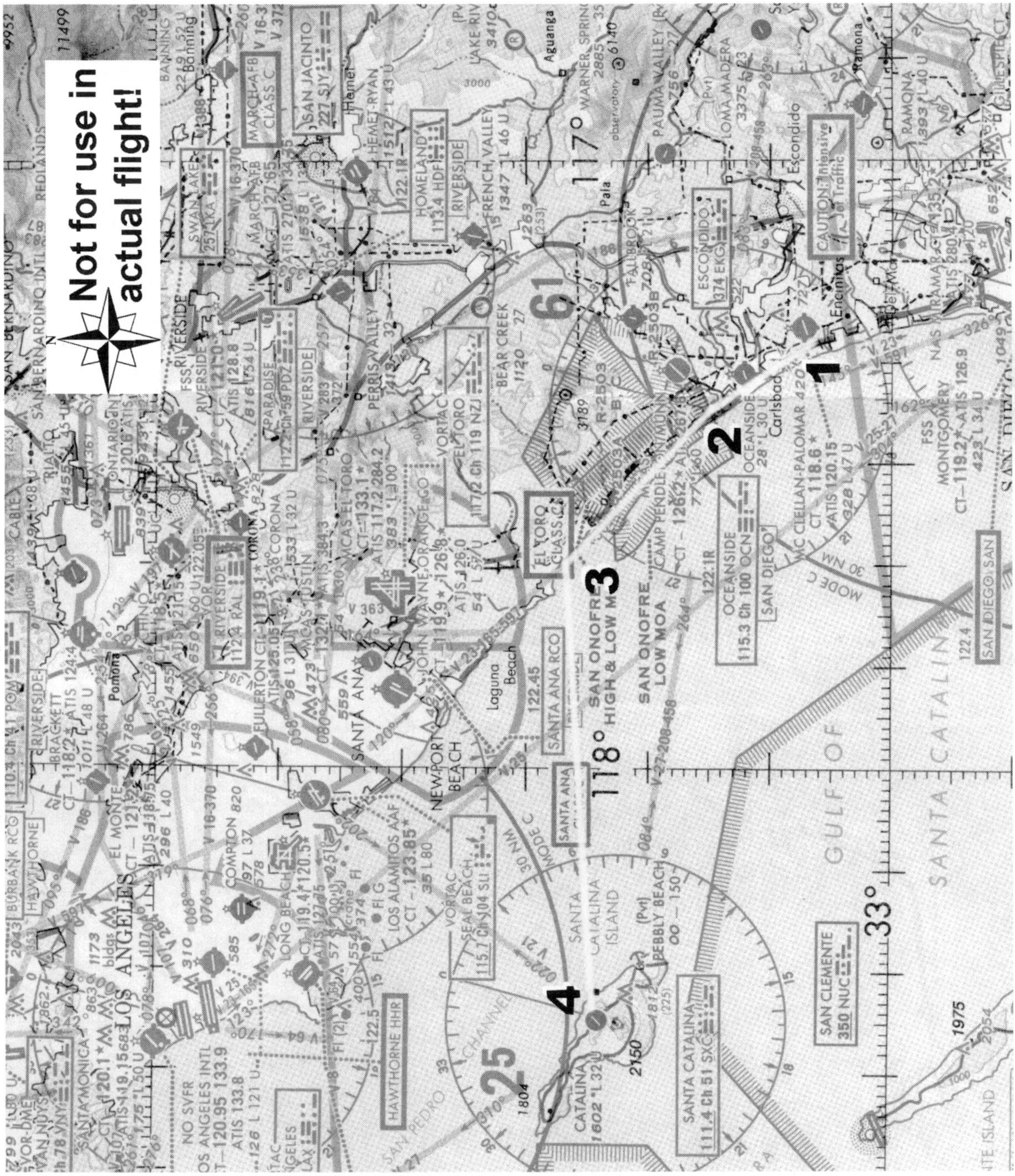

Not for use in actual flight!
1
2
3
4
SAN ONOFRE HIGH & LOW MOA
SAN ONOFRE LOW MOA
EL TORO CLASS C
LOS ANGELES
GULF OF SANTA CATALINA
SANTA CATALINA ISLAND

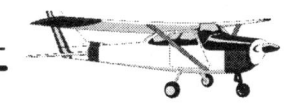

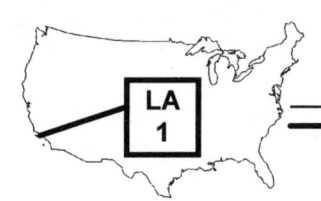

Note that there are hatched-lines just north of the Oceanside VOR. These lines surround two areas, marked "R-2503" and "R-2533". The R stands for "Restricted" and these are airspaces that have been reserved for military operations. Even if you're only puttering along at 100 to 120 knots, your closing rate with an F-18 traveling at 500 knots or faster will be about 10 nautical miles per minute—you'll have 15 seconds to react to one just 2.5 miles away, if you even see it. So, aside from the dim view that the FAA and military take of unauthorized entry into restricted airspace, you also have some real self-interest in not straying where you shouldn't be.

The chart legend has details on the restricted airspaces (though in the real world, you should also check on the status of the airspaces when you get a weather briefing as part of your planning.) R-2503 extends from the surface to 15,000 feet—a little too high for a Cessna C-182RG to climb over in just 10 miles—but the one along the beach, R-2533, only covers from the surface to 2,000 feet. So we'll plan to climb above that one, and stay over the shoreline to make certain that we stay clear of the other restricted airspace to the northeast.

After you take off from McClellan-Palomar, you will climb to about 1,000 feet before turning right and heading for the Oceanside VOR. Watch your DME readout for the VOR, and make sure that you have reached 2,500 feet before you get to it. Your heading will be about 300° but you can also simply follow the coastline if you prefer.

Notice that there is another shaded area just north of the restricted airspaces. There is a notation with a "44" over a "25", indicating that this is a special airspace from 2,200 feet to 4,400 feet on the approach to John Wayne/Orange County Airport, and a note on the chart indicates that you need to contact Air Traffic Control before entering this airspace. To make communications easier, I've planned for you to climb above the upper limit before you get there. I'll explain why in a moment.

VFR Flight Log

Departure: McClellan-Palomar (CRQ)
Destination: Catalina (AVX)

FIXES	ROUTE		ESTIMATED		ACTUAL
	MAG COURSE	NAUT. MILES	GROUND SPEED (KT)	TOTAL TIME	TIME
1. Depart McClellan-Palomar	310°			1 (1)	
2. Cross Oceanside VOR	305°	9	80	8	
3. Turn at Dana Point	247°	18	80/130 (2)	17.5	
4. Arrive Catalina airport		37		34.5 (3)	

(1) Take-off, climb-out, and turn
(2) Climb for about 3.5 minutes on this leg to reach cruise altitude, then transition to cruise flight.
(3) Plus 3 to 5 minutes to enter pattern and land.

McClellan-Palomar
Coordinates: 33-07.5; 117-16.8
Elevation: 328 feet MSL
Pattern altitude: 1500 MSL
Runways: 6-24 4,700x510
Tower: 118.6

Catalina Airport
Coordinates: 33-24.3; 118-24.8
Elevation: 1602 feet MSL
Pattern altitude: 2600 MSL
Runways: 4-22 3,240x100
UNICOM/CTAF: 122.7

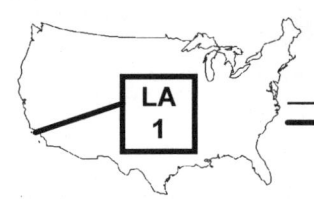

FLYING THE LOG

The flight log for this trip has only three checkpoints. After taking off, you proceed to the Oceanside VOR. From there, you follow the coast to Dana Point where the highway turns inland and you turn toward the water. There aren't any good visual references on the ocean, so your third and final checkpoint will be the island itself.

Earlier, we mentioned that by climbing over some of the special use airspace, you could simplify your communications requirements. The main reason for climbing, however, is because a Cessna is not a duck. Unless you have floats on your plane, it won't land well on the water in an emergency, so you should do everything you can to make sure you have a chance to come down on *terra firma*.

The Cessna C-182RG is no sailplane with the engine turned off, but it does glide better than a brick. Figure that you can glide at least a mile for every 1,000 feet of altitude you have. If you start your crossing before you enter the El Toro Class C airspace around John Wayne, the route will take you over about 32 nautical miles of water, shore to shore. In order to guarantee that you could glide to a shore from the midpoint, you'd need to be up at 16,000 feet. We won't plan to climb that high on this flight; at 8,500 feet, we will be out of gliding distance for about 15 miles, or at a 130 knot airspeed, for less than seven minutes. This altitude also complies with the hemispheric rule for VFR flights where westbound flights should travel at even thousands plus 500 feet, though you won't actually spend much time at that altitude.

Note: I have planned this flight with no winds—which would be highly unlikely in the real world. A headwind or tailwind would not affect the distance you would be out of gliding range from land, but any crosswind will increase your at-risk period. If you set up your flight with a wind, consider going even higher for your crossing.

To reach 8,500 feet, you'll be climbing for the first 15 to 20 minutes of your flight. After you reach about 1,000 feet AGL (above ground level) after take off, convert to a cruise climb (aim for about 80 to 85 knots and a 500 fpm climb rate) to help keep the engine cool, and just keep climbing as you turn onto your course up the coast. When you reach 8,500 feet, level out, throttle back to 2350 to 2400 RPM and trim for level flight—you should end up at about 130 knots.

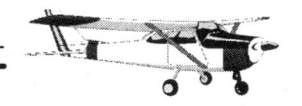

But where should you make your turn to leave the mainland behind? Use a combination of good old-fashioned pilotage and radio navigation to make sure you turn before the El Toro Class C airspace. It's a little difficult to see on the chart, but there is a highway—Interstate 5—that runs along the coast right where you're headed. At Dana Point, the road makes a right-angle turn to the right; you go left. You should be able to see Santa Catalina Island awaitin' for you across the sea, but follow the 247° radial of the Santa Catalina VOR as a backup.

The field elevation at Catalina is 1,602 feet, and pattern altitude is at 2,600 feet. You'll need to lose about 6,000 feet from your cruise altitude, and under normal circumstances, you'd start a 500 fpm descent when you're 12 minutes from the field. This would mean giving up your gliding distance cushion, however, so you're better off waiting until you're eight miles from the island, then starting a 500 fpm descent, and make some circles to lose the remaining altitude once you get over the island.

The VOR is south of the field, and you'll use Runway 22 for your landing. There's a right-hand traffic pattern for 22, so the easiest approach is to cross over at mid-field (traveling south to north) and make a left-hand 270° turn to enter a right-hand downwind for 22. Make sure you're down to pattern altitude before you enter the pattern.

BEFORE YOU TAKE OFF

All that's left is to set up the instruments and some other details. First, let's get in position.

Choose the World menu item, then Set Exact Location. On the screen that appears, enter the following items:

    North/South Lat.:   N033 07 45.4995
    East/West Lon.:   W117 16 24.9711
    Altitude: 331
    Heading: 246

Choose OK. This should place you at the start of runway 24, ready to roll.

Now set the radios. Set NAV1 to 111.4 for the Santa Catalina VOR, and set the OBS to the 247° radial. Set NAV2 to 115.3 for the

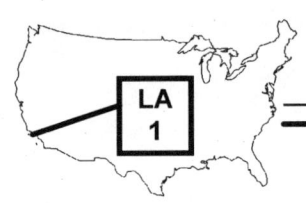

Oceanside VOR; no need to set the OBS at this point, though you can set it for 310° if you want, since that will be close to your course for it after your initial climb on take off.

Set COM1 to 118.6, which is the frequency for the McClellan-Palomar control tower. And set your transponder squawk code to 1200, which indicates a VFR flight.

If you want to use the engine leaning feature (discussed in Appendix C), choose the Sim menu, then the Realism and Reliability item. Put a check in the box for Mixture Control to enable that feature, and then choose OK.

And finally, since we want to get a jump on the day, go to the World menu, choose Set Time and Season, and pick Dawn under the Time of Day setting.

You'll be flying over water, so you should have a life jacket in the unlikely event that you have to ditch. The time to put it on is now, before you take off, rather than wait and have to struggle into it while you are also trying to fly a plane with an engine problem. So don your Mae West along with your Ray-Bans before you fire up the engine.

You should be all set to take off for a great day at the beach. And watch your DME carefully as you head across the water to the island; as it ticks down past 23 miles, you will have entered that stretch where you're out of gliding distance from land. You might find it helps the seven minutes to pass if you sing a little. Hmmm... "26 miles across the sea, Santa Catalina is a waitin' for me, Santa Catalina, the island of romance, romance, romance, romance!"

💾 Situation file: XC-LA1

Los Angeles Flight 2

Wedding Cake Blues

Los Angeles! City of Angels! City of Lights! And City of Freeways! The stories of monumental traffic jams on the asphalt maze that makes up the L.A. road system abound—who hasn't heard at least one account of the overcrowded driving conditions of Southern California?

The ground-bound citizens may not realize it, but the situation in the air over the greater Los Angeles area is no less crowded. Due to controlled airspace restrictions, standard routes for commercial airliners serving the various major airports in the region, and operations from a handful of military air bases, a lowly little VFR bugsmasher may find it difficult to find a route that goes from here to there without busting an FAA regulation or meeting another pilot face to face at 3,000 feet.

Undaunted by this challenge, I have decided to help you thread the eye of this needle, and have planned a flight that cuts right through the middle of some of the busiest airspace in the country. So put your head on a swivel, dust off your altitude control skills (because you're going to *need* them!) and get ready to go flying.

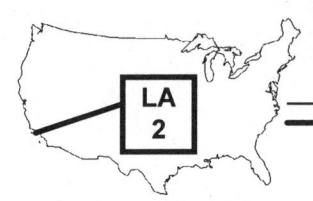

FROM THE ISLAND TO THE MOUNTAIN

Picking up where you left off in the last flight in the Los Angeles area, this flight will start at Catalina Island. Your destination is El Monte Airport, a mere 45 nautical miles (direct) from Catalina; you could just head directly for the mountains and you'd come out close to your destination. But flying direct is not a practical option.

As with every *Cross Country* flight, I lay out the route so that you will comply with all FAA regulations (or at least, as much as possible). I assume that you'll be able to use your radio to talk to the control tower at your departure and destination fields, but I try to pick routes that do not require that you contact Air Traffic Control in order to fly through controlled airspace en route.

The portion of the Los Angeles sectional chart shows your highlighted route. Most of the shaded lines indicate the borders of controlled airspace. The marks are extremely crowded; if you want to see them in a more legible format, I strongly recommend that you get a copy of the Los Angeles Terminal Area Chart (TAC) which uses a larger scale and provides greater detail than the sectional. Another advantage of the TAC is that it has special VFR corridors printed on the reverse side, making it easier to find your way.

One of your main obstacles is the Los Angeles Class B airspace (formerly known as a Traffic Control Area, or TCA). Right around Los Angeles International (LAX), this area goes from the ground to 12,500 feet MSL. As you get further from the airport, the "floor" of the airspace rises, first to 2,000 feet MSL, then 2,500, then 4,000. The limitations are shown in hundreds of feet, with the ceiling listed above the floor with a horizontal line separating the two numbers. These sections are loosely based on concentric rings centered on the airport, so a cross-section looks a little like a wedding cake placed upside-down on the airport.

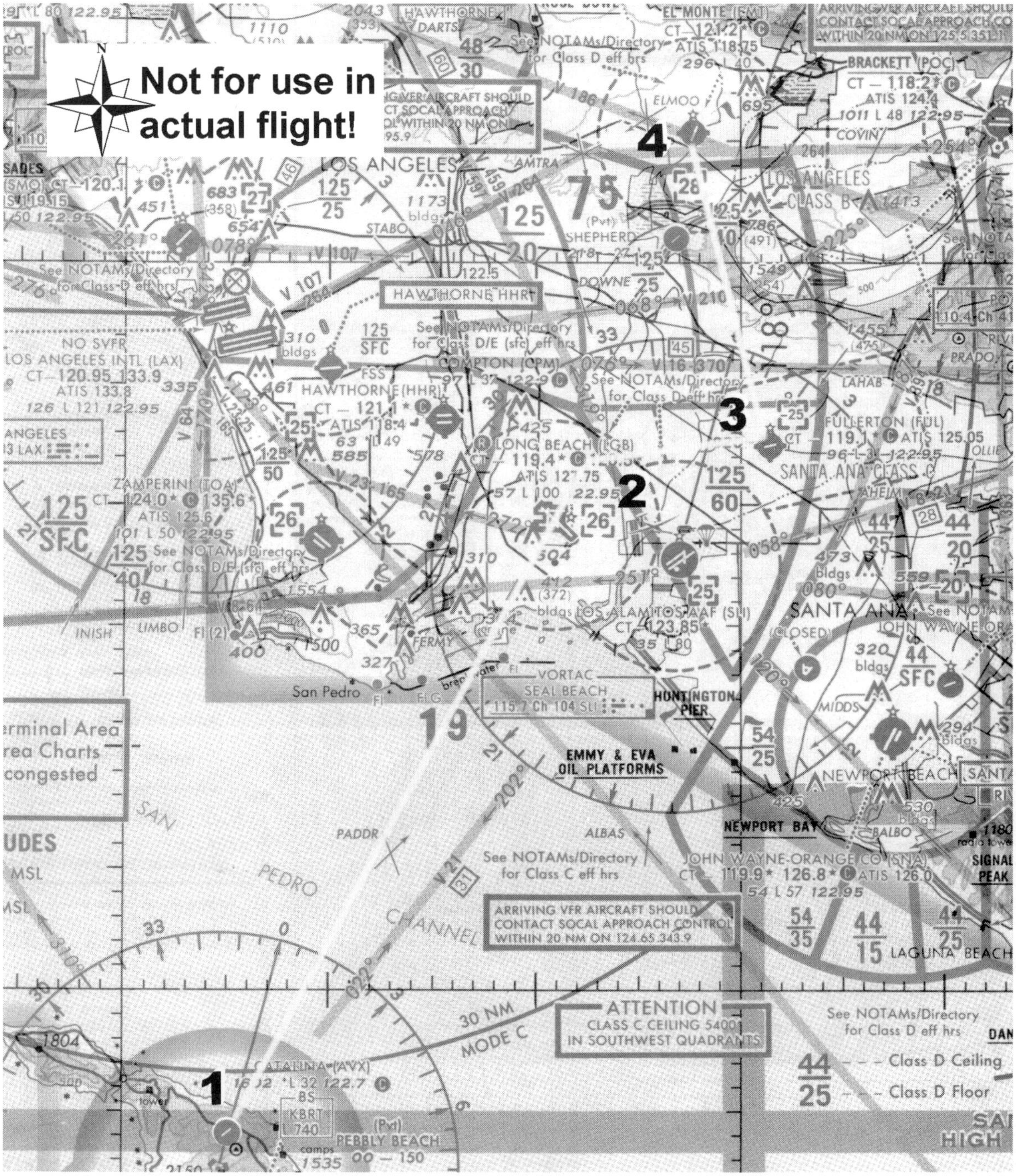
Not for use in actual flight!
N
1
2
3
4
LOS ANGELES
HAWTHORNE HHR
See NOTAMs/Directory for Class D/E (sfc) eff hrs
NO SVFR
LOS ANGELES INTL (LAX)
CT — 120.95 133.9
ATIS 133.8
HAWTHORNE (HHR)
CT — 121.1
ATIS 118.4
COMPTON (CPM)
LONG BEACH (LGB)
CT — 119.4
ATIS 127.75
ZAMPERINI (TOA)
CT — 124.0 135.6
ATIS 125.6
LOS ALAMITOS AAF (SLI)
CT — 123.85
FULLERTON (FUL)
CT — 119.1 ATIS 125.05
SANTA ANA CLASS C
SANTA ANA
JOHN WAYNE-ORANGE CO (SNA)
CT — 119.9 126.8 ATIS 126.0
EL MONTE (EMT)
CT — 121.2
ATIS 118.75
BRACKETT (POC)
CT — 118.2
ATIS 124.4
LOS ANGELES CLASS B
SHEPHERD
San Pedro
VORTAC
SEAL BEACH
115.7 Ch 104 SLI
HUNTINGTON PIER
EMMY & EVA OIL PLATFORMS
NEWPORT BEACH
NEWPORT BAY
SAN PEDRO CHANNEL
PADDR
ALBAS
See NOTAMs/Directory for Class C eff hrs
ARRIVING VFR AIRCRAFT SHOULD CONTACT SOCAL APPROACH CONTROL WITHIN 20 NM ON 124.65 343.9
ATTENTION
CLASS C CEILING 5400
IN SOUTHWEST QUADRANTS
30 NM
MODE C
CATALINA (AVX)
PEBBLY BEACH
LAGUNA BEACH
SIGNAL PEAK
See NOTAMs/Directory for Class D eff hrs
44 — Class D Ceiling
25 — Class D Floor
Terminal Area
Area Charts
congested

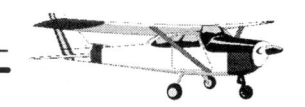

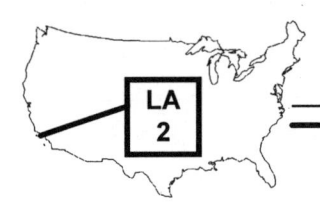

You need clearance to enter the Class B airspace, so I had to find a route that either goes under one of these cake layers, or around the cake altogether. A direct route would take you through a section with a 2,500 foot floor, which is a little lower than I want to plan for, so I chose a different route.

I can't send you too far to the east, however, because there is the John Wayne Orange County Airport Class C airspace (which requires radio contact with air traffic control before you can enter). Portions of it has floors as low as 2,500 feet, and the tops reach up to 5,400 feet, so going over or under this airspace would be more trouble than it's worth.

But wait; there's more. The various airports with control towers have their own Class D airspace, which extends from the ground to an altitude shown in a broken box. For example, the top of this zone is at 2,600 feet over Long Beach airport, and 2,500 feet over Los Alamitos AAF. We'll need to find a route that avoids these as well.

The solution is to climb to 2,800 feet after taking off from Catalina and flying right over Long Beach airport. This altitude is a little low for the water crossing, but you will be flying under IFR routes that start at 3,000 feet.

After you pass Long Beach airport, you will turn right. The VFR portion of the Los Angeles TAC shows that you could follow the Riverside Freeway at this point, but this road is not included in the FS5.1 default scenery, so you'll have to follow a compass heading. The 2,800 foot altitude will give you just a 200 foot clearance above the Long Beach Class D zone, and you'll be under a portion of the LAX Class B airspace that has a floor of 6,000 feet.

If you don't make the right turn at this point, you would have to descend to get under the 2,500 floor of the LAX Class B airspace, but that would be tricky to do since you would almost certainly have to clip the top of the Long Beach Class D zone to get down in time. Instead, I'll head you east for a bit, until El Monte is directly off to your left. You can then turn and head for the airport and travel under a section of the LAX Class B that has a 4,000 foot ceiling. All that you have left to do then is start your descent in time to enter the traffic pattern for a landing at El Monte.

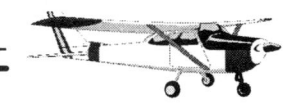

NAVIGUESSING

By about this point, you may be wondering just how you're going to be able to find your way through this maze of restrictions, especially if you don't have visual references like the Riverside Freeway to guide you.

The answer is that you will use a combination of three different navigating techniques. For the first leg, you will use a VOR beacon as a guide. For the second leg, you'll use old-fashioned ded reckoning ("ded" is short for "deduced"). And for the final leg, you get to home in on a non-directional radio beacon (NDB) on the field at El Monte. The three legs are detailed for you in the flight log, which I have filled in for you.

The VOR for the first leg is the Catalina VOR, located about a mile and a half from the airport. By tuning the OBS to a 12-degree heading, you can fly the outbound radial which will take you straight over the Long Beach airport. I will assume that you are flying in calm conditions, and that you will take off from Catalina using Runway 4. As soon as practical, go to a cruise climb (about 80 knots at full throttle) and fly the runway heading until the VOR needle centers on the gauge. Then turn to a 12-degree heading and keep the needle centered. Don't forget to level off at 2,800 feet when you reach that altitude, then throttle back and trim your aircraft for straight and level flight at 130 knots at that altitude. You'll want to get the trim settled down before you make landfall, because you will be busy enough navigating without worrying about busting an altitude at the same time.

VFR Flight Log

Departure: Catalina (AVX)
Destination: El Monte (EMT)

FIXES	ROUTE MAG COURSE	NAUT. MILES	ESTIMATED GROUND SPEED (KT)	TOTAL TIME	ACTUAL TIME
1. Depart Catalina and join SXC VOR 12° outbound radial	12°			1 (1)	
2. 2 miles past Long Beach Airport	60°	30	80/130 (2)	12	
3. Turn toward El Monte		39	130	16	
4. Arrive El Monte Airport		51		21.5 (3)	

(1) Take-off, climb-out, and turn
(2) Climb for about 4 minutes to cruise altitude, then transition to cruise flight
(3) Plus 3 to 5 minutes to enter pattern and land

Catalina Airport
Coordinates: 33-24.3; 118-24.8
Elevation: 1602 feet MSL
Pattern altitude: 2600 MSL
Runways: 4-22 3,240x100
UNICOM/CTAF: 122.7

El Monte Airport
Coordinates: 34-05.2; 118-02.1
Elevation: 296 feet MSL
Pattern altitude: 1300 MSL
Runways: 1-19 3,995x75
Tower: 121.7
Notes: Right-traffic for Runway 19

You will pass over the Long Beach airport when the DME read-out for the Catalina VOR reads about 29 miles. (NOTAM: in some of my test flights, the scenery for Long Beach did not appear; instead it remained a rectangular gray patch next to a freeway. This may be caused by a low-memory condition.) Continue two miles past the airport, until the DME reads about 31 miles or until you can see the airport out the back window of your Cessna.

The second leg starts with a right turn to a magnetic heading of 60 degrees. This takes you along the edge of the LAX Class B airspace that has the low floor, with plenty of room to spare. There are no landmarks you can use for this leg (though you will be flying directly to Fullerton Airport, but this is not included in the default scenery).

You will make your turn onto the third leg based on the El Monte NDB radio beacon, using your ADF (automatic direction finder) gauge. The ADF arrow always points to the beacon. So you will fly on your 60-degree heading until the ADF arrow points to 270-degrees, indicating that El Monte is at right angles to your left. Turn to a 330-degree heading, and continue on until you see the airport.

This third leg is about 12 nautical miles long, and you will need to descend to 1,300 feet by the time you reach the airport so that you are at pattern altitude when you get there. Since you will be cruising at 2,800 feet, you must lose 1,500 feet, which will take three minutes at a typical 500 foot per minute descent rate. Since you will be traveling at 130 knots, you will need to start your descent at least 6.5 miles from the airport, so plan on starting down (by reducing your throttle) a minute after you make your turn onto the third leg.

Once you arrive at the airport, assume that the tower clears you to enter a right downwind for landing on Runway 19, and then clears you to land. This means you will fly past the near end of the runway when you reach the airport, then turn to parallel the field with it off your right side. Turn base and then final to set up for your landing.

There's one more surprise lurking for you. When you are on final approach, you will see that there are some arrows painted at the start of the runway. These indicate a "displaced threshold" and you may *not* land on this section of the runway. Keep the plane in the air until after you pass over the solid line that indicates the start of the landing zone. (You are permitted to use a displaced threshold for take-off runs, however.)

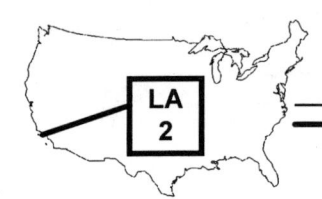

READY TO FLY

You can use the World Airports menu to go directly to Catalina. Choose the "USA - Los Angeles" scenery area, and then "Avalon - Catalina - Runway 4" from the list of airports.

You then need to set your radios and other equipment. Since you are going to be flying under VFR rules, you want to make sure that your transponder is "squawking" 1200, the VFR code. Your NAV1 radio should automatically be tuned to the Catalina VOR (111.40), but you will need to adjust the OBS setting to 12 degrees. This will set up the gauge so you can intercept the radial after takeoff.

Finally, you need to set up the ADF. Choose the ADF option from the Nav/Com menu. Enter the frequency for El Monte, which is 359, and then check the "Activate ADF Gauge" box. The ADF gauge will replace the second NAV gauge on the Cessna panel. Choose OK to return to your cockpit, and you're ready to fly. If you're looking for an extra challenge, set the time of day to Dusk, and pretend that you're flying home after a great day at the beach.

Los Angeles may be crowded both on the ground and in the skies, but with a little careful planning, and a lot of attentive piloting, you can wind your way through the different types of airspace and make much better time than the folks stuck on the freeways.

💾 Situation file: XC-LA2

Los Angeles Flight 3

What You Can't See...

The Cross Country flights in this book are designed to be easy enough for novice pilots to fly, while offering the opportunity to more experienced pilots to get their palms a little sweaty. Even though this flight is planned for clear and calm conditions, it is probably the most challenging flight yet in the book. The reason it's so difficult is that you'll be flying by a combination of visual and radio navigation, but it's what you *can't* see that can hurt you on this trip.

For this flight, you'll be traveling from El Monte to Riverside Airport—just a short 30 nautical miles to the east. As you discovered in the last flight in this area, the LA basin is a patchwork quilt of special-use airspace, with Class B and C areas towering over pillars of Class D space, forming a maze of obstacles for a small plane trying to navigate without entering airspace that requires contact with Air Traffic Control—so I plan these flights to keep you clear of those areas so that you don't bust special airspace regulations.

A look at the Los Angeles sectional shows that the Class C airspace over Ontario International sits right in the way of a direct route from El Monte to Riverside. (The information on the sectional is very dense; for a better look at it, you might want to get a Los Angeles

LA 3

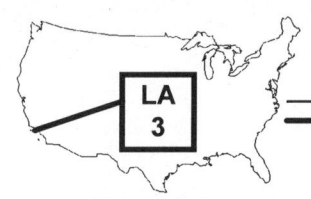

VFR Terminal Area Chart that uses a scale twice as large as the sectional.) To the south of this, there is a hunk of Class D airspace over Chino airport, and if you go further south, there are the combined Class C spaces over John Wayne Airport and the military El Toro base. It clearly gets hairy if you try to take a southern detour.

Now look north of the route and Ontario International; there's nothing out there. Nothing, except for all that dark shading, that is. (The shading is harder to see in this black and white image than it is on a real chart, where it is printed in brown ink.)

The shading represents mountains, and they rise up rapidly from the floor of the LA basin. Elevations rise from 296 at El Monte and 943 at Ontario to peaks above 4,000 feet just a couple of miles north of the edge of the Ontario airspace. All you have to do is keep those mountains at a safe distance to your left as you fly eastward along their edge, then you can turn southeast to Riverside once you have cleared the edge of the Class C space.

Now here's the catch; you won't be able to see the mountains because you're going to make this flight at night. (If this seems like too much of a challenge to start with, fly it in the daytime once or twice, and then see if you can do it at night.)

The mountains are big, brown monsters in the daylight, but at night, the lack of houses and roads on their steep surfaces make them darker than the starlit sky. So you'll have to be careful not to hit what you can't see as you fly at night.

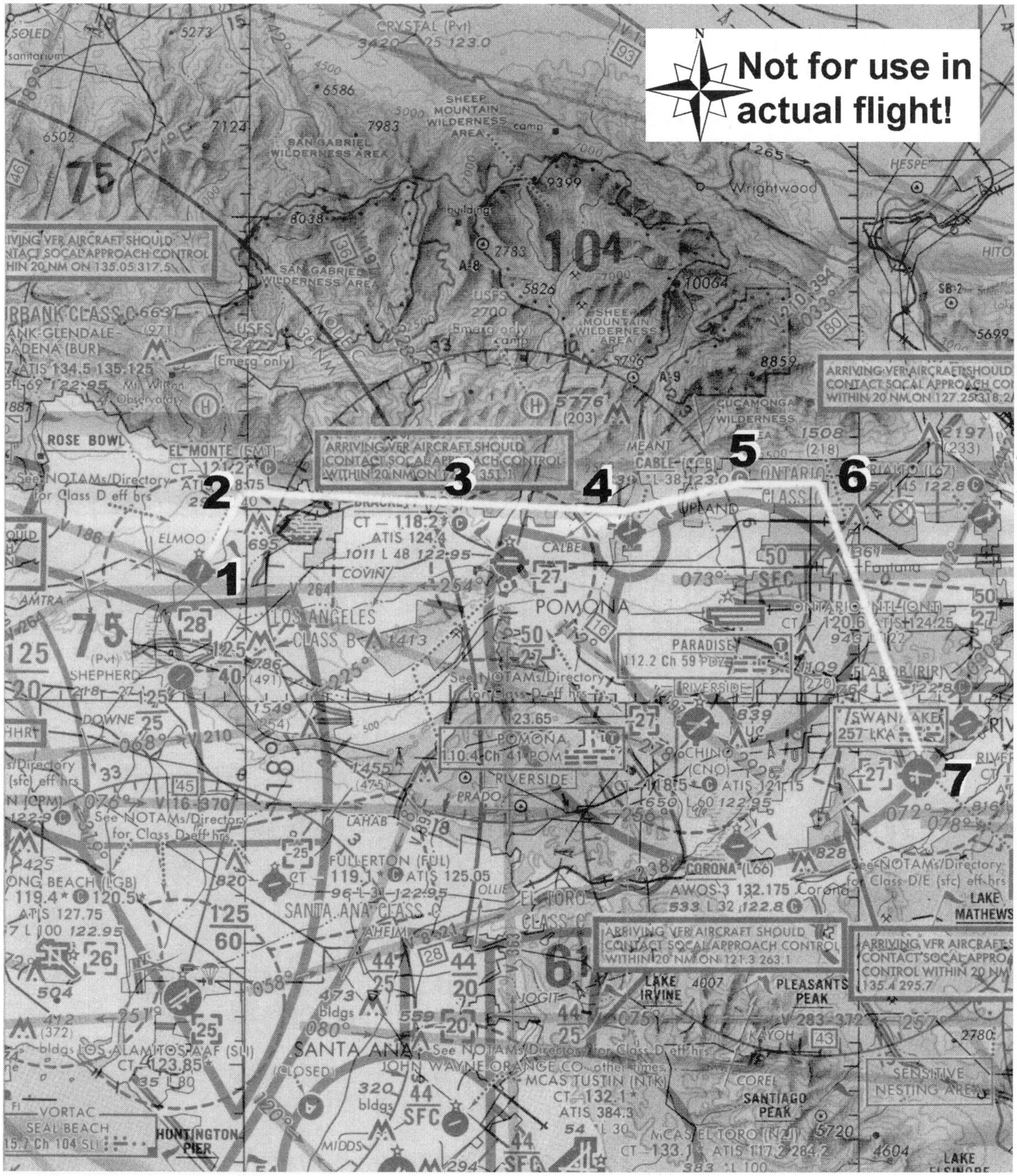
Not for use in actual flight!
1
2
3
4
5
6
7
SHEEP MOUNTAIN WILDERNESS AREA
SAN GABRIEL WILDERNESS AREA
Wrightwood
ROSE BOWL
EL MONTE (EMT)
ARRIVING VFR AIRCRAFT SHOULD CONTACT SOCAL APPROACH CONTROL WITHIN 20 NM ON 127.25 318.2
ARRIVING VFR AIRCRAFT SHOULD CONTACT SOCAL APPROACH CONTROL WITHIN 20 NM ON 121.3 263.1
CABLE (CCB)
UPLAND
POMONA
ONTARIO INTL (ONT)
PARADISE
RIVERSIDE
CHINO (CNO)
CORONA (L66)
AWOS-3 132.175 Corona
LOS ANGELES CLASS B
SANTA ANA CLASS C
EL TORO CLASS C
FULLERTON (FUL)
LONG BEACH (LGB)
LOS ALAMITOS AAF (SLI)
SANTA ANA
JOHN WAYNE-ORANGE CO
MCAS TUSTIN (NTK)
MCAS EL TORO (NZJ)
LAKE IRVINE
PLEASANTS PEAK
SANTIAGO PEAK
SENSITIVE NESTING AREA
LAKE MATHEWS
SEAL BEACH
HUNTINGTON PIER
SWAN LAKE 257 LKA

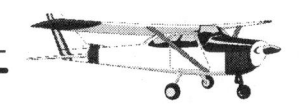

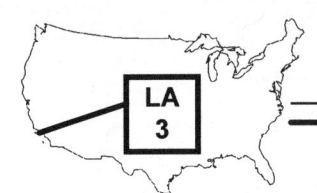

PLANNING THE FLIGHT

The flight log that I have prepared for your trip lists the key points along your route. The main trick on this flight will be to stay under or outside the Ontario airspace. You'll also have to either go around the Class D airspace at Pomona, or over it. There's only a little space between the dotted circle and the dark bad stuff, so we'll plan to fly over it. Note the "27" in a broken box inside the dotted circle around Pomona; this indicates that the Class D airspace ends at 2,700 feet, so we'll plan to climb to 2,800 feet before you get there.

In the rectangular section east of Ontario, the Class C space is marked with a fraction: 50 over 27. This means that the special use airspace extends from 2,700 feet up to 5,000 feet. Since Riverside is just under the southeastern curved portion of this space, you'll have to be down to about 2,500 feet by the time you get to this point.

So now we know what altitude you'll fly at (more or less), but what about headings? Well, since you'll be departing from Runway 1 at El Monte, you can just fly the runway heading until you reach Interstate 210 (which is the east-west road north of the airport), and then you can follow the road to the east. (At night, the roads have orange-yellow lights as if from sodium-vapor lamps, making them easier to distinguish from house lights in the FS 5.1 night landscape.) But how can you tell when you get to the Pomona Class D airspace?

One way to do this is use the VOR beacon at Pomona. The edge of the airspace intersects I-210 along the 115° radial, so to be safe, you need to be at 2,800 feet by the time the VOR is about 110° from your position over the road.

It would be great if you could follow the highway right past Ontario, but soon after it turns into Foothill Boulevard, it goes right through the portion of the Class C airspace that extends from 5,000 feet right down to ground level. So you'll have to deviate to the north.

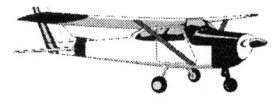

VFR Flight Log

Departure: El Monte (EMT)
Destination: Riverside (RAL)

Fixes	Route Mag Course	Naut. Miles	Estimated Ground Speed (Kt)	Total Time	Actual Time
1. Depart El Monte	11°			1 (1)	
2. Cross I-210; turn right to follow it	about 75°	3	80	3.5	
3. Climb to 2,800 feet before intercepting Pomona VOR 110° radial		9	80/130 (2)	8	
4. Intercept and follow Pomona VOR 50° radial	270°	17	130	11.5	
5. Intercept Riverside VOR 130° radial; begin descent		22		14	
6. Intercept Riverside VOR 145° radial and follow it		26		16	
7. Arrive Riverside		39		26 (3)	

(1) Take-off, climb-out, and turn
(2) Climb for about 5 minutes to cruise altitude, then transition to cruise flight
(3) Plus 3 to 5 minutes to enter pattern and land

El Monte Airport
Coordinates: 34-05.2; 118-02.1
Runways: 1-19 3,995x75
Tower: 121.7

Riverside Airport
Coordinates: 33-57.1; 117-26.7
Elevation: 816 feet MSL
Pattern altitude: 1816 MSL
Runways: 16-34 2,850x50; 9-27 5,400x100
UNICOM/CTAF: 121.0

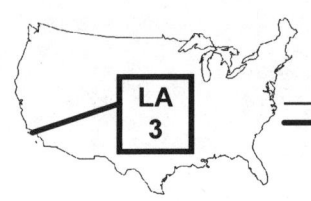

Again, the VOR can help you with this; before you reach Pomona, head about a mile north of I-210, and set the NAV radio OBS to a 50° setting. Fly along north of the highway until the needle centers, and then fly out along the radial. As long as you stay to the left of the highway and on or to the left of this radial, you'll stay clear of the Class C airspace.

You can't fly this heading forever without climbing or you'll hit something solid, however. If you use your other NAV radio to track the Riverside VOR, you can fly out along the 50° radial from Pomona until it intersects the 130° radial toward the Riverside VOR. This will place you halfway between the mountains and the Ontario airspace, and you can turn east to a heading of about 75° to remain clear of them both.

Finally, when you reach the 145° radial for the Riverside VOR, you can follow it down to the airport; remember to start to descend to 2,500 feet when you make your turn. This route will keep you clear of the Class C airspace to the west and the little bump of rocks to the east (it has a peak at 2,217 feet). Keep on descending until you reach the Riverside pattern altitude of 1,816 feet.

Once you have the airport in sight, enter a left downwind leg for Runway 9. The tower closes at 8 o'clock at night, so you can use the CTAF frequency of 121.0 to announce your intentions. You'll have 5,400 feet of runway to work with, so don't be too worried about planting the gear right on the numbers. Remember that everything looks different at night, including how a runway looks on final, so take your time and be sure to set up a nice, stable approach.

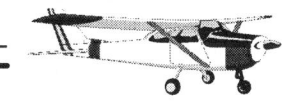

GETTING READY TO FLY

El Monte Airport is not on the FS 5.1 World Airports list, so you'll have to use the Set Exact Location feature to put yourself at the starting point for the flight. Here are the values you will need to enter:

      North/South Lat.: 034 04 54.5
      East/West Lon.: 118 02 14.1
      Altitude (ft): 299
      Heading: 11°

This will put you right at the number for Runway 1 at El Monte.

In the World menu, set the time of day to 20 hours 00 minutes local time; that's 8:00 o'clock at night. You may want to turn on your landing light at this point; press L to turn it on.

Next, tune your NAV radios. Set NAV1 to 110.4, which is the Pomona VOR. Set the OBS to 110° initially; remember that you want to be at 2,800 feet and about a mile north of the highway before the needle centers. After it does center, you'll want to reset the OBS to 50°; this is the radial that you'll follow to stay northwest of the Ontario Class C airspace.

Then set your NAV2 radio to 112.4, which is the Riverside VOR. Adjust the OBS to 130° for the initial setting; when you're following the 50° radial for the Pomona VOR, you'll want to come right to a heading of 75° when the needle centers for the Riverside VOR 130° radial. After you have made your course change, readjust the OBS on NAV2 for the 145° radial. When it centers, turn to follow it right to the Riverside Airport.

Make sure that your transponder is set to 1200, the VFR squawk code.

Take off and climb out at a cruise climb of 75 to 80 knots. You'll still be climbing after you turn to follow I-210, so you may need to use your side views to know where to turn and to keep track of your position. (And the view out the window as you climb out from the airport is going to be mostly black, so you may want to make sure that you're familiar with your panel's gauges since you won't have a horizon or other ground references.)

Once you reach your initial altitude of 2,800 feet, throttle back to a 130 to 135 knot cruise. Remember to start your descent about the time you turn to a 75° heading after intercepting the Riverside VOR

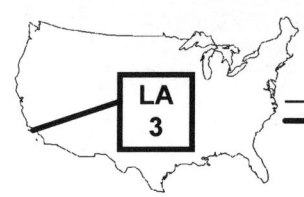

130° radial, but don't descend below 1800 feet. It's a clear night for flying, and you'll be able to see the Riverside Airport from miles away. If for some reason you should lose sight of the airport as you follow the 145° radial to it, keep in mind that the only reason would be that something has come between you and the field—like perhaps that "little bump of rocks" mentioned earlier.

Remember—when flying at night, it's what you *can't* see that can cause you the most trouble.

Situation file: XC-LA3

Section C: New York

The Big Apple: the city of bright lights and endless nights has a reputation around the world. New York also has a reputation with pilots of small planes; with its three international airports, the air traffic is so congested right around New York City that most pilots give the area a wide berth on their way from one point to another. In this section, you'll find one flight that shows off Manhattan, but the other two give you a taste of what nearby New England has to offer.

New York Flight 1

Hudson River Tour

Cross country trips are part of the training requirements for a private pilot's license, and any student pilot should be able to tell you the requirement for a cross country flight: a landing 50 or more nautical miles from your starting point. So as far as the FAA is concerned, this flight doesn't qualify, even though you'll be covering more than 70 nautical miles.

Why won't it qualify? Because you'll take off and land from the same airport: Westchester County (HPN) in White Plains, New York. And your flight plan is going to take you on one of the most impressive sight-seeing trips that you can enjoy from a single-engine private aircraft: down the Hudson river which separates Manhattan Island from the New Jersey shore.

In real life, this is one of the most popular flights for private pilots in the northeast. You get to cruise over the George Washington Bridge, look down on the Big Apple including the theater district along Broadway, look up at the Empire State building and the impressive twin World Trade Towers, dip a wing in honor of the Statue of Liberty, and then head toward the boundless Atlantic Ocean that stretches beyond the Verrazano Narrows Bridge.

Whoa! Back up a minute! What was that about looking *up* at the Empire State and World Trade Center? This trip is for a plane, not a tour bus, right?

Well, you're right, you will be flying down the river, but as with all Cross Country flights, you're going to follow the real world rules for navigation and airspace restrictions. The Hudson is a narrow strip of water that is less than 10 miles from three of the busiest commercial airports in the country: Newark (EWR) in New Jersey and La Guardia (LGA) and Kennedy (JFK) on New York's Long Island. As a result, the FAA has created a Byzantine Class B airspace (formerly a Terminal Control Area, or TCA) over the three airports.

Fortunately, the FAA has also taken touring private aircraft into account when designing the airspace, so there is a corridor for VFR (Visual Flight Rules) aircraft that follows the Hudson's path along a roughly north-south course. You can fly the length of it without once being obligated to contact any air traffic controller along the way.

However, the heavy iron gets most of the airspace over New York, and the little planes have to settle for a low level limit for their sight-seeing lane. How low? A large part of the corridor is below Class B airspace that has a floor of 1100 feet. So I'll plan your flight to remain at 900 feet—this gives you a 200-foot leeway to avoid busting the Class B limits. And "bust" is the correct word; poking through the floor of the Class B airspace without a clearance is likely to earn you an introduction with an FAA inspector.

Now, I don't want to add to the pressure, but keep in mind that there are lots of other pilots with the same idea as you. In good weather, there's more traffic along the corridor than you'll find at most airports. So plan on keeping your landing light on (for increased visibility) and your head on a swivel to watch for traffic while you make sure you maintain your altitude as close to the planned 900 feet as possible (and stay to right hand side of the river to fit in with the traffic flow) and you'll do fine. Oh yes, and don't forget to enjoy the scenery!

NY
1

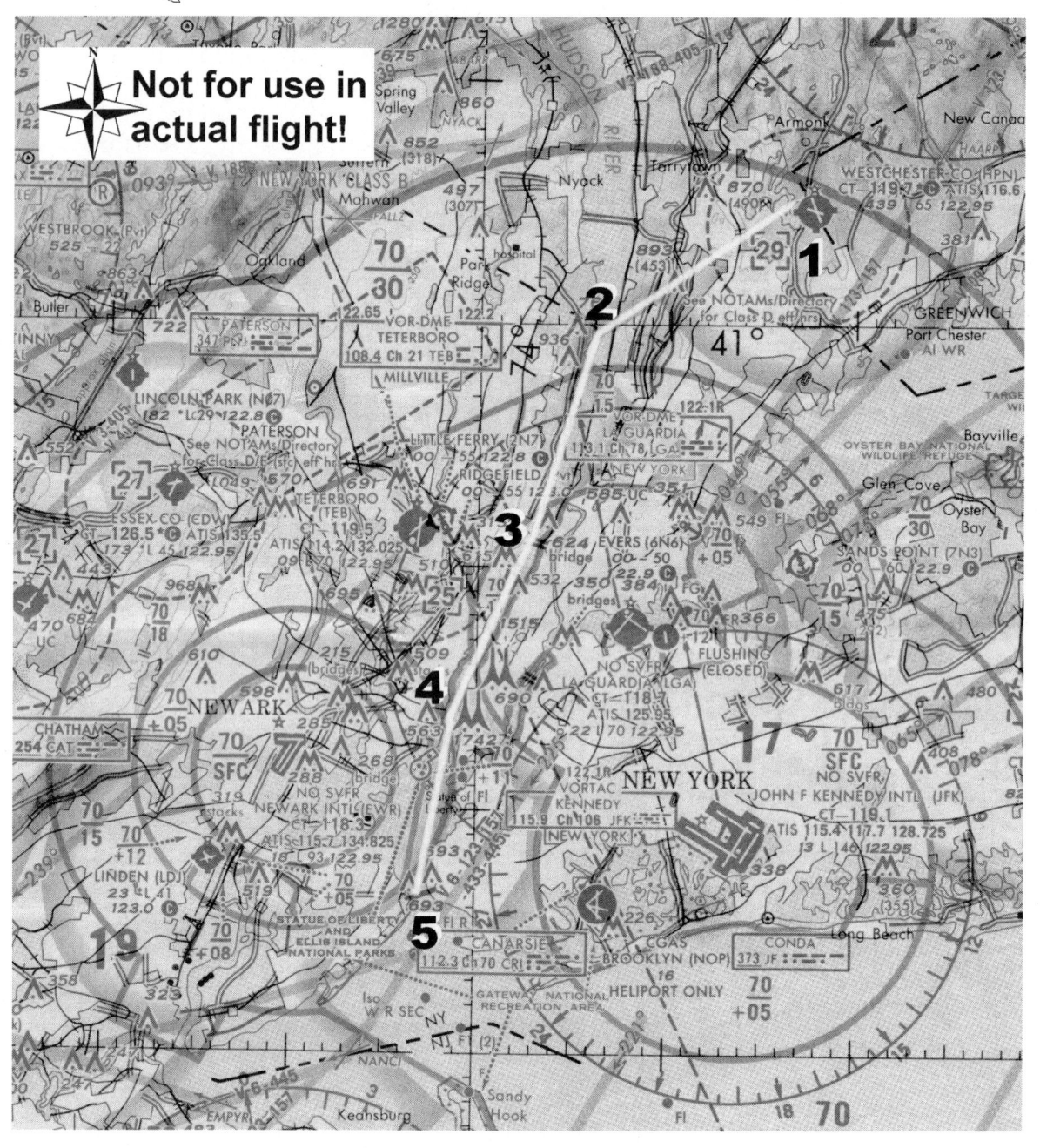

Not for use in actual flight!

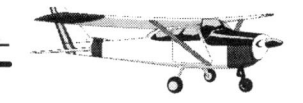

PLANNING THE FLIGHT

I'll plan the flight using pilotage techniques (relying on visual ground references) backed up by VOR radio navigation techniques. As mentioned at the start, you depart from and return to Westchester Airport in White Plains, which is northeast from Manhattan.

The portion of the New York sectional covering the area for your flight shows your highlighted course with checkpoints. This chart uses a scale of about 7 nautical miles to the inch. You can also use a VFR Terminal Area Chart for the New York area which uses a 3.5 nautical mile per inch scale, which means that it shows more detail. Westchester County has two runways, and I'll plan on using Runway 29 (since that will head you in the right direction.)

As your plotted route indicates, you'll fly a heading a bit south of west on a heading of 255 degrees so that you reach the river south of the Tappan Zee Bridge. In the real world (or if you have the Microsoft New York scenery collection) you could head to the Tappan Zee and turn south from there, but the FS5.1 default scenery thinks that the Hudson River dead-ends a few miles south of the bridge. Unfortunately, the default scenery does not include I-287 or the Saw Mill River Parkway or any of the other major roads in the area, so you can't use roads for pilotage, either. Once you get to the river, you will make certain that you're at your 900 foot cruising altitude, cross over to the right hand (western) shore, and turn south.

From here on, it's strictly a matter of pilotage. Stay over the water, but on the right-hand half of the river. When you get to the Statue of Liberty, you can proceed to the western end of the Verrazano Bridge, where you turn around, cross to the right hand shore (now the eastern side) and retrace your steps.

To make sure that you stay out of Newark's airspace on the southward leg once you reach the Statue, you'll use the NAV1 radio tuned to the Colt's Neck VOR (located south of Sandy Hook in New Jersey) on a frequency of 115.4. If you set the OBS to 205 degrees, and keep the needle deflected to the right of center, you'll stay in the clear.

VFR Flight Log

Departure: Westchester County (HPN)
Destination: Westchester County (HPN)

FIXES	ROUTE MAG COURSE	NAUT. MILES	ESTIMATED GROUND SPEED (KT)	TOTAL TIME	ACTUAL TIME
1. Depart Westchester, head west	255°		130 knots	3 (1)	
2. "End" of Hudson River	205° (2)	9		5	
3. George Washington Bridge		18		9	
4. World Trade Towers	205°	26.5		13	
5. Verazzano Narrows Bridge		36		19 (3)	
4. World Trade Towers		45.5		23	
3. George Washington Bridge		54		27	
2. "End of Hudson River	75°	63		31	
1. Arrive Westchester		72		35	

(1) Take-off, climb-out, and turn
(2) Initial heading; follow shoreline
(3) Includes 1 minute for 180° turn

Westchester County Airport
Coordinates: 41-04.0; 073-42.5
Location: 14 nm from Carmel VOR (CMK) 116.6, 216°
Elevation: 439 feet MSL
Pattern altitude: 1499 MSL
Runways: 11-29 4,451x150; 16-34 6,548x150
Tower: 119.7

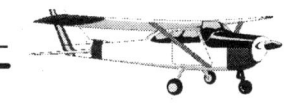

After you complete your trip back up the river and reach the end of the river, you'll turn north of east on a heading of 75°, and then watch for the airport. To make sure that you don't overshoot it, you'll use the NAV2 radio tuned to the Carmel VOR on 116.6. Set the OBS to 40 degrees, and the needle should center just before you reach the airport. If the needle centers and you don't see the airport yet, it is either to your right or left. Look out the side windows or fly along headings of 40 and 220 degrees with the NAV2 OBS needle centered and you should find the airport sooner or later. When you do find it, you can assume that the tower has cleared you to make a left-hand pattern approach and landing for Runway 29, so you can plan on entering the pattern on the downwind leg.

A LOOK AT THE LOG

I have prepared a flight log for you. The Fixes column lists the departure and destination points, as well as turning points and visual checkpoints along the route. The Route columns list the magnetic course for the leg, and the cumulative distance (in nautical miles) between points in the log.

The Estimated columns include the Ground Speed and Total Time entries. Since I've planned this flight for calm wind conditions, the ground speed will equal the airspeed, so there's only one entry in that column. You want to enjoy the scenery, so I've planned on 130 knots for the Cessna 182.

Note that I only planned one minute for your take-off and climbout; you won't need much more than this because your cruise altitude will be so low and because you'll be launching in your direction of travel.

The Actual column is for you to use. Use a stopwatch or the clock on the airplane's panel to keep track of the elapsed time, and enter the time at each point of the trip. You'll know when you should be coming up on the next checkpoint or turn, which helps you stay "ahead of the airplane" by anticipating the next step before its time comes. Keep in mind that the estimated times are based on when you *pass* the point, not when you first see it.

The flight log also helps you measure your performance, by seeing how well your times match the predicted times. If you can touchdown at Westchester within a few minutes of the predicted time, you're doing very well.

The four checkpoints are straightforward for this trip. The "end" of the Hudson marks the end of the river in the default scenery. The George Washington Bridge is the only road that crosses the Hudson to Manhattan, and the World Trade Towers are a pair of skyscrapers that are close together near the southern tip of Manhattan. The Verrazano Narrows Bridge is at the mouth of the Hudson where it meets the Atlantic.

READY TO ROCK AND ROLL

Before you can blast off, you need to set a number of items, the first of which is your location. You could take off from Meigs and fly all the way to Westchester first, but that would take a rather long time. You could also use the menu command World Airports to put your aircraft directly at Westchester if the airport were listed there, but it's not. So you'll have to use the World Set Exact Location menu command, which will open a dialog box on the screen. Make sure that the top line reads "Set Location of: Aircraft" and then enter the following:

      North/South Lat.: N041 03 52.5
      East/West Lon.: W073 42 2.8
      Altitude (ft): 442
      Heading: 300°

When you choose OK on the dialog box, you should find yourself positioned at the end of Runway 29 in Westchester.

Next, set the radios. To be absolutely faithful to reality, you would have to contact Ground Control and the Tower at Westchester in order to take off, but we'll skip that for now. Instead, tune your COM1 to 123.05 which is the frequency for self-announcing your position as you fly along the corridor. In real life, you'd also be paying close attention to the position calls of other aircraft on that frequency. Set NAV1 to 115.40 and the OBS to 205, and NAV2 to 116.6 with the OBS at 040—notice that the needle on NAV2 is deflected to the left of center, which means you'll cross that radial soon after you take off. Because this is a VFR flight, set your transponder to the VFR squawk code of 1200. You'll also want to be as visible as possible, so make sure that both your Strobe and Lights are on.

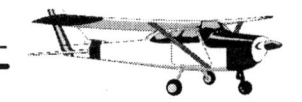

Finally, let's add a little spice to the flight. The Manhattan skyline is impressive during the day, but it gets positively breathtaking from sunset to dusk. (Incidentally, this is the time of day that I first flew this route, as I was finishing off my final preparation for my pilot's license checkride.) So use the World Set Time and Season menu command to open its dialog box, and use Set Exact Time to set Hours to 18 (which is 6 PM) and Minutes to 15. Check the Set Season box and make sure it is set to the default setting, Spring.

RUNNING THE RIVER

So now you should be all set to launch. Take off, follow your flight log, and be prepared for a sight-seeing treat. Remember to watch your altitude and to look out for other traffic, pay close attention to your ground track so you stay out of restricted airspace, and be prepared for it to get a bit dark before you get back to the airport—night landings can be a bit trickier than daylight landings.

If you want to add to the challenge, dial in 10 to 15 knots of wind out of the west (270° magnetic) so you have to compensate for drift as you travel up and down the river.

In any event, you're likely to find that you have your hands full on this flight. Don't forget to take the time to enjoy the sights, however, and wave to all those tourists stuck on the ground at the Statue of Liberty. They'll be wishing they could enjoy the view from your seat!

🖫 Situation file: XC-NY1

New York Flight 2

Buzz Over to Block Island

The Massachusetts vacation spots of Cape Cod, Martha's Vineyard, and Nantucket are internationally known. Not as many people know about Rhode Island's little gem in the Atlantic Ocean, which has some of the most delightful beaches in the northeast: Block Island. It's easy to reach by air, however, and is a favorite spot for area pilots.

STRONG, SILENT TYPE

In a departure from most of the flight plans in this book, you won't be departing from the same place you ended the last flight; since that one started and ended at Westchester, I decided that you should get to see a different starting point for this flight. You'll begin this trip at Bridgeport in Connecticut where you'll want a COM radio to chat with Bridgeport Ground and Tower, but you won't need any navigation radios for this flight—you'll be relying on the Mark I Eyeball to find your way to the destination.

The only tricky part is tracking your course with a wind present. There is a steady breeze blowing out of the west (not unusual for the area in some seasons), and you'll have to compensate on some legs.

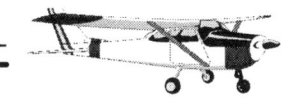

I've set the wind to be "straight down the numbers" at Block Island, but if you want a more realistic experience landing at the Crosswind Capital of New England (and you have a set of rudder pedals to give you the control you'll need), try swinging the wind around to the northwest—a more accurate heading for the region's winds.

The other concern that governs the routing for this trip is the fact that Block Island shares one attribute with most other islands; it is surrounded by water. While you could just launch and head straight for it, I'll keep you flying over land as much as possible so that you have a chance at finding a dry place to set down in the unlikely event of an emergency.

PICKING A ROUTE

The scanned section of a chart is from the WAC (World Aeronautical Chart) for Long Island Sound, and I've marked the chosen route and major checkpoints along the way. Note that the scale is twice that of a normal sectional chart, and you may find it easier to navigate with a sectional if you can get your hands on one.

In order to stay near dry land, there are two routes you could pick. First, you could stay over the Connecticut shoreline until you reach New London, and then cross over to Block Island. Another option is to cross over to Long Island first, then fly out to the tip of Montauk and on to Block Island.

The second route has a few strikes against it. First, it involves two over-water legs of about a dozen miles each, compared with a single 16 mile leg (which you could make as short as eight miles if you want to minimize the over-water time). Second, you'd be flying over some densely-populated portions of Long Island, and could encounter some traffic congestion over Long Island Mac Arthur (ISP) airport in Islip (with its Class C airspace), Francis Gabreski airport in Westhampton Beach (FOK) and the Navy Calverton Peconic field (CTO) near Riverhead. So I'll stick with the simpler route and stay over Connecticut.

NY 2

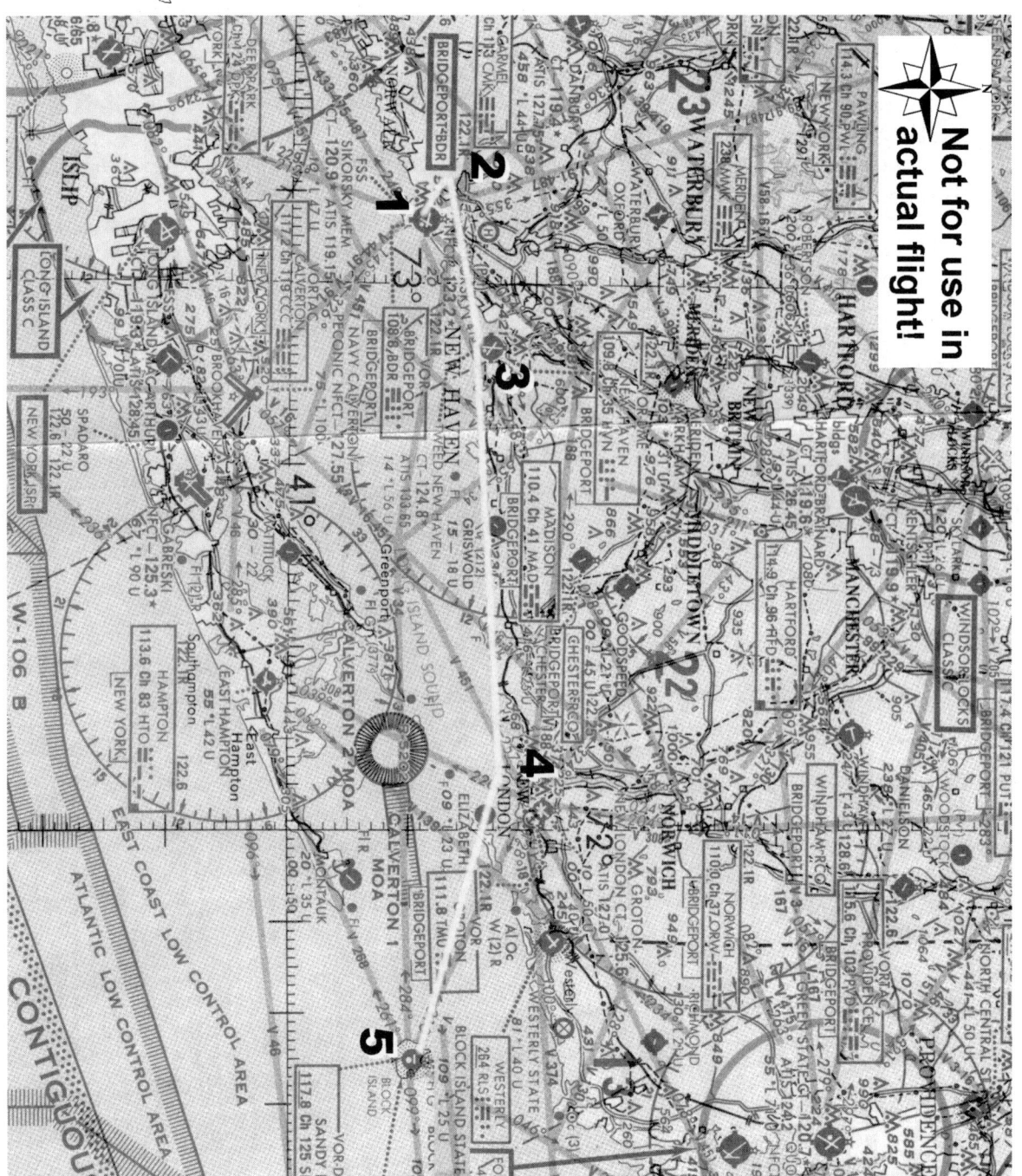

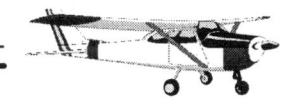

If you have a sectional to refer to, you'll see blue dotted circles around Bridgeport and Tweed New Haven airports that are not shown on the WAC here; these indicate Class D airspace. The New Haven circle has a broken box with the number [25] inside it, which signifies that the Class D area extends up to 2,500 feet above sea level; if you are higher than that, you don't need to communicate with the New Haven Tower. I'll plan the flight to be above that level before you get to New Haven. (In the real world, it would be a good idea to check in with New Haven anyway, just to let them know that you're passing overhead.)

I have prepared a flight log for this trip that shows your route and the checkpoints; it's pretty simple compared with some of the other flights in this book. You'll take off from Bridgeport's Runway 29 (which will be the active if the winds are from 280 magnetic), climb to 1,000 feet before starting a turn to the right, then continue climbing as you fly toward New Haven. Make sure you're above 2,500 feet before you get within five miles of New Haven, and continue climbing to your cruise altitude of 5,500. I picked that altitude because when traveling between 0 and 180 degrees, you should fly at an odd thousand plus 500 feet. 3,500 feet is a bit low because it can make spotting your checkpoints more difficult, and you don't want to be too low when it comes time for your water-crossing. On the other hand, it's not really worth climbing all the way up to 7,500 feet for this short a flight, so 5,500 feet is a good choice.

I've already entered the headings and estimated ground speeds based on an 80 knot climbing airspeed, 130 knot cruise, and a 15 knot wind at 280 degrees magnetic. If you change any of these parameters for your flight, you will need to recompute the wind corrections and ground speeds.

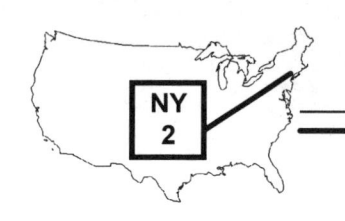

VFR Flight Log

Departure: Bridgeport Sikorsky (BDR)
Destination: Block Island (BID)

Fixes	Route Mag Course	Naut. Miles	Estimated Ground Speed (Kt)	Total Time	Actual Time
1. Depart Bridgeport, climb to 1,000 feet	290°		65		
2. Right turn toward New Haven	65°	2	92	2	
3. Tweed New Haven Airport; follow coastline east	100°	14	145	12	
4. New London, Fisher's Island	120°	51	143	27	
5. Arrive Block Island Airport		65		37 (1)	

(1) Plus 3 to 5 minutes to enter pattern and land

Bridgeport Sikorsky Airport (BDR)
Coordinates: 41-09.81; 073-07.57
Location: Bridgeport VOR (BDR) 108.0 on the field
Elevation: 10 feet MSL
Pattern altitude: 1010 MSL
Runways: 11-29 4,761x150; 6-24 4,677x150
Tower: 120.9 (6:30 am to 10 pm); CTAF: 120.9
Notes: Right traffic Runway 29

Block Island Airport (BID)
Coordinates: 41-10.09; 071-34.67
Location: NDB 117.8 on field
Elevation: 105 feet MSL
Pattern altitude: 1105 MSL
Runways: 10-28 2,501x100
UNICOM/CTAF: 123.0
Notes: Deer reported in vicinity.

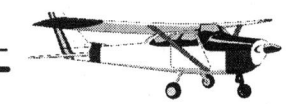

Over New Haven, turn and follow the shoreline to the east. In real life, you would have Interstate 95 visible to follow, but in the default FS5.1 scenery the road peters out somewhere near Guilford. Just stick to the shoreline, and watch for the large physical features to mark your route. About 25 miles after New Haven, you'll find a sharp inlet that marks the mouth of the Connecticut River (near Old Lyme). And 12 miles further on, you'll come to the mouth of the river at New London and Groton; you'll also see Fisher's Island to your right. Turn and cross over Fisher's Island and you should see Block Island to the southeast. Don't be fooled by Montauk point which will be to your south—that's not where you want to go.

The pattern altitude at Block Island is 1,105 feet, so you'll need to descend to that altitude before you get there. Assuming that you set up a 500 foot per minute descent rate while maintaining the same cruise airspeed (which you can do by cutting back on the throttle instead of pushing the nose over), you'll need about 9 minutes to make the descent. Since the estimated time for the last leg is 10 minutes, plan on making your turn at Fisher's Island and then starting your descent once you get settled on course. Once you get to the island, set yourself up for a left downwind entry for Runway 28, and take it on in for a landing.

PREFLIGHT PREPARATION

Positioning your aircraft is easy; simply choose the World Airports command from the menu, then Choose USA - New York as the scenery area, and then Bridgeport Sikorsky - Runway 29 as the airport you want to fly from, and choose OK.

Then use the World Weather command to set the winds. Choose the Winds button, then the Create button. Choose the Surface Wind option and these settings:

    Type: Steady
    Depth (ft): 10000
    Speed (kts): 15
    Direction (Mag): 280
    Turbulence: 1

Note that if you choose Winds Aloft instead of Surface Wind, you will be asked to specify the direction in terms of True instead of Magnetic.

If you want to add some challenges to this flight, try changing the wind direction as mentioned earlier. Or change your take-off time to 6:00 PM (1800 hours) and see if you can find Block Island before it gets too dark. Or add a broken cloud deck between you and the ground to provide an extra challenge. Enjoy your trip, and don't get too much sand in your picnic!

🖫 Situation file: XC-NY2

New York Flight 3

Confronting A Fog

"Time to spare, go by air."

That's the credo of the small airplane pilot—because there are myriad details that can slow you down or delay your progress. Another important saying to remember is "It's better to be on the ground wishing you were up in the air, than the other way around!"

This Cross Country flight will provide a new test for your VFR flying skills. The last flight ended on Block Island, which is surrounded by Block Island Sound. As is sometimes the case with bodies of ocean water, weather conditions frequently create low clouds and fog. For your departure from Block Island, you'll be faced with a real go/no go decision, and should you decide to launch, you may find yourself wishing you were back on the ground.

WEATHER OR NOT

For this trip, you'll be flying to Southbridge Municipal Airport, just over the northeast corner of Connecticut in Massachusetts. The town is southwest of Worcester, but is perhaps best known for its exit on the Mass Turnpike where I-84 branches off towards Hartford and New York. And don't confuse it with Stockbridge, MA, of "Alice's

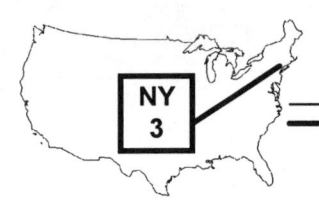

Restaurant" fame; if you want a meal at the Southbridge Airport, try the Windsock Diner located right on the field.

The route is fairly straightforward. Since there are not a lot of pilotage landmarks to use on this trip, I'll plot a simple course with two legs—both based on the same VOR. But navigation is not going to be the issue, at least not at the start. Before you can get off the ground, you'll have to cope with the weather.

So here you sit on Block Island, staring up at the sky and not liking what you see. What you'll see is not the standard Flight Simulator "severe clear"; instead, there are clouds above you and not that far above you, for that matter. Look to the west, and the weather doesn't seem to be that bad—there seem to be plenty of holes in the cover—but looking to the north where you want to go, it looks like the cloud deck may be filling in.

Checking the current weather observations, you find out that it's clear in Hartford and Boston, and there's a low, thin, broken layer over Providence. So it sounds a lot like this is a localized condition. Sitting around the pilots' lounge, you find that the opinions range from forget flying today, to wait a few hours and maybe it will burn off, to go for it—find a hole to climb through and you'll be able to fly on to your destination without a hitch.

Now, if you're a student pilot, you are not allowed to fly solo without being able to see the ground. This is generally a good idea for non-instrument rated pilots as well, even though it is legal to fly VFR over a solid deck of clouds. The reason that you might want to be more cautious than the law requires is that an engine failure or other emergency could leave you with no way out except through the clouds—and you have no idea what's under them.

Fortunately, a few pilots have just landed after completing IFR approaches to the island, and they all tell you that there seem to be plenty of holes to get up and down through, and the tops of the clouds seem to be at around 1,000 feet, so you should be able to climb and cruise above them with no problem.

You decide to take a look for yourself. What will you find?

Not for use in actual flight!

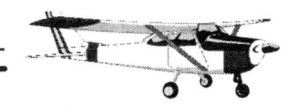

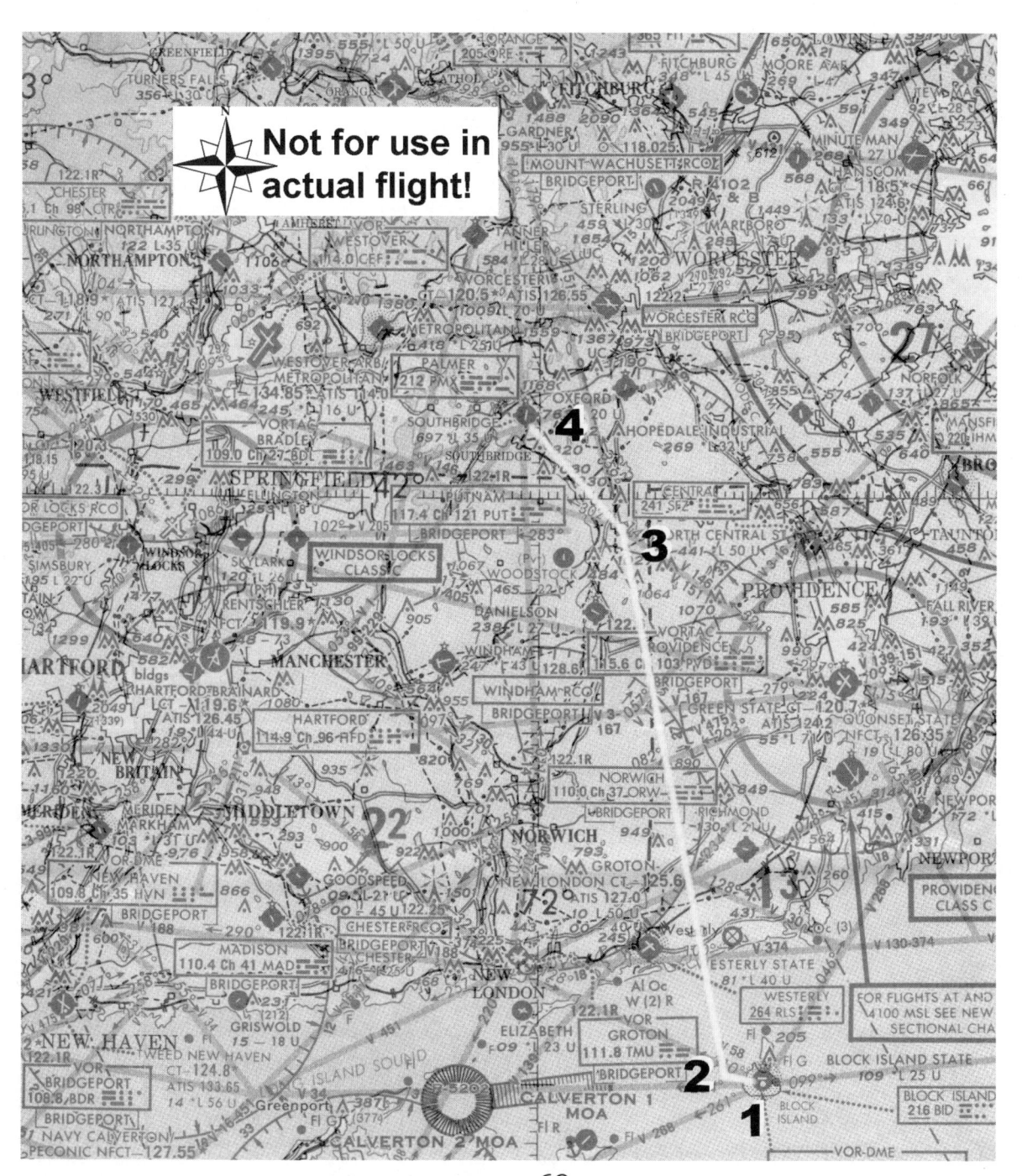

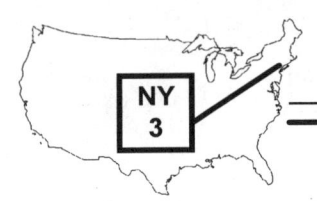

PLANNING A ROUTE

The portion of the World Aeronautical Chart (WAC) for the area shows your route. At this scale, the crowded New England region results in a fairly cluttered chart; for more detail and a clearer picture, you might prefer to use the New York sectional instead, though that chart has its own problem in that you have to flip from one side to the other midway through your flight.

The only special-use airspace that you have to be concerned with in our planning is the Class C circle around Green State Airport in Providence, Rhode Island. (The airport is not included in the default scenery for the floppy disk version of FS 5.1, but it is present on the CD-ROM version in the North American scenery. If you should see the airport as you fly past it, it might be because you have the CD-ROM scenery enabled.)

Fortunately, a straight shot from Block Island to the Putnam VOR (117.4 PUT) keeps you well to the west of the Providence Class C. Before you take off, you'll tune your NAV2 radio to this beacon, and set the OBS to 360, since that will be about the correct heading. Once you have completed your climb out and managed to get clear of the clouds, you can then center the needle using the OBS adjustment and fly direct to the VOR.

Once you reach the VOR, you'll turn to a heading of 329° magnetic, and Southbridge will be 12.3 miles ahead. Watch the DME readout for NAV2 as you fly along; if it gets to 12 miles and you haven't spotted the field yet, you might want to double-check your navigation.

Southbridge has a grass Runway 10-28 and a paved 3,500-foot Runway 2-20 that is 75 feet wide. Field elevation is 697 feet, with pattern altitude at 1,697 MSL. I'll plan on a relatively low cruising altitude—3,500 feet—for the trip and our standard Cessna 182 cruise of 130 knots. This means that you'll need to lose nearly 2,000 feet, and at a standard 500 fpm descent rate, this means that you'll need to start letting down four minutes from the pattern, or about 10 miles from the field. Since the airport is just 12.3 miles from the VOR, you may as well plan to start your descent right when you make your turn so you are stabilized at pattern altitude well before you get to the field. When you reach the field, enter on a 45-degree angle for a left-downwind leg for Runway 20.

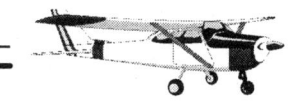

I have worked up a flight log for the flight; it's a bit simple compared with some of our other flights in the past. But don't worry; you still have the weather to confront.

GETTING READY TO FLY

The troublesome weather on this trip is made possible by the FS5.1 weather area feature, but it does take a bit more setting up than most Cross Country flights.

Start by choosing the Airport command on the World menu. Pick "USA - New York" as the scenery area, and then pick "Block Island State - Runway 28" from the list. This will place you at the end of Runway 28, ready to take off.

Next, choose Weather on the World menu. Then pick the Add Area button, which will open the Add Weather Area window. Give the area a name; I decided to use "Block Island Sound". In the "Beginning Lat:" box enter 41, and in the "Beginning Lon:" box, enter 71. For the "Width", enter 50, and for the "Transition", enter 5. Don't enter anything for any of the other fields on this window; just choose OK to close it.

Now make sure that you have Block Island Sound selected as the Weather Area on the Weather window. Make sure that the Clouds option is selected, then choose the Create button to create a new cloud layer. Leave the Type as "User-Defined", and give the layer a Base of 500 feet and Tops of 1,000 feet, with Coverage of "Broken 6/8" and a Deviation of 50 feet. (If you're feeling brave, increase the coverage to 7/8.) Then choose OK.

VFR Flight Log

Departure: Block Island (BID)
Destination: Southbridge Municiple (3B0)

Fixes	Route Mag Course	Naut. Miles	Estimated Ground Speed (Kt)	Total Time	Actual Time
1. Depart Block Island, climb to 1,000; remain clear of clouds	280°		65		
2. Right turn toward Putnam VOR (1)	360°	2	130	2	
3. Turn toward Southbridge, start descent	329°	51		25	
4. Arrive Southbridge		63		31 (2)	

(1) Continue climb to cruise altitude of 3,500 feet
(2) Plus 3 to 5 minutes to enter pattern and land

Block Island Airport (BID)
Coordinates: 41-10.09; 071-34.67
Elevation: 105 feet MSL
Pattern altitude: 1105 MSL
Runways: 10-28 2,501x100
UNICOM/CTAF: 123.0
Notes: Deer reported in vicinity.

Southbridge Municipal Airport (3B0)
Coordinates: 42-06.06; 072-02.30
Elevation: 697 feet MSL
Pattern altitude: 1697 MSL
Runways: 2-20 3,500x75 asphalt; 10-28 1,450x100 turf
UNICOM/CTAF: 122.8

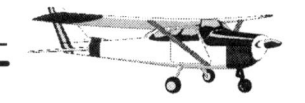

Back in the Weather window, pick Visibility, and set it to 20 miles for both the Global and the Block Island Sound weather areas. Choose OK when you're finished to close the Weather window.

On your cockpit panel, the NAV1 should be set to 117.8, which is the Block Island VOR. Leave this set as it is, just in case you decide you want to return to the island instead of continuing your trip. Set NAV2 to 117.4 for the Putnam VOR and set the OBS to 360.

You may also want to check your Scenery Complexity choices from the Scenery menu; View 1 should be set to Very Dense for best effects. If you have the CD-ROM version, you can also use the Scenery Library command to turn off the North American extra scenery if you want.

There's one more option you might want to change at this point. Under the Preferences command on the Options menu, the Display screen has a Scenery Display Options button. Here you can select Wispy Cloud Effects and Cloud Thickness Effects. The Wispy Cloud Effects causes your view to be gradually obscured as you enter the edge of a cloud, just as it would in real life.

The Cloud Thickness Effects show how high the clouds rise above the base altitude; without this effect, you only see a "footprint" of the clouds, but cannot tell when you might fly into a portion of cloud rising about that footprint. Unfortunately, the thickness is portrayed using blocks that look like they were left strewn about by some celestial toddler, which is not realistic at all. In this particular case, however, you might want to enable this feature since you will need to know just where the clouds are so that you can avoid them as you climb out from the island.

If you want to add some more challenge, make your take-off time about 7:00 PM, so that you have dusk and darkness to deal with as well before you finish your trip.

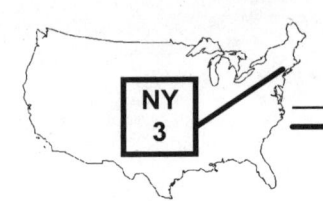

TAKE OFF!
    The weather reports say it's clear inland, and it sure looks like you should be able to climb out through one of these holes. So stay out of the clouds, and give them plenty of clearance to the sides and above so that you stay in legal VFR conditions. Make sure that you have some place in sight where you can set down in an emergency, and hope that the weather reports are true!

        🖫 Situation file: XC-NY3

Area D: San Francisco

If you left your heart in San Francisco, here are some trips that will let you search the area. With San Francisco International and Oakland Airports handling a steady stream of commercial jets, the Bay area is a bit congested for general aviation flights. Head out a bit towards the Sierra Nevada mountains, and you'll find wilderness and beautiful vistas to explore.

San Francisco Flight 1

Gold Rush!

Simulated flight may not be inexpensive—especially once you start adding flight controls and add-on scenery and all those other goodies—but it's nothing compared with flying in the real world. An hour in a Skyhawk at many airports costs more than the FS5.1 CD-ROM program. Wouldn't it be great to strike it rich, find the Mother Lode, and have all the flight time you wanted—both real and simulated?

Well, I can't promise you riches, but here's an entertaining diversion instead. Take a trip to California's gold country, and maybe some of the good fortune will rub off on you!

At first blush, this flight is remarkably straightforward. Take off, turn to a heading and climb to cruise altitude, turn at a VOR, descend, enter the pattern, and land. There are a few twists in store, however, and you'll find out just how precisely you can control your plane.

The flight starts at Reid-Hillview airport, just south of San Francisco Bay in San Jose. The destination is Columbia Airport, nestled in the foothills of the Sierra Nevada mountains. The town of Columbia has a colorful history; it was one of the richest placer-mining centers during second half of the last century. A state park in the old business district includes renovated buildings of the period. As for lodging during your visit, you can follow the example of the miners of the old days—just bring along a bedroll, because you can camp beneath the wing of your airplane at the airport for just $5 a night.

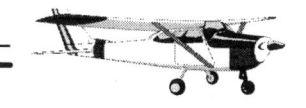

PLANNING THE FLIGHT

You'll be departing from Runway 31R at Reid-Hillview. While you could head directly for Columbia, I'll plan your flight to use a VOR near the mid-point just to make the navigation easier. (There are not a lot of visual checkpoints available in the default scenery along this route.) The Manteca VOR near Stockton makes a perfect mid-point.

Runway 31R has a right-hand traffic pattern, which is just as well since you want to head northeast, and you'll also want to avoid the San Jose International Class C airspace to the west.

The scanned section of the chart shows your planned route. Since you will be flying more than 80 nautical miles—almost in a straight line—I do not have room on the page to show the regular sectional chart to scale. Instead, I have used a World Aeronautical Chart (WAC) that has twice as big a scale.

Even at this larger scale, you can see a lot of light-colored areas northeast of the Reid-Hillview. This indicates high terrain, and in this case, it's the Diablo Mountain Range. You could take the time to go around it to the north or south, but that would add time. If you're careful, and can accurately control your airspeed in the Cessna 182, you can climb right over the range and take a direct route to the Manteca VOR.

SF 1

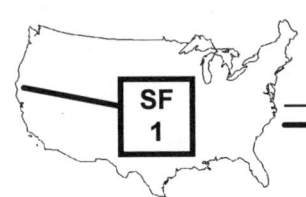

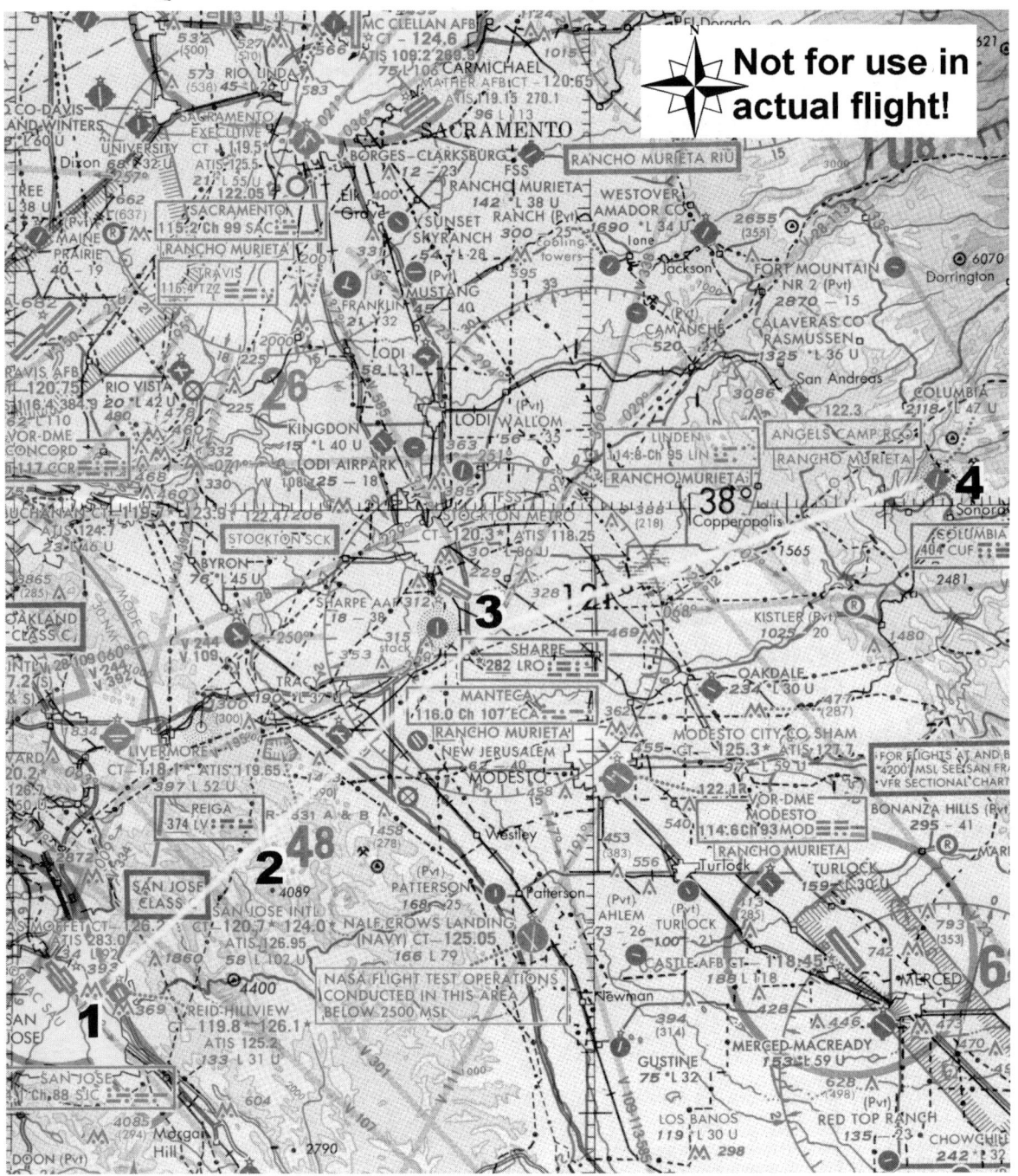

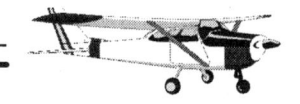

The course from Reid-Hillview to the Manteca VOR is 30 degrees magnetic, so once you're close to pattern altitude after take off, you can turn to that heading. The next question is how high to climb.

The highest point in the Diablo Range is Mount Hamilton at 4400 feet, but you'll pass north of that. You will still have to clear a 4089 foot high spot, however. But you'll want to climb even higher that.

In getting the weather briefing for this flight, you have received information about the winds aloft. These are reported in terms of altitude, direction, and true heading (as opposed to magnetic heading). I'll get to the details later, but there are some strong winds out of the west and they get stronger as you go higher, so we should plan to take advantage of them.

The hemispheric rule for VFR flights calls for eastbound flights to travel at odd thousands plus 500 feet. You could stop at 5,500 feet, but to take full advantage of the wind, I've planned on an altitude of 7,500 feet.

There's a second advantage to the higher altitude; engine efficiency. The air is thinner, so you experience reduced drag, but this also means that there are fewer oxygen molecules available to burn in the engine. For maximum efficiency, you can lean the gas/air mix so you get the most miles per gallon. (In real planes, the goal is to minimize the gallons burned per hour, rather than miles per gallon, since the miles can be affected by external factors such as winds.) You'll take advantage of that on this flight, too.

Once you reach the Manteca VOR, you'll turn toward Columbia. I have planned on using the VOR for a back-bearing, but how can you find the field? It may be difficult to see in the figure, but the Columbia Airport symbol is surrounded by tiny magenta dots, which indicates the presence of a non-directional radio beacon, or NDB. You can track this using an automatic direction finder, or ADF. Unlike the VOR indicator which tells you whether or not you are on track, all the ADF can do is point toward the NDB. Go where the arrow points, and you'll find the airport.

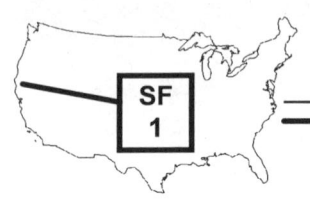

VFR Flight Log

Departure: Reid-Hillview (RHV)
Destination: Columbia (O22)

FIXES	ROUTE		ESTIMATED		ACTUAL
	MAG COURSE	NAUT. MILES	GROUND SPEED (KT)	TOTAL TIME	TIME
1. Depart Reid-Hillview	30°		70	1 (1)	
2. Cross the Diablo Range		17	130	15.5	
3. Cross Manteca VOR	55°	43	150	27.5	
4. Arrive Columbia		81		42.5 (2)	

(1) Take-off and, climb-out
(2) Plus 3 to 5 minutes to enter pattern and land

Reid-Hillview Airport (RHV)
Coordinates: 037-20.0; 121-49.1
Elevation: 136 feet MSL
Pattern altitude: 1133 MSL
Runways: 13L-31R 3,101x75; 13R-31L 3,099x75
Tower: 119.8

Columbia Airport (O22)
Coordinates: 038-01.9; 120-24.9
Elevation: 2118 feet MSL
Pattern altitude: 3112 MSL
Runways: 17-35 4,660x75 asphalt; 11-29 2,600x100 turf
UNICOM/CTAF: 123.0

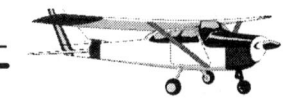

Finally, when you arrive at Columbia, you'll have a choice of runways. If you want to practice soft field landings, try Runway 29, a 2,600 foot long turf strip. Otherwise, take Runway 35 which is paved. The pattern altitude is 3112 feet, with standard left-hand traffic. Oh yes, one more detail—try not to fly too far east past the airport; the Linden MOA (Military Operations Area) starts about five miles east of the field, and you don't know if it is "hot" or not.

FLYING THE LOG

The flight log is unusually short for this flight, mainly because there are not many visual checkpoints available along the route. The few points that do exist deserve some additional comments and advice, however.

First, you will need to trim your airplane for 70 knots on the initial climb if you are going to make it over the mountain range. You can use the side view to see when you cross over the top, but you won't want to waste any altitude pushing the nose over for a peek on the way up. (There should be plenty of mountain filling your windshield to keep the palms moist, even without nosing over.)

Start leaning the engine once you pass about 3,000 feet, and check it again every 1,000 to 1,500 feet you climb. (See Appendix C for information on how to use the mixture control.)

When you reach 4,500 feet, you know that you will safely clear the top of the mountain range; transition to a cruise climb by trimming for an airspeed of 80 knots. This gives better visibility over the nose so you can spot other traffic more easily, and increases the airflow through the engine which helps keep cylinder temperatures down.

As you get up into the wind, you'll have to account for drift. In order to keep the OBS needle lined up, you'll actually have to aim a bit to the north of your intended track—by as much as 15 to 20 degrees. If you notice the needle starting to edge away from the center, change your course by five to ten degrees in the direction it has moved. Once you stop the movement, you know how much correction is required. Then overcorrect until the needle centers, and then swing back to the corrected heading.

When you reach the cruise altitude of 7,500, throttle back to around 2300 rpm or so and trim your plane for 130 knots and level flight. See if you can get it stable enough to fly steady without your touching the controls. By the way, it can be interesting to see just how much of kick in the tail you're getting from the winds aloft. If you are flying directly toward (or away from) a VOR with DME capability, you can read your ground speed on the DME readout. Assuming that you are heading for the VOR tuned on NAV1, press F then 1 to select the DME readout, then press the Equal Sign key to toggle back and forth between distance from the VOR (in nautical miles) and ground speed to or from the VOR (in knots). The speed readout can take a little while to settle on a number (and it helps to be flying straight and level to get an accurate reading) but you'll soon see your true speed over the ground.

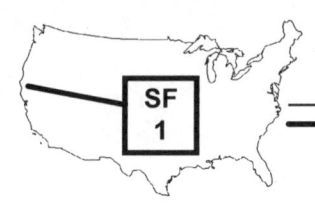

As you approach the Manteca VOR, you'll see colorful fields in the San Joaquin River Valley. When you reach the VOR, Stockton Metro airport will be close by on the left side; it's easy to recognize by its parallel runways of different lengths. Note that VOR DME measures actual distance, so at your cruise altitude, you will still register as more than a mile away even when you are directly over it. If your DME reads less than 1.5 miles from the VOR as you pass it, you've done very well.

Then you'll turn to a heading of about 50 degrees (again, correcting for the wind drift) and should set the OBS on NAV1 to 55 degrees which you can use as a back-bearing. Your ADF needle should be pointing straight ahead, or a little to the right (again, compensate for the wind that is pushing you to the right). The wind will be mostly behind you at this point, so check the DME for your ground speed. (Wow! A Cessna with afterburners!)

Olympia is 38 miles from the VOR, so you can use the DME distance readout for an indication of when you get to the airport. However, you'll want to be at pattern altitude when you get there, so you need to figure out when you should start a standard 500 foot per minute (fpm) descent. Pattern altitude at Olympia is 3112 feet, so you have roughly 4,500 feet to lose, which will take nine minutes, so add one more to slow down for the pattern, and you should start your descent 10 minutes from the airport. If you are traveling at 150 knots, this would be 25 miles out, or 13 miles after turning at the VOR. Descend by slowing your engine by about 100 or 200 rpm without changing the trim; you should be able to find an engine speed that provides a 500 fpm descent while the plane continues to fly with an airspeed of 130 knots.

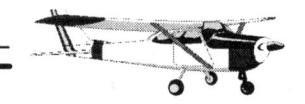

Don't forget to make sure you have the engine mixture full rich (handle all the way up) by the time you get into the pattern. When you get to the airport, enter a left downwind for your chosen runway, land, and break out the bedroll! Oh, and watch out—there have been reports of deer on the runway, so look carefully when you're on short final.

BEFORE YOU TAKE OFF

All that's left is to set up the instruments and some other details. First, let's get your airplane in position. Choose the World menu item, then Set Exact Location. On the screen that appears, enter the following items:

    North/South Lat.:   N037 19 48.3328
    East/West Lon.:   W121 48 59.4561
    Altitude (feet):   136
    Heading: 310

Choose OK. Now set the radios. Start by choosing the Nav/Com menu option, then ADF. On the screen that appears, enter a frequency of 404 (the NDB at Olympia) put a check in the box for Activate ADF gauge, then choose OK. When you see the panel again, you'll see that the NAV2 gauge has been replaced with the ADF.

Set COM1 to 126.1 (Reid-Hillview tower frequency), NAV1 to 116.00 (Manteca VOR) with the OBS heading 30. And set your transponder squawk code to 1200, which indicates a VFR flight.

Choose the Sim menu, then the Realism and Reliability item. Put a check in the box for Mixture Control to enable that feature, and then choose OK.

Now, the remaining tricky part is to set the winds aloft. Choose the World menu item, then Weather. On the screen that appears, choose Winds, then choose create. A new screen appears. Leave the Type as Steady, and enter a Base of 2500, Tops of 4500, Speed of 20 knots, and Direction of 270. Note that Direction is True, not Magnetic North. Leave the Turbulence setting at 1 for no turbulence). Then choose OK. Then use Create to make two more layers (all with a Type of Steady and no Turbulence):

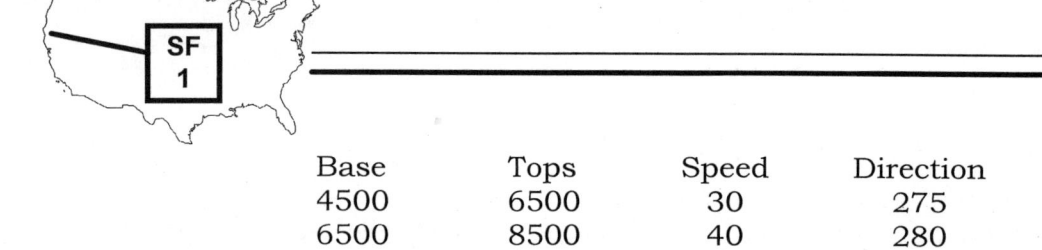

Base	Tops	Speed	Direction
4500	6500	30	275
6500	8500	40	280

So now you should be ready to head for them thar hills, and who knows? Maybe you'll find your pot of gold waiting for you when you land.

💾 Situation file: XC-SF1

San Francisco Flight 2

Lake in the Mountains

People often ask me whether it's easier or more difficult to fly FS5.1 than it is to fly a real plane. The answer is "both", and this cross-country flight demonstrates my ambivalent response. Some aspects of the flight will be much easier on your computer because you won't have to deal with some of the terrain and wind problems you would encounter in the real world, but the absence of topographical detail for the section you will fly over makes navigation a lot more difficult.

The previous flight ended up in Columbia, California—site of an old gold-mining town—and this flight will take you from there to the emerald in the state's sight-seeing treasures: Lake Tahoe.

The default scenery includes a number of airports in the region, including two near Reno, Nevada. We'll head for the one at the southern end of the lake, in the California town of South Lake Tahoe. Lake Tahoe airport has only one runway, 18-36, but it is 8,544 feet long—which is just as well given the field's 6,264 MSL elevation. The air is much less dense at that altitude, so you need more runway for take-off and landing than you would at sea level.

When you get to Lake Tahoe, there are plenty of things to do: excellent skiing conditions in the winter, and lots of summer outdoor activities such as a hike in to Vikingsholm, a recreation of a 9th-century Viking fortress. Or if you just want to take it easy by the largest alpine lake in North America, try camping at South Lake Tahoe City Beach.

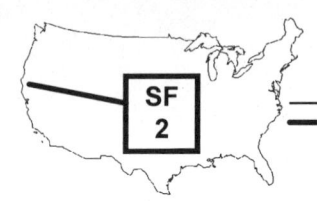

PLANNING A ROUTE

As the old commercial said, however, "getting there is half the fun" and this trip is no exception. The portion of the WAC (World Aeronautical Chart) for this region shows your route marked out on it. There are a number of important details to notice.

First and foremost, check out the dark, shaded land regions. Those indicate areas of high terrain. Right by the bend in the course there is a notation "6070". That is the altitude of a peak on a ridge at that location. Closer to Lake Tahoe, there's a peak near the route marked at 10,400 feet. So one of your first concerns will have to be gaining sufficient altitude.

Here's one place where real world flying is a little easier. The FS5.1 default scenery does not show the mountainous terrain. In the real world, you could simply keep track of ridges and fly up valleys and through passes to get where you want to go, but the FS5.1 scenery doesn't show these. Nor does it show the various roads and rivers indicated on the chart. As a result, you will have no visual checkpoints that you could use for pilotage. Since there is a 36 mile stretch that you have to fly by ded reckoning, this will be harder than it would be for real.

Also in the real world, you'd have a 22-mile long lake as a landmark, but the FS5.1 scenery doesn't include this either.

Not for use in actual flight!

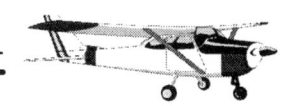

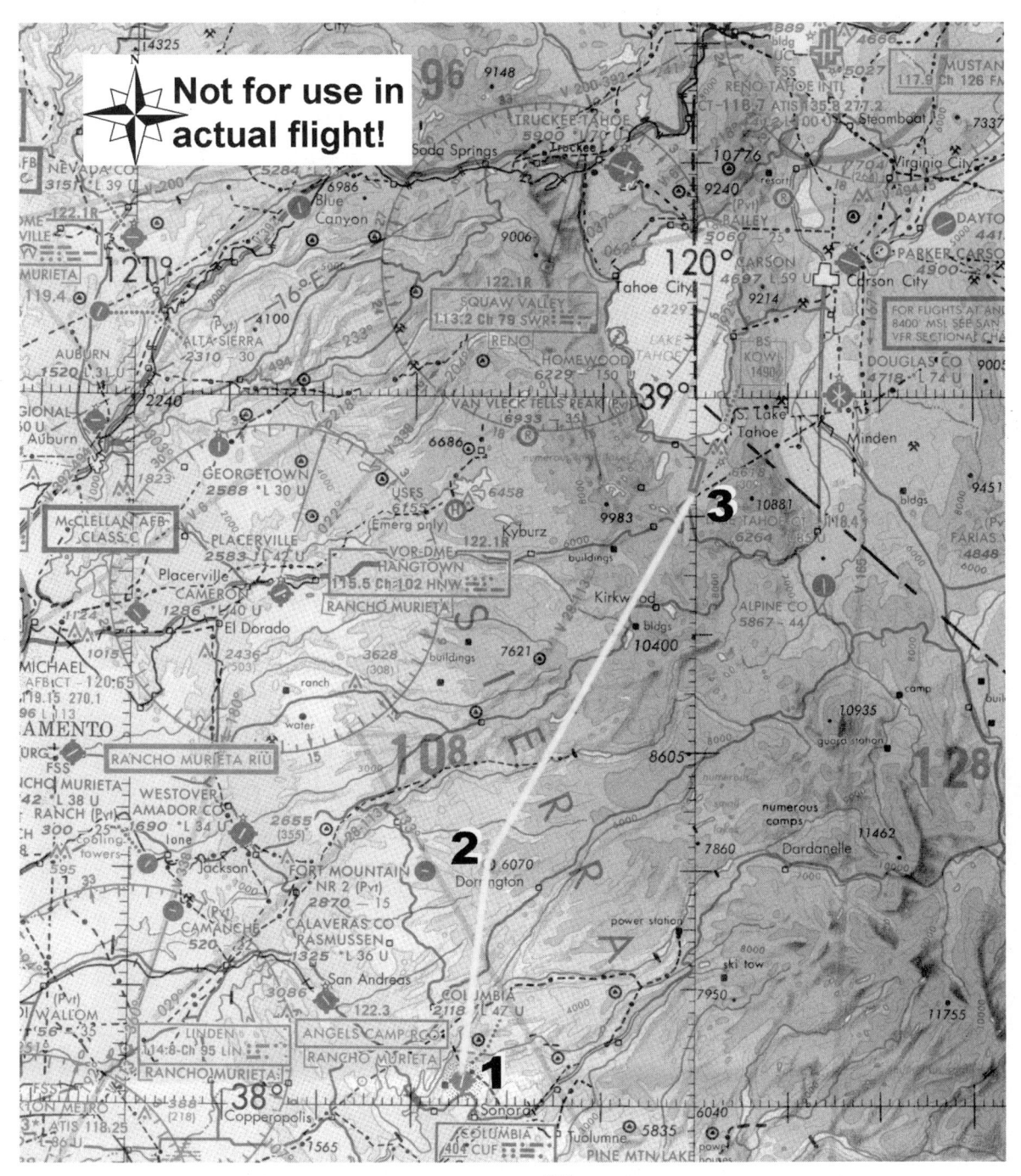

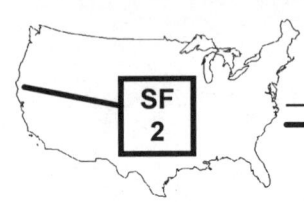

So if you can't use pilotage, how are you going to find your way from Columbia to Lake Tahoe? If there were a radio beacon (NDB or VOR) on the field at Lake Tahoe, you could just fly right to it... but there isn't. You could fly to a VOR and then head out on a course that would take you to the field, but that involves a lot of extra flying; the VOR nearest Lake Tahoe Airport is more than 21 nautical miles away.

The answer is that you can use the closest VOR, Squaw Valley (SWR 113.2), and your DME readout on your panel to find the airport. Consulting the AOPA Aviation USA airport directory (available from Sporty's), you can find a notation marked "Waypoint: SWR-113.2 127° 21.4". This indicates that the airport is located 21.4 nm from the Squaw Valley VOR along the 127° radial. By setting up your NAV radio correctly, you can pick an approximate course and then use the radio beacon to home in on the location.

There are other points to consider on the chart. For example, there is a large, cross-hatch bordered section northeast of Columbia, marked "LINDEN MOA". This is a military operations area. According to a notation elsewhere on the chart, it is active from 0500 to 2000 Monday through Friday and starts at 12,000 feet. You could probably cut across underneath this area, but to be extra cautious, I've planned the route to go around it instead. It only adds a few miles to the flight, and means that you won't have to be quite as concerned about encountering a jet fighter closing on your nose at rates exceeding 500 knots during your climb out.

To do this, you'll take off and head for the Squaw Valley VOR. When you have gone 18 miles, you will be able to turn and head for Lake Tahoe without cutting the corner on the Linden MOA. You can measure how far you have flown using the DME readout for the NAV radio. When you reach the turning point, Lake Tahoe should be on about a 10° Magnetic heading. The flight log that I have worked out for the flight shows these details.

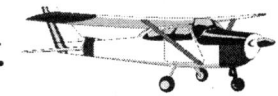

VFR Flight Log

Departure: Columbia (O22)
Destination: Lake Tahoe (TVL)

	ROUTE		ESTIMATED		ACTUAL
FIXES	MAG COURSE	NAUT. MILES	GROUND SPEED (KT)	TOTAL TIME	TIME
1. Depart Columbia	350°		65	1 (1)	
2. Turn toward Lake Tahoe	10°	18	140	17.5	
3. Arrive Lake Tahoe		54		33 (2)	

(1) Take-off and climb-out
(2) Plus 3 to 5 minutes to enter pattern and land

Columbia Airport (O22)
Coordinates: 038-01.9; 120-24.9
Elevation: 2118 feet MSL
Pattern altitude: 3112 MSL
Runways: 17-35 4,660x75 asphalt; 11-29 2,600x100 turf
UNICOM/CTAF: 123.0

Lake Tahoe Airport (TVL)
Coordinates: 038-53.63; 119-59.72
Elevation: 6264 feet MSL
Pattern altitude: 7500 MSL
Runways: 18-36 8,544x150
Tower: 118.4

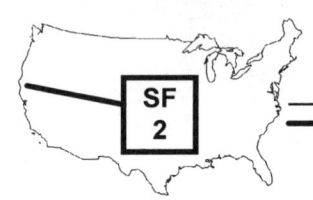

And finally, there's the question of how high to fly. Columbia is only at about 2,000 feet MSL, but Lake Tahoe is more than a mile up at 6,264, and is surrounded by hills as well. Since you'll be flying east of a northerly heading, and the VFR rule is odd thousands plus 500, we'll plan for 9,500 feet for your cruise altitude. (In real life, you'd use a sectional instead of the WAC to get better detail about terrain elevation, and you would plan the flight to follow contours and passes, but neither the WAC nor the FS5.1 default scenery provide this level of detail, so I will assume that this is a sufficiently safe altitude for your route—which is just one more reason why you should never use these flight plans for real-world flying.) Remember that the rules for altitudes don't start until you are 3,000 feet above ground level, but we'll follow the rule anyway.

Now here is a point where the simulator is easier than the real world. Flying in the mountains is tricky; you'll find updrafts on the upwind side of a ridge, and downdrafts on the downwind side, and often more turbulence than you want all around. FS5.1 ignores the effect of terrain on air masses, so you can settle down and enjoy a smooth flight.

LET THE WINDS BLOW

I am going to add some weather to complicate matters, however. Since you have to fly that long stretch without anything to guide you, calm conditions would mean that you could just point your nose on a heading and go for it. Instead, I'll add some winds aloft to give you a crosswind component to contend with.

I'll set up winds from 2,500 feet MSL to 10,000 MSL at a brisk 30 knots from 270°. Since Winds Aloft are entered as True headings, that translates to about 254° Magnetic (since the magnetic variation is about 16° East in that area).

This crosswind will have an impact on the courses you must fly. The first leg—toward the Squaw Valley VOR—requires a ground track of 350° Magnetic. Since you will be climbing out for most of this leg to reach altitude, we have planned on an airspeed of 70 knots. When you hit the level with the winds, that 30-knot breeze from the side is going to require a hefty correction; I estimate you'll need to head 333° Magnetic to keep the VOR needle centered.

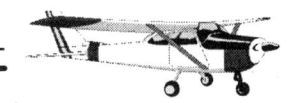

Once you reach cruise altitude and make the turn toward Lake Tahoe, I have planned on a cruise speed of 130 knots. The winds will be behind you giving a push, but you will still need to use a heading of about 357° Magnetic to maintain the desired 10° Magnetic heading for your ground track. The flight log reflects these wind corrections.

Note that I said you should use the east-of-north VFR altitude for your cruise altitude before, even though here the plan tells you to head *west* of north. The reason is that it doesn't matter where the pointy end of the plane is *headed*, what matters is where it *goes*. In this case, you are headed west of north, but your ground track will (or at least, should) be east of north, thus I chose the odd thousand plus 500 altitude.

And when you arrive at Lake Tahoe, the wind will be just about sideways to the runway, but slightly favoring Runway 18, so expect to enter a left downwind when you get to the pattern.

GETTING READY TO FLY

Start by putting your plane at Columbia Airport. Since there is no entry for this field in the World Airports menu, you will have to use the Set Exact Location command on the World menu to enter the following values:

```
North/South Lat.:    N038 01 27
East/West Lon.:      W120 24 51.9
Altitude (feet):     2121
Heading:             345
```

Using the Weather command on the World menu, choose Winds, then Create to create a new layer. Make sure that the Wind Aloft setting is checked, then choose Type as Steady, Base of 2500, Tops as 10000, Speed as 30, and Direction 270. Dial in as much or as little turbulence as you wish; but since you'll be landing in this wind layer when you reach Lake Tahoe, we recommend that you leave Turbulence set to its lowest setting for now.

On your control panel, set your transponder to the code for VFR flight: 1200. Tune your NAV1 radio to the Squaw Valley VOR, at 113.2, and turn the OBS heading to 350 which should center the needle with a "TO" indication on the gauge.

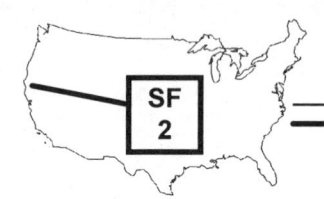

MAKING THE FLIGHT

You'll take off headed straight for the VOR. Note that the DME reading for the VOR is about 69 miles when you are at the field. As mentioned earlier, climb out at about 70 knots, and when you get to 51 miles from the VOR, you can make your turn to the north to go on course. At that point, adjust the OBS setting on your NAV1 so that it is at 307° (the reciprocal bearing for the 127° radial). When the needle is centered and your DME reads 21.4 miles, you should be right over the airport. Make sure that you descend to the 7500 foot pattern altitude before you get to the runway, and enter a left downwind for Runway 18.

One word of warning: FS5.1 has a magical "elevator" scenery effect, so be prepared for it. As you fly near the field (about pattern distance), the terrain will rapidly rise up to meet you. Fly away from the runway, and it will just as rapidly move back down. Don't let it throw you; just pay attention to your altimeter and don't be distracted by this weird visual effect.

And once you make it on the ground, prepare to park your plane and have some fun in the sun at Lake Tahoe.

Situation file: XC-SF2

San Francisco Flight 3

Big Mountains, Little Mountains

The last San Francisco area flight is a fairly simple, one-leg trip. The last flight ended up at Lake Tahoe, nestled among the mighty Sierra Nevada mountains. For this flight, you will head to Yuba County Airport in Marysville, California. One of the attractions in the Marysville area is the Sutter Butte, located about 15 miles from the airport. Sometimes billed as "the world's smallest mountain range", this is a collection of dark volcanic rock that rises nearly 2,000 feet above the otherwise level Sacramento Valley that surrounds it.

PLANNING A ROUTE

The detail from a WAC (World Aeronautical Chart) that we'll use for our flight planning shows your route. For more detail, use the San Francisco Sectional chart, which uses a scale twice as large as the WAC.

The first thing you may notice is the dark shading all around Lake Tahoe at the right of the chart. This represents ground with high elevation, which pilots sometimes refer to as "cumulo-granite"; trying to fly through mountains is not recommended. The mountain range rises to nearly 10,000 feet above Lake Tahoe Airport—your departure point—and you'll have to climb from the field elevation of 6,200 feet before you can head off over the mountains.

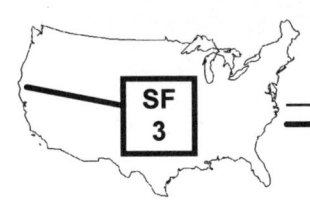

After you clear that first ridge, everything is downhill from there, to coin a phrase. The only other complication you'll have to contend with is not physical, but legal. Notice that near your destination airport, Yuba County, there is a magenta circle around Beale Air Force Base. This indicates that there is a Class C airspace surrounding this field, and you cannot enter this airspace unless you are in contact with the air traffic controller for that area.

Since we don't have simulated two-way radio for Microsoft Flight Simulator (well... at least we don't have it *yet!*), you won't be able to call up Beale Approach, and so you can't go into that Class C airspace.

A look at the sectional provides some useful additional information, however. The Class C airspace goes down to the ground surface only for a five mile radius (that's nautical miles) from the center of the Beale airfield, and for the next five miles, the airspace only starts at an altitude of 1,600 feet. So as long as you're down to about 1,500 feet altitude before you get to within 10 miles of Beale, you'll be okay. But in order to clear the five mile radius, you'll have to approach Yuba County from the southeast at a heading of 290° or greater. Yuba County is relatively easy to find, since it has the Marysville VOR right on the field.

Finally, you'll have to plan to start your descent well in advance. You'll have to lose more than 10,000 feet between the time you cross the mountain ridges and when your wheels finally touchdown at Yuba County, so we'll allow time for that in our flight plan as well.

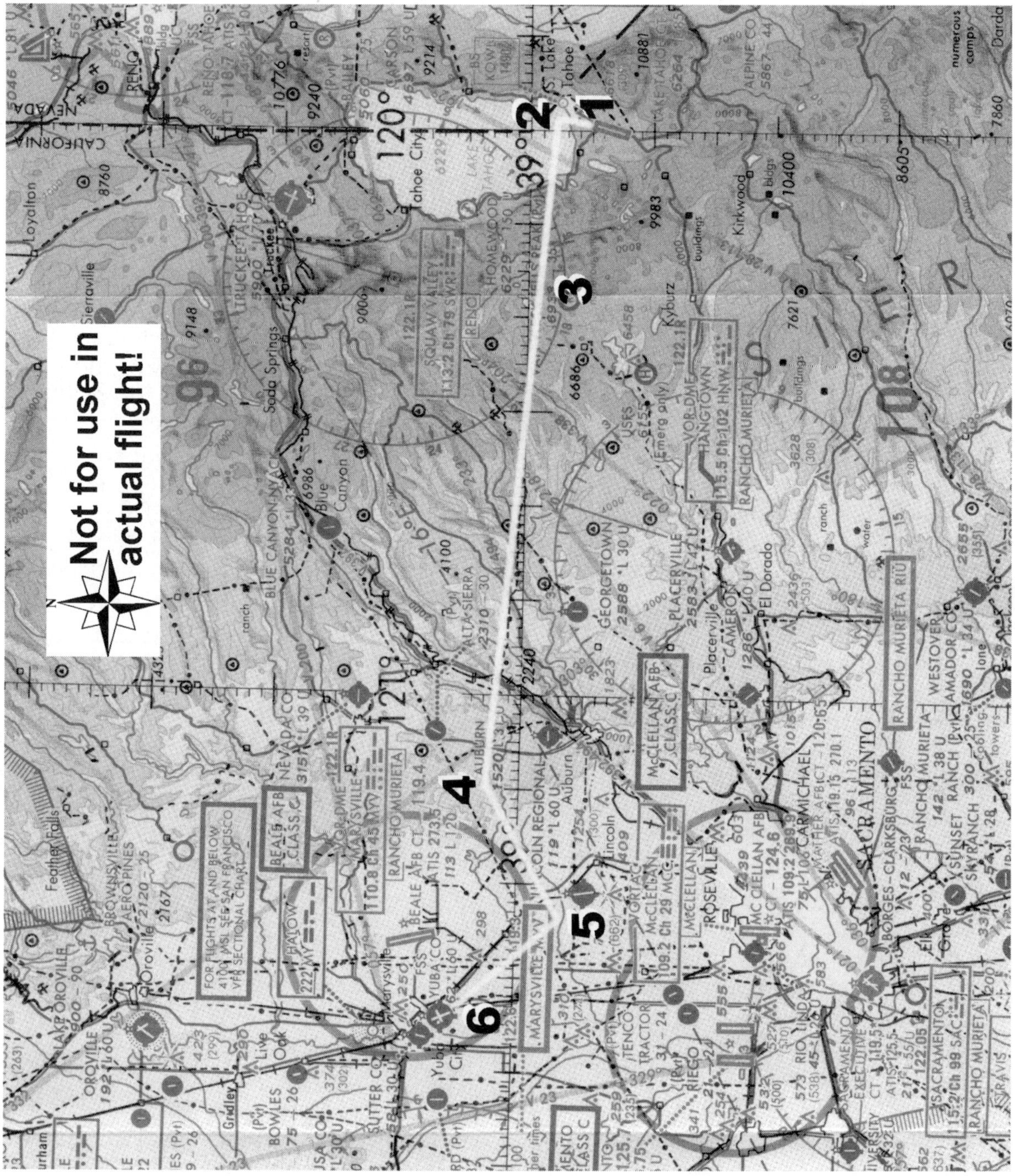
Not for use in actual flight!
1
2
3
4
5
6

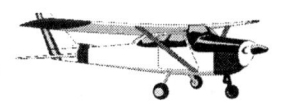

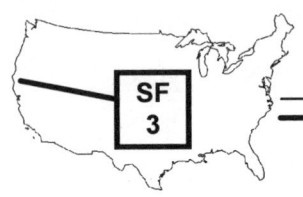

THE FLIGHT LOG

I have prepared a flight log for your trip. You'll start on Runway 36 at Lake Tahoe, taking off towards the lake. (The lake is not present in the FS 5.1 scenery, but you can pretend that it is there.) The field elevation is 6,200 feet, so don't be surprised if your take-off roll is longer than you are used to; the air is thinner at this altitude, so it takes a longer run to get up to speed.

You'll also need to manage your speed carefully if you are going to make it over the mountain ridge to the west of Lake Tahoe. Trim the airplane so it flies at 70 knots, which should give you a climb rate of about 500 feet per minute or better.

Head out over the lake, and climb to at least 7,200 feet before turning on course—your heading will be about 260° or so. Maintain your 500 fpm climb rate as best you can, because you have a lot of altitude to gain before you can get over the mountains.

If you have the Mixture Control feature turned on in the Realism and Reliability command on the Sim menu, be sure to lean your engine every thousand feet or so in your climb. If you don't, you might not generate sufficient power to make it over the mountains. Lean the engine by pulling back on the mixture control (the red knob) until the exhaust gas temperature (indicated by the EGT gauge on your control panel) hits a peak. Don't lean too much, or you'll reduce power instead of increasing it. And if you do adjust the mixture, don't forget to put it back to full rich before you get down to your landing pattern altitude at the end of the trip.

(If you see mountains around Lake Tahoe, then you probably have the FS 5.1 CD-ROM scenery enabled. If you don't have this scenery enabled, you won't see any mountains in the scenery, but you better climb anyway.)

How high should you climb? For VFR flights higher than 3,000 feet above the ground, you should travel at even thousands plus 500 when your heading is in the western half of the compass, and odd thousands plus 500 when headed in the eastern half of the compass. Since you'll be flying west, the first altitude that will get you over the rocks is 10,500, so climb to that altitude before leveling off.

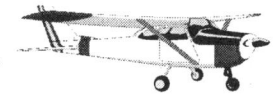

VFR Flight Log

Departure: Lake Tahoe (TVL)
Destination: Yuba County (MYV)

FIXES	ROUTE		ESTIMATED		ACTUAL
	MAG COURSE	NAUT. MILES	GROUND SPEED (KT)	TOTAL TIME	TIME
1. Depart Lake Tahoe	360°		65	1 (1)	
2. Climb to 7,200 feet; turn toward Marysville VOR	260°	2	70	2	
3. Level off at 10,500 feet		10	130	10	
4. 20 miles from Marysville VOR, turn to stay clear of Class C airspace	245°	54		30	
5. Intercept Marysville VOR 295° radial	295°	66		35.5	
6. Arrive Yuba County		74		39 (2)	

(1) Take-off, climb-out, and turn
(2) Plus 3 to 5 minutes to align with Runway 32 and land

Lake Tahoe Airport (TVL)
Coordinates: 038-53.63; 119-59.72
Elevation: 6264 feet MSL
Pattern altitude: 7500 MSL
Runways: 18-36 8,544x150
Tower: 118.4

Yuba County Airport (MYV)
Coordinates: 039-05.87; 121-34.19
Elevation: 62 feet MSL
Pattern altitude: 1063 MSL
Runways: 14-32 6,006x150; 5-23 3,281x150
CTAF: 119.3

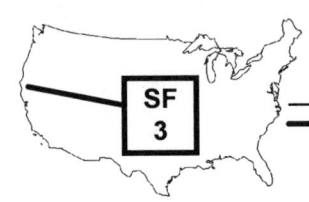

Watch out as you climb; if you use the default weather, there will be a broken cloud layer at 10,000 feet. Since you are flying under Visual Flight Rules (VFR), you must remain clear of the clouds. Find a hole to climb through in order to get on top of the layer, and then be careful not to fly over any clouds. (Unless you have the Cloud Thickness feature turned on, you won't be able to see how high they stick up, and you can fly into them inadvertently.)

Continue on at this heading at this altitude for about 10 minutes or until you are clear the mountains. Then descend back down to 8,500 feet so that you get back under the cloud layer and don't have to zigzag across the sky.

The pattern altitude for Yuba County is just over 1,000 feet, so you'll have to lose 7,500 feet of altitude before you get there. It's best to do this gradually over time rather than do an imitation of a falling brick at the last minute. A 500 fpm descent is a reasonable rate, so you will need to start at least 15 minutes before you reach the field. At 130 knots, this means starting about 35 miles from your destination. When the VOR DME readout for the Marysville VOR indicates 30 miles, just reduce your throttle to get the 500 fpm descent rate.

When the VOR DME readout shows about 20 miles, change the OBS setting to 295°; the needle will swing to the left of center. Change your course to 245° and continue straight until the OBS needle swings to the center of the gauge; it should start to show some movement after a few minutes on the new course.

When the needle centers, turn to a heading of 295° to follow the radial to the airport. When you see the field, you can swing over to the west a bit and line up for a straight-in approach for runway 32. Set up for your landing, and grease it on the runway to complete your trip.

GETTING READY TO FLY

There is no entry for Lake Tahoe on the World Airports list, so you'll have to use the Set Exact Location feature. Here are the values you will need to enter:

North/South Lat.:	038 52 58.1
East/West Lon.:	119 59 54.9
Altitude (ft):	6266

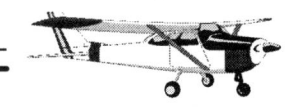

Heading: 360

These settings will put you on the displaced threshold of runway 36 at Lake Tahoe. While you are not supposed to land on a displaced threshold, you can use it for your takeoff run, and at this altitude, you'll want to use all the runway you have.

Tune your NAV1 radio to the Marysville VOR frequency of 110.80 (in the real world, you wouldn't be able to receive the signal until you clear the mountains, but FS 5.1 makes it a bit easier for you.) Set the OBS heading to 260°—the needle should be approximately centered on the gauge. And make sure that you have the DME readout for NAV1 showing nautical miles (and not speed in knots).

And with this, you should be ready to fly. Double check your settings, and then when you're ready, advance the throttle and take off! Just remember that if you can get over these big mountains in the beginning of the trip, you can go sight-seeing and visit the little ones at the other end.

▢ Situation file: XC-SF3

Section E: Seattle

What do you think of when you think of Seattle? Computer people tend to think of Microsoft. Aviation people tend to think of Boeing. Although it is true that I spend time with both computers and airplanes, I must confess that the fresh beer from the Pacific Northwest microbreweries and the wonderful seafood top the list of my favorite Seattle features. On the other hand, the incredible amounts of rain and cloudy weather that you get there makes one wonder when anyone gets enough VFR weather to learn to fly. If Microsoft could figure out a way to let Seattle residents pick their weather as easily as FS5.1 pilots can control their simulated weather, Bill Gates would become an even richer man.

Seattle Flight 1

Airport Hopscotch

It's a beautiful day in the Pacific Northwest; too good a day to waste indoors. So you decide to drive on over to Olympia Airport and go flying. When you check in at the local FBO, you discover that your favorite Cessna is due back from a lesson any minute now, and it is not booked to go out again until noon. It's almost 11:00 am, however, so you will have to have it back on the ground in an hour.

Sounds like a perfect day to play "airport hopscotch"!

THE ART OF GOING NOWHERE

Airport hopscotch is a game with loosely-defined rules. The basic object is to try to land at as many airports on one trip as you can. Some pilots add their own restrictions, such as it only counts if you land at an airport where you have never landed before. In this case, we've added the one-hour trip limit, and we'll impose some other restrictions in a minute.

The portion of the sectional shows a lot of airports located to the north and east of Olympia. Fortunately, most of these are also included in the FS5.1 default scenery for the Seattle area. The two major exceptions are the Gray and McChord military airfields. Since the residents of these two locations might take exception to being included in your game of hopscotch, it is just as well that they are not included in the scenery. Notice, however, that there are Restricted and MOA (Military Operations Area) airspace indications associated with these two airfields on the sectional, so you will have to take them into account in your planning.

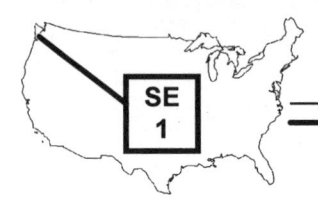

Unlike most Cross Country flights, I will not provide a VFR Flight Log for this trip. It is your responsibility to figure out which airports you are going to try to fly to, and in which sequence. To help you figure out your route, I have included a table of information about the four airports that are within reach that you might want to consider. The listings are arranged in alphabetical order. To simplify matters, I will assume that all landings (except your return to Olympia) and take-offs will be made on northerly runways.

MAKING PLANS

You'll depart from Runway 35 at Olympia, which will start you off in the right direction. But where will you go from there?

Spend a moment with the sectional and the airport table to plan your route. If you decide to go for Tacoma Narrows first, you can take a straight shot at it after take-off; the heading should be about 15° or so. If you decide to head for one of the other three fields first, however, you will need to skirt the MOA and Restricted airspaces. (According to the Seattle sectional, the MOA is only in use intermittently from 2,000 to 9,000 feet, but the Restricted areas extend from the surface to 5,000 or 14,000 feet, and some parts are in use from 7:00 am to 11:00 pm on weekdays, so I'll just play it safe and advise that you simply stay away from there.) If you stay to the northwest of the 25° outbound radial of the Olympia VOR (113.4) until you cross Interstate I-5, you'll stay clear of the restricted space. Then you can turn to a heading of about 60° to head for the airports in that direction.

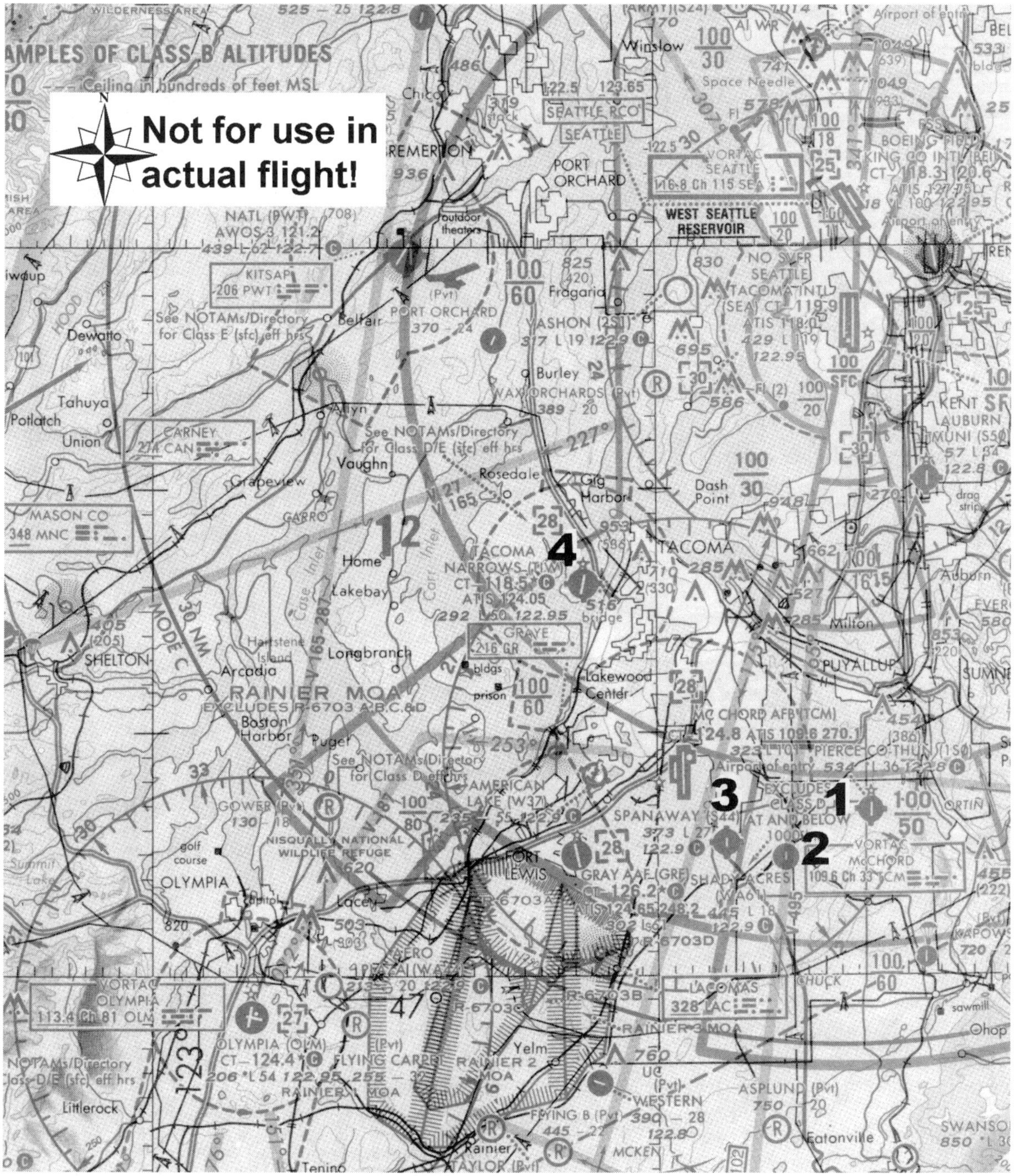
Not for use in actual flight!
N
1
2
3
4
EXAMPLES OF CLASS B ALTITUDES
Ceiling in hundreds of feet MSL
WILDERNESS AREA
Winslow
Space Needle
SEATTLE RCO
SEATTLE
PORT ORCHARD
BREMERTON
Chico
VORTAC SEATTLE
WEST SEATTLE RESERVOIR
BOEING FIELD KING CO INTL (BFI)
NATL (PVT)
AWOS-3 121.2
KITSAP
outdoor theaters
Fragaria
VASHON (2S1)
SEATTLE TACOMA INTL (SEA)
See NOTAMs/Directory for Class E (sfc) eff hrs
Belfair
Dewatto
Burley
WAX ORCHARDS (Pvt)
KENT
AUBURN MUNI (S50)
Tahuya
Potlatch
Union
CARNEY
Allyn
See NOTAMs/Directory for Class D/E (sfc) eff hrs
Vaughn
Rosedale
Gig Harbor
Dash Point
Grapeview
MASON CO
Home
TACOMA NARROWS (TIW)
TACOMA
Lakebay
Auburn
Milton
SHELTON
Arcadia
Longbranch
GRAYE
Lakewood Center
PUYALLUP
RAINIER MOA
Boston Harbor
Puget
prison
MC CHORD AFB (TCM)
PIERCE CO-THUN (1S0)
See NOTAMs/Directory for Class D eff hrs
AMERICAN LAKE (W37)
SPANAWAY (S44)
EXCLUDES CLASS D AT AND BELOW
VORTAC McCHORD
GOWER (Pvt)
NISQUALLY NATIONAL WILDLIFE REFUGE
golf course
OLYMPIA
FORT LEWIS
GRAY AAF (GRF)
SHADY ACRES (WA61)
Lacey
LACOMAS
VORTAC OLYMPIA
OLYMPIA (OLM)
FLYING CARPET
RAINIER 2 MOA
RAINIER 3 MOA
Yelm
WESTERN
ASPLUND (Pvt)
Littlerock
FLYING B (Pvt)
Eatonville
Rainier
Tenino
SWANSON
sawmill
Ohop
MCKENNA

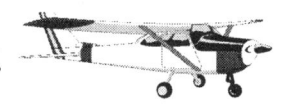

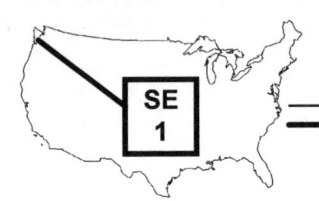

Notice also that the Seattle Class B airspace sits above all four target airports, but the floor is at 6,000 feet (3,000 over Tacoma Narrows) so it should not be a factor since you won't want to waste time climbing up that high. There is a Class D airspace associated with the two military airfields and Tacoma Narrows, going up to 2,800 feet, but since we would need to enter those airspaces in order to reach Spanaway or Tacoma Narrows, we'll assume that the controllers will give us free passage when we need it. In real life, you would have to contact the tower each time you wanted to pass through, or you'd have to climb over the airspace.

You also need to consider in which sequence you will visit the airports. Here are some tips to keep in mind. You can't make it to all four and still get back in time (at least, not without breaking some of the other rules we'll set for your flight). Since we will require that you obey traffic patterns, think about which sequence will put you on the correct side for the next airport's pattern. For each approach (except the last), you must join the downwind leg on a 45-degree angle starting from outside the pattern (no crossing, mid-field entries permitted).

On your return leg, remember to stay clear of the Restricted airspace, and as you approach Olympia, you can assume that the Tower has cleared you for a straight-in landing on Runway 17. If you're down and stopped (and in one piece) before the clock ticks over to 12:00, then you've successfully completed your game of hopscotch.

RULES OF THE GAME

Okay, now for the extra rules. You'll start at Olympia, ready for take-off on Runway 35, at 11:00 am. For all take-offs, you must fly the runway heading until you are at least 500 feet AGL (above ground level) before leaving the pattern and turning onto your course heading. You should then climb to the pattern altitude for your next destination before leveling off.

Airport Hopscotch Airports

Airport (1)	Runway Hdg	Runway Dimensions	Elev.	Pattern Alt. (2)
1. Pierce Co. /Thun Field	34	3650 x 60	530	1500
2. Shady Acres	34	1800 x 20	425	1225 Right
3. Spanaway	34	2724 x 20	385	985 Right
4. Tacoma Narrows	35	5002 x 150	292	1300

(1) Numbers correspond to airports marked on the sectional.

(2) Note that Runway 34 at both Shady Acres and Spanaway calls for a right hand traffic pattern; the other two use a standard left hand pattern.

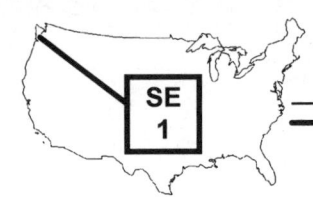

Even though this is a rental plane and you're only paying by the hour for "wet" time (which means that the cost of fuel is included—you don't pay extra for the gas you burn), the FBO is not going to want to rent to you again if you burn up the engine or bend any metal. Therefore, you must not exceed 140 knots (indicated) at any time during your trip.

Also in the interest of safety, you may not make any turns steeper than a 30° angle. Honor your aircraft's limitations, and do not lower the flaps until the airspeed is in the white arc of the indicator (95 knots or lower).

Each landing must be to a full stop, and you must remain on the pavement from the time you touch down until you come to a stop. (And a full-stop landing that results in an airplane in many pieces does not count.) Some of the runways are narrow, and since you must take off in the same direction as you land—to the north—you may have to leave the pavement to back taxi to the end where you landed.

TIPS FOR SUCCESS

Aside from working out a careful plan in advance, the most important factor for success is precise flying skills. Don't waste time by wandering off your heading or altitude. Trim your airplane for maximum (permitted) speed in cruise, then adjust your engine controls to maintain the desired altitude.

And don't rush your approach. Give yourself plenty of time and distance to set up a stabilized approach on final. Landing at Pierce County or Tacoma Narrows isn't too difficult, since they are long and wide. But Shady Acres and Spanaway are narrow, and Shady Acres is also short. If you come in with excess airspeed or are not lined up, you'll almost certainly have to go around and lose precious time. A successful slow approach takes much less time than two high-speed attempts.

Keep in mind that the visual cues for narrow and short runways are different from the air than for bigger ones, so you may find yourself lower and faster than you intend to be. Pay close attention to your instruments as well as what you see out the window, and fly by the numbers.

BEFORE YOU FLY

Now all you have to do is set your location and instruments, and you'll be ready to go. First, let's put your plane at the end of Runway 35 at Olympia. Choose the Set Exact Location... command from the World menu. In the resulting dialog box, enter the following items:

North/South Lat.:   N046 57 51.0728
East/West Lon.:   W122 54 21.3902
Altitude (feet):   209
Heading: 350

Choose OK. Also on the World menu, choose the Set Exact Time and Season... command. In the resulting dialog box, choose Set Exact Time, and then set Local Hours to 11 and Local minutes to 00.

Choose OK. Now, using either the mouse, keyboard shortcuts, or menus, set your flight instruments. Set NAV1 to 113.4 (the Olympia VOR) and its OBS heading to 25. (If you want some help finding Spanaway, set NAV2 to 109.60—the McChord VOR—and its OBS heading to 110, since Spanaway is located near that radial, about 4 nm. from the VOR.) And since you'll be flying within the 30 nm. veil of the Seattle Class B airspace, make sure that you have your transponder on and set for the correct squawk code for VFR flight: 1200.

TAKE-OFF!

Good luck at your game of airport hopscotch; it's a great way to learn to fly your airplane precisely and have fun at the same time. Remember that you can use the same objective and rules for other areas of the FS5.1 scenery to play the game there.

Situation file: XC-SE1

Seattle Flight 2

A Sound Plan

There's an old folk song about Puget Sound, with a final refrain that goes "surrounded by acres of clams". If you're a fan of fresh seafood, from salmon to shellfish, then you'll want to head on out to the Pacific Northwest for a visit.

For this flight, you'll take a scenic tour of Puget Sound, flying up to Harvey Field in Snohomish, Washington. You can camp right on the field and then take the short trip to nearby Everett for a tour of the Boeing aircraft factory.

PLANNING A ROUTE

You can turn off the radios on this flight because you'll be relying solely on your DG (directional gyroscope) and your Mark I Eyeball to find your way. And in the process you'll get an up-close and personal tour of Puget Sound.

How close? Well, the Seattle area is not known for its sunshine or arid climate. It does rain there a bit, and it's often cloudy. For this flight, I've set you up with a solid overcast to fly under—there's still plenty of room for safe VFR flight, but don't let your altitude drift away from you or you'll end up in the soup above or the drink below!

The route from Olympia to Harvey Field is highlighted on the section from a WAC (World Aeronautical Chart); in order to see more detail, you might want to use either a Seattle sectional chart or a Seattle Terminal Area Chart which show the same area in a larger scale.

You will start from Runway 26 at Olympia, then fly up towards the Tacoma Narrows Bridge. You could continue on in a straight line to go to Harvey, but this route would take you close to the heart of the Seattle Class B airspace, and you'd have to get down below 1,800 feet to avoid busting this special airspace. Instead, let's cut you some slack so you can enjoy the flight while remaining clear of the most active airspace.

After passing the bridge, you'll turn north and fly along the Colvos Passage between the mainland and Vashon Island. Once you reach the northern tip of Vashon Island, you will turn a bit to the left and fly past Bainbridge Island. This is easy to spot because it has three distinct bays along its eastern shore. Just beyond Bainbridge Island, there is a large point sticking out into the sound towards the east. Once you reach this, you can safely turn back to the northeast and head toward Harvey. One convenient checkpoint along this leg is Martha Lake Airport; Harvey Field is just six miles further on. The airport is nestled into a bend in the Pilchuck River, and as the old saw goes, "when you cross the river, you've gone too far."

This route is all laid out for you in the flight log. Note that the headings are approximate; you'll be relying on visual references to make adjustments to your course headings.

Next comes the question of how high to fly. The Class B airspace is arranged in layers, and the portion over Vashon Island and the Sound where you will be flying has a floor of 3,000 feet MSL. You can tell this by the "fractions" on the chart; the indication of 100 over 30 means that the airspace extends from 3,000 feet (30 hundred feet) to 10,000 feet (100 hundred feet) above mean sea level.

SE
2

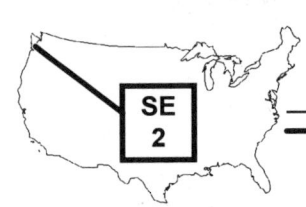

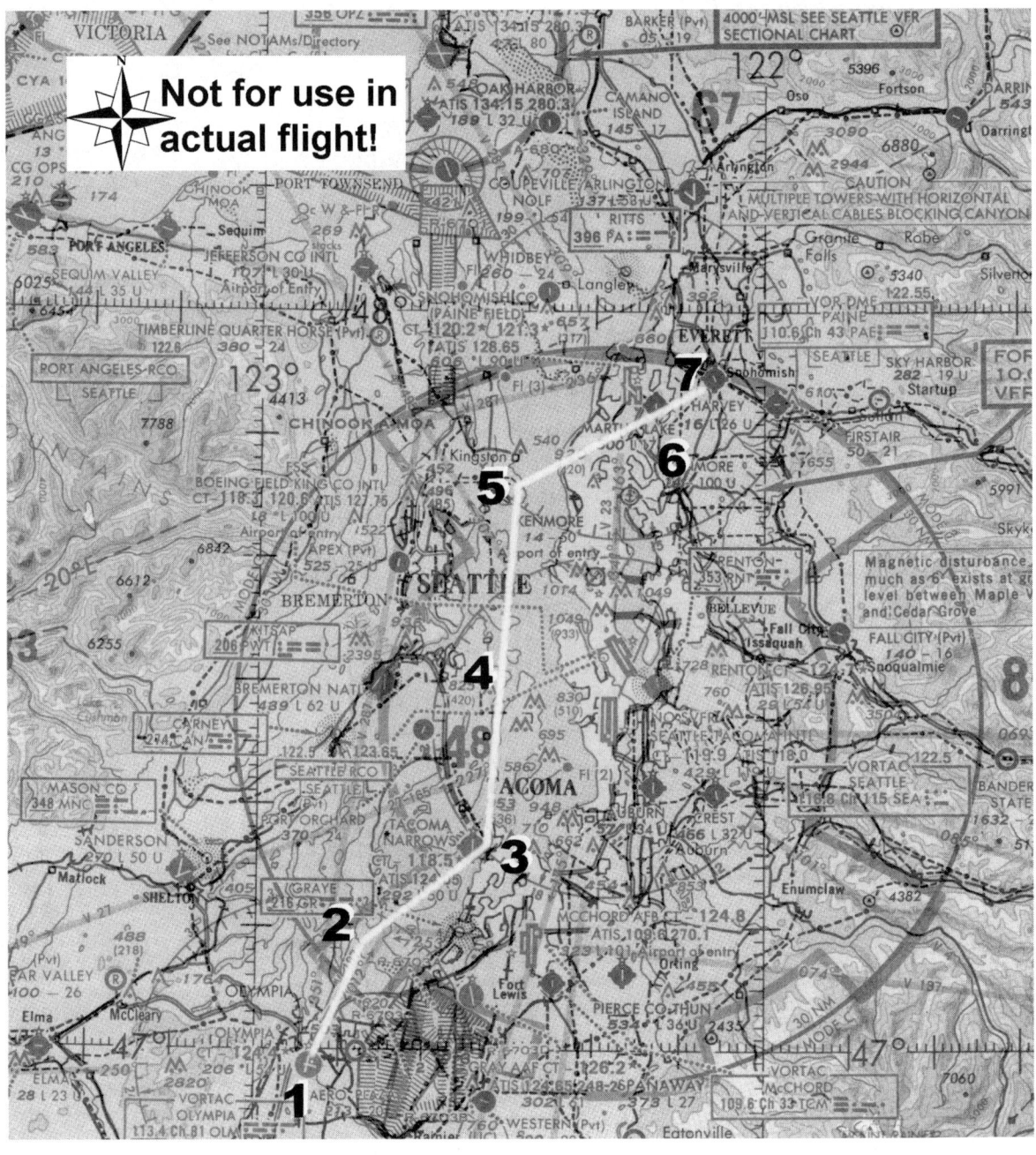

Not for use in actual flight!

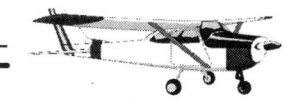

You're not going to fly over that—not without spending an inordinate amount of time climbing and circling outside the Class B airspace—and even if you did, you'd be faced with a 10,000 foot descent at the other end to get to Harvey Field which is just under the outer edge of the airspace on the other side.

As a result, the only practical approach is to go under the airspace. Since this is Seattle, we have also dialed in a low overcast for the flight to add some realism and to help you visualize the Class B airspace; stay out of the clouds, and you stay clear of the airspace.

With a ceiling of 3,000 feet, Visual Flight Rules require that you remain at least 500 feet below the clouds (or 1,000 feet above, or 2,000 to the side). This is designed to give you and the other pilot a moment to react when a plane flying under instrument rules (IFR) pops out of the clouds headed in your direction. A look at the chart shows that there are no obstacles along your route that are higher than 1,000 feet, but you want to fly high enough to give you some gliding distance in the unlikely event that something goes wrong. So plan to cruise at 2,250 feet. (Note that the "hemispheric rule" that dictates cruise altitudes based on your course does not apply, since you will be flying less than 3,000 feet above ground level.)

We are ignoring one airspace requirement on this flight, but you can act it out if you want to remain strictly legal. The dashed line around the Tacoma Narrows Airport indicates that it is Class D airspace with a tower. The airspace extends up to 2,800 feet MSL, and you will be flying right through it. (You also have McChord Air Force Base with its own Class D airspace to the right of your course, and the Tacoma Narrows Class D airspace extends pretty far to the west, which make a detour impractical.) To stay legal, you need to be in radio contact with the Tacoma Narrows Tower before you enter the airspace. So tune your COM1 to 118.5, and give out your airplane's N-number and your position, and ask for permission to transition the Class D airspace over the bridge. All you need to hear is the controller repeat back your N-number and you can continue on your merry way.

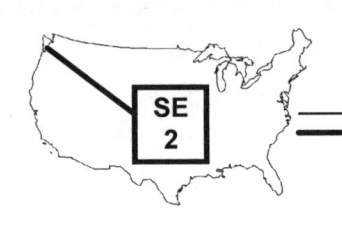

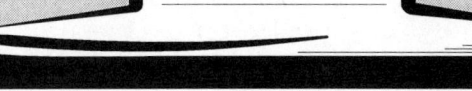

VFR Flight Log

Departure: Olympia (OLM)
Destination: Harvey Field (S43)

FIXES	ROUTE MAG COURSE	NAUT. MILES	ESTIMATED GROUND SPEED (KT)	TOTAL TIME	ACTUAL TIME
1. Depart Olympia, climb to 700 feet, then turn on course	10° (1)		70	2 (2)	
2. Cross the coastline	20°	10		7.5	
3. Tacoma Narrows Bridge	355°	32		16	
4. Northern tip of Vashon Island	340°	47		22.5	
5. Pt. north of Bainbridge Island	35°	61		29	
6. Martha Lake Airport		73		34.5	
7. Arrive Harvey Field		79		37.5 (3)	

(1) Navigate using pilotage; all headings are approximate
(2) Take-off, climb-out, and turn
(3) Plus 3 to 5 minutes to enter pattern and land

Olympia Airport (OLM)
Coordinates: 41-51.33; 087-36.47
Elevation: 206 feet MSL
Pattern altitude: 1200 MSL
Runways: 17-35 5,419x150; 8-26 5,001x150
Tower: 124.4 (8 am to 8 pm); CTAF: 124.4
Notes: Right traffic Runways 35 and 8

Harvey Field (S43)
Coordinates: 047-54.49; 122-06.32
Elevation: 16 feet MSL
Pattern altitude: 800 MSL
Runways: 13-31 2,400x75 turf; 14-32 2,660x36 asphalt
UNICOM/CTAF: 123.0
Notes: Right traffic Runways 13 and 14

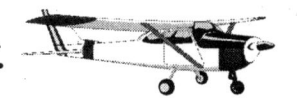

The only other point to consider is your descent at the other end. The pattern altitude for Harvey Field is 800 feet, which means that you will need to lose 1,450 feet. At a standard 500 fpm descent rate, that means you will want to start down three minutes (or more) before you enter the pattern. At 130 knots—the airspeed I used for the flight plan—that means starting 6.5 nautical miles out. Conveniently, this is almost exactly the distance from Martha Lake Airport to Harvey Field, so set up your descent before you cross Martha Lake and you should be ready to enter the pattern at your destination.

I'll assume for this flight that the winds are light and variable out of the northwest, so you will depart from Runway 26 at Olympia, and land on Runway 32 at Harvey Field. There are a couple of details to note about your destination, by the way. First is the fact that pattern altitude is just 800 feet, which is lower than the standard 1,000 feet used at most airports, so your view of the field will be a little different than you are used to seeing. You may have a tendency to fly the pattern too close to the field. The other detail is that the paved runway is just 36 feet wide—only 25% the width of Olympia's runways. This narrow landing strip can also mess up your visual picture of the situation, and you may find yourself flaring too late on the landing. (No, you cannot log each bounce as a separate landing, either!) You'll be a safer pilot if you think ahead about details such as these before your flights.

GETTING READY TO FLY

Set up for this trip is easy. Start up FS5.1 and choose the Airports command from the World menu. In the "Choose a scenery area:" box, select "USA - Seattle". Then pick "Olympia - Runway 26" from the list of airports.

Next, you need to set up the cloud cover. Choose Weather from the World menu, and then Edit the cloud layer. Change the Base setting to 3000 feet, and the Coverage to Overcast. Choose OK twice to return to the simulator.

If you want to make the trip more challenging, here are two modifications. First, you can add some wind. Try a 15 knot breeze from 270°, in a layer from 1,000 to 3,000 feet. (You can even bring it down to ground level if you want to practice cross-wind take-offs and landings.) Also, you can add some patchy fog to the Sound by Creating an extra cloud layer; try a global layer from 100 feet to 1000 feet with a 100 foot deviation. You won't have any trouble getting up and down while remaining clear of the clouds, but it can make spotting your visual references a little more difficult.

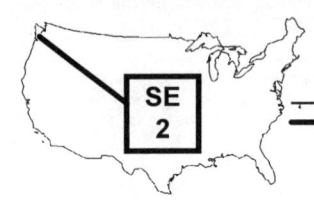

TAKE OFF!

That's it—you're ready to go sight-seeing over Puget Sound. Have a great flight, and enjoy the view. But be sure to get your seafood *after* you get to the airport, and not en route—unless you have floats mounted, a Cessna makes a pretty poor fishing boat!

▫ Situation file: XC-SE2

Seattle Flight 3

Head for the Mountains

I guarantee that you'll have a fair flight for this trip, no matter what the weather.

How can I be so certain? Because you're going to the Fair—the Puyallup Fair. The last flight in this area ended at Harvey Field, north of Seattle, and on this flight you'll backtrack down to Pierce County-Thun Field which is nearly due south of Seattle. This airport is located outside of Puyallup; the town name comes from a pair of native American words that mean "friendly people".

You might want to visit Puyallup for its annual Daffodil Parade, but the big draw is the Puyallup Fair—first held in 1900—that runs for 17 days each fall, attracting more than 1.3 million visitors to its farm exhibits, crafts, food, rides, and free entertainment. Plan on riding the Ejection Seat or the Skycoaster, and then enjoying a few Fisher scones—dripping with butter and raspberry jam—that have been a tasty part of the fair since 1915.

PLANNING A ROUTE

Your route is highlighted on a portion of the Seattle sectional chart. Notice the patchwork of blue lines surrounding Seattle-Tacoma

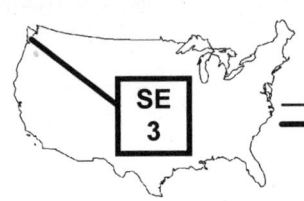

International Airport (SEA). These lines mark the Class B airspace that surrounds the airport, and you cannot enter it without air traffic control's (ATC) permission. Since we don't have interactive voice communications with ATC in the default version of FS5.1 (well, at least not in *this* version), I plan your flights so you don't have to talk to the controllers.

The "fractions" in the different Class B segments indicate the ceiling and floor of the airspace. For example, the "100/80" indicates that the Class B airspace starts at 8,000 feet (80 hundreds) and ends at 10,000 feet (100 hundreds). Right around the airport itself, the airspace extends down to "SFC": the surface of the ground itself. Because the Harvey and Pierce fields are both under the Class B space, it makes no sense to climb over the ceiling, so instead I'll plan a route that goes under it.

If you travel due south (true, not magnetic) from Harvey Field, you'll notice a line running north and south. The Class B airspace extends down to 3,000 feet to the west of that line, but has a floor of 5,000 or 6,000 just to the east of it. Fortunately, there is a major landmark you can use to stay on the east side of that line: Sammanish Lake. There are also some hills—maximum elevation of 3004 feet—just east of the town of Issaquah, which should make a big target.

Once you cross the highway at Issaquah (Interstate 90), you could turn directly toward Pierce County-Thun Field, but just to make certain that you don't tangle with any approach or departure traffic from SEA, I'll keep your route a bit to the east. How can you know when it's okay to turn toward your destination? You can use the VOR beacon at McChord Air Force Base; by tuning the OBS on your NAV radio to 255, you'll know when you have crossed the 255° radial, which you can then follow until you see the airport.

Not for use in actual flight!

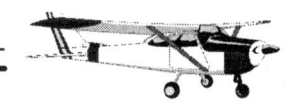

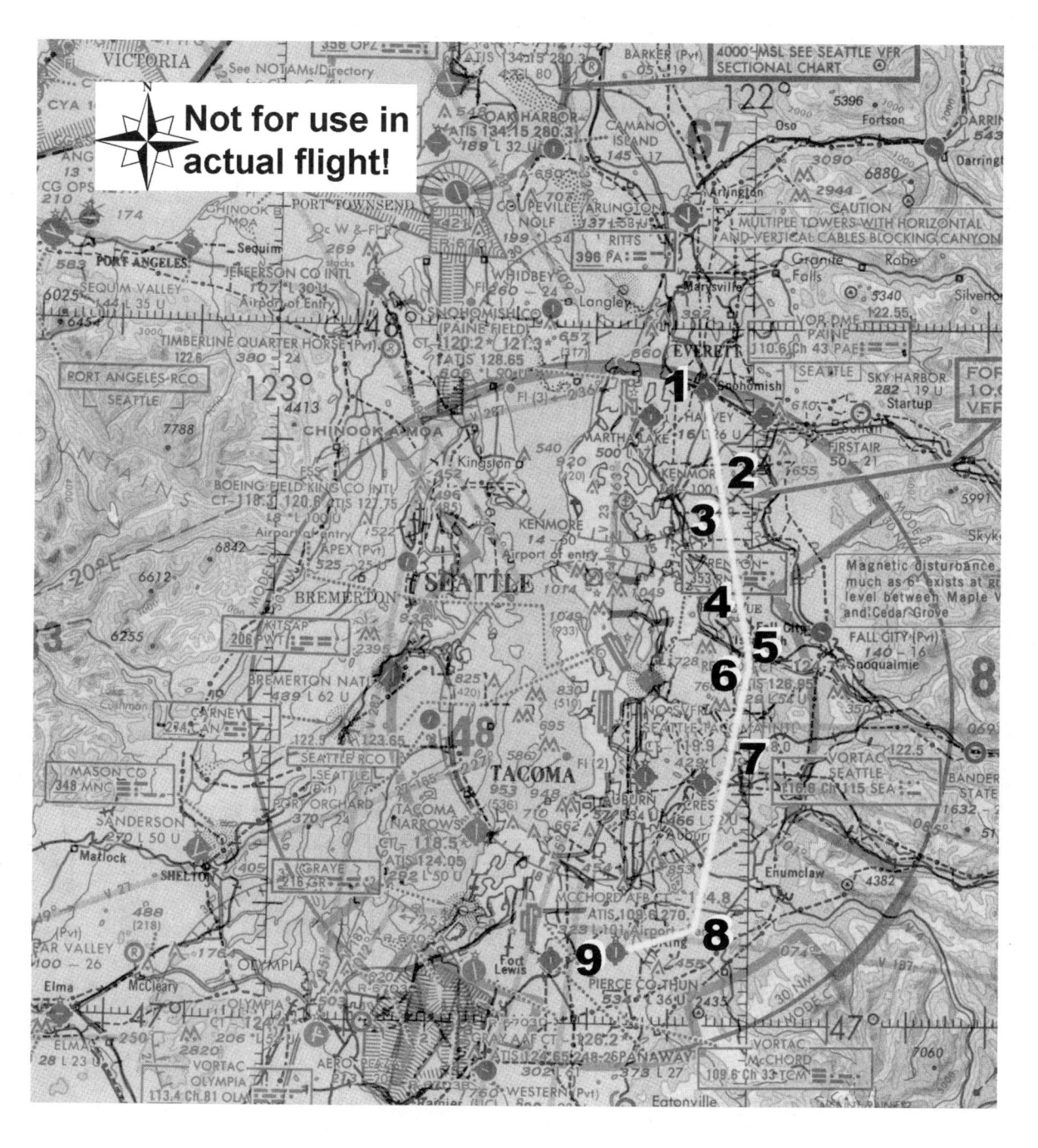

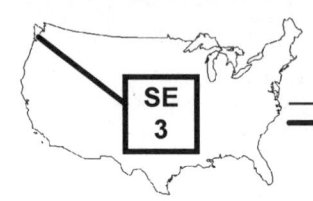

The next question is how high you should fly. You want to make sure that you have room to spare when you near the high ground at Issaquah, but this is a short flight and there's no sense in climbing up to the base of the Class B airspace. So I've planned a cruise climb (at 80 knots) to 3,500 feet for the first leg; this complies with the hemispheric rule that states that VFR traffic on a heading between 0 an 179 degrees should cruise at altitudes of odd thousands plus 500 feet, and you'll be headed slightly east of south.

Once you make it through the pass at Issaquah, you'll need to descend to 2,500 feet, since the floor of the Class B airspace is only at 3,000 feet in places along the second leg. (The hemispheric rule does not apply here because you will be less than 3,000 feet above ground level.) And when you turn toward the airport for the final leg, descend further so that you are at the pattern altitude of 1500 feet by the time you are ready to enter your downwind leg for a landing.

SETTING YOUR COURSE

I have prepared a flight log for your flight, which lists a series of visual checkpoints that you will be able to use to keep track of your position as you make your way along the route.

You'll depart Harvey Field on Runway 14, and after you climb to 1,000 feet, turn to a heading of about 155°. This should point you roughly at the western edge of the hills at Issaquah; you're aiming for the pass between the last two peaks on the right, but remember to stay to the left of Sammanish Lake.

You may wonder about that 155° heading; the course on the chart looks like it's nearly vertical, which would lead you to expect a heading of somewhere between 170° and 180°. Magnetic north is not in the same location as the north pole, however, so there is what's called a "variation" between true and magnetic headings. In some parts of the country, this variation can be quite small, or even zero. In the Seattle area, however, the variation is extreme; magnetic north is nearly 20° to the east of true north. Thus a magnetic heading of 155° will point you almost due south.

VFR Flight Log

Departure: Harvey Field (S43)
Destination: Pierce County-Thun Field (1S0)

Fixes	Route		Estimated		Actual
	Mag Course	Naut. Miles	Ground Speed (Kt)	Total Time	Time
1. Depart Harvey, climb to 1,000 feet; turn on course	155° (1)		80	2 (2)	
2. Cross Rt. 522		4		5	
3. Cross Woodinville to Duvall Rd.		8	130	8	
4. North end Sammanish Lake		14		11	
5. Cross I-90		22		14.5	
6. Through pass; change course	170°	24		15.5	
7. Junction Rt. 169 and Rt. 18		29		18	
8. Intercept McChord VOR 255°	255°	47		26.5	
9. Arrive Pierce County-Thun Fld.		55		30 (3)	

(1) Navigate using pilotage; headings are approximate
(2) Take-off, climb-out, and turn
(3) Plu 3 to 5 minutes to enter pattern and land

Harvey Field (S43)
Coordinates: 047-54.49; 122-06.32; Elevation: 16 feet MSL
Pattern altitude: 800 MSL
Runways: 13-31 2,400x75 turf; 14-32 2,660x36 asphalt
UNICOM/CTAF: 123.0
Notes: Right traffic Runways 13 and 14.

Pierce County-Thun Field (1S0)
Coordinates: 047-06.21; 122-17.29; Elevation: 530 feet MSL
Pattern altitude: 1500 MSL
Runways: 16-34 3,650x60
UNICOM/CTAF: 122.8

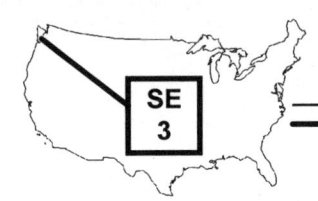

Your first checkpoint will be Route 522. Next, you'll cross the road between Woodinville and Duvall. There's a road that you'll cross near Sammanish Lake, but the north end of the lake makes a better checkpoint. Past the southern end of the lake, you'll cross Interstate 90 at Issaquah, and then head between the two hills. Once through the pass, turn to a heading of 170°, and start to descend. You'll cross Route 169 near Cedar Grove, and then Route 18 near Maple Valley. Continue on course until the OBS needle centers on your NAV1 radio, and then head 255° until you see the field. Then swing to the west to make a 45-degree entry on a left-downwind leg for a landing.

GETTING READY TO FLY

Harvey Field isn't on the World Airports menu list, so you'll need to place your airplane there yourself. Use the World Set Exact Location command, and enter the following values:

North/South Lat.:	N 47 54 31.9
East/West Lon.:	W 122 06 11.7
Altitude (ft):	19
Heading (deg magnetic):	140

This will place you at the end of Runway 14, ready for take-off.

Then tune your NAV1 radio to 109.60, and set the OBS to 255; this will set the radio to the McChord VOR, and you can make the turn from the second to third legs when the OBS needle centers. (If you want, you can tune your NAV2 radio to 116.80, which is the SEA VOR; you can then use the DME readout for NAV2 to monitor your distance from the airport, which can help you locate your position relative to the boundaries of the Class B airspace.

Make certain that your transponder is set to 1200, the squawk code for VFR flights. This would be a good time to use the Options Save Situation command to save these settings so that you can load them again when you want to fly this flight again.

And now you're ready to roll. Head for those mountains, and enjoy a "Fair" day when you reach your destination.

Situation file: XC-SE3

PART II:

Optional Scenery Areas

The trips in Part II require the use of optional scenery collections. These commercial scenery collections give you many more airports and detailed areas in which to fly, giving you a bigger flying world to enjoy.

Section A:
Hawaii

Aloha! Welcome to the Pacific paradise of the Hawaiian Islands. Microsoft's Hawaii scenery collection includes a host of wonderful sights for the sim flight tourist. While Diamond Head and Waikiki may be the most familiar locations ("Book 'em, Danno!"), your cross country flights will take you to some of the less-familiar islands. In real life, you have to contend with tropical winds, turbulence on the lee side of the many mountains, rapidly-changing weather, and even reduced visibility due to "vog" (smog from volcanic activity). And then there's the problem of understanding Air Traffic Controller instructions; it can take a while to master the correct pronunciation of landmarks such as "Kaunakakai"! The weather is always as perfect as you want it with FS5.1, however, and these flights don't require radio communications, so prepare to enjoy the stunning scenery as you fly around the islands.

Hawaii Flight 1

A Spin Around Niihau

Kauai Island anchors the northwest end of the Hawaiian archipelago, with little Niihau dangling off its western tip. There are four airfields on the island, but only two without control towers. And one of those two is a private field.

For your first flight in Hawaii, I have planned a simple sightseeing jaunt around this left-end of the island chain. You'll start at the private Princeville airport on the north shore of Kauai (we'll assume that you have permission from the owners to be there), and you'll fly around the island of Niihau, and on around to Port Allen on the south shore of the Kauai.

PLANNING A ROUTE

There are not many radio navigation aids on the island, but it's easy enough to use standard pilotage techniques in this feature-rich environment—there's something identifiable just about everywhere you look.

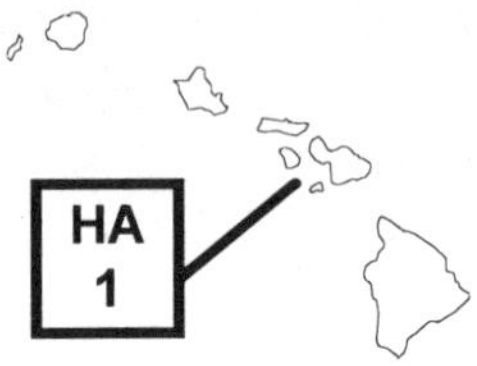
HA
1

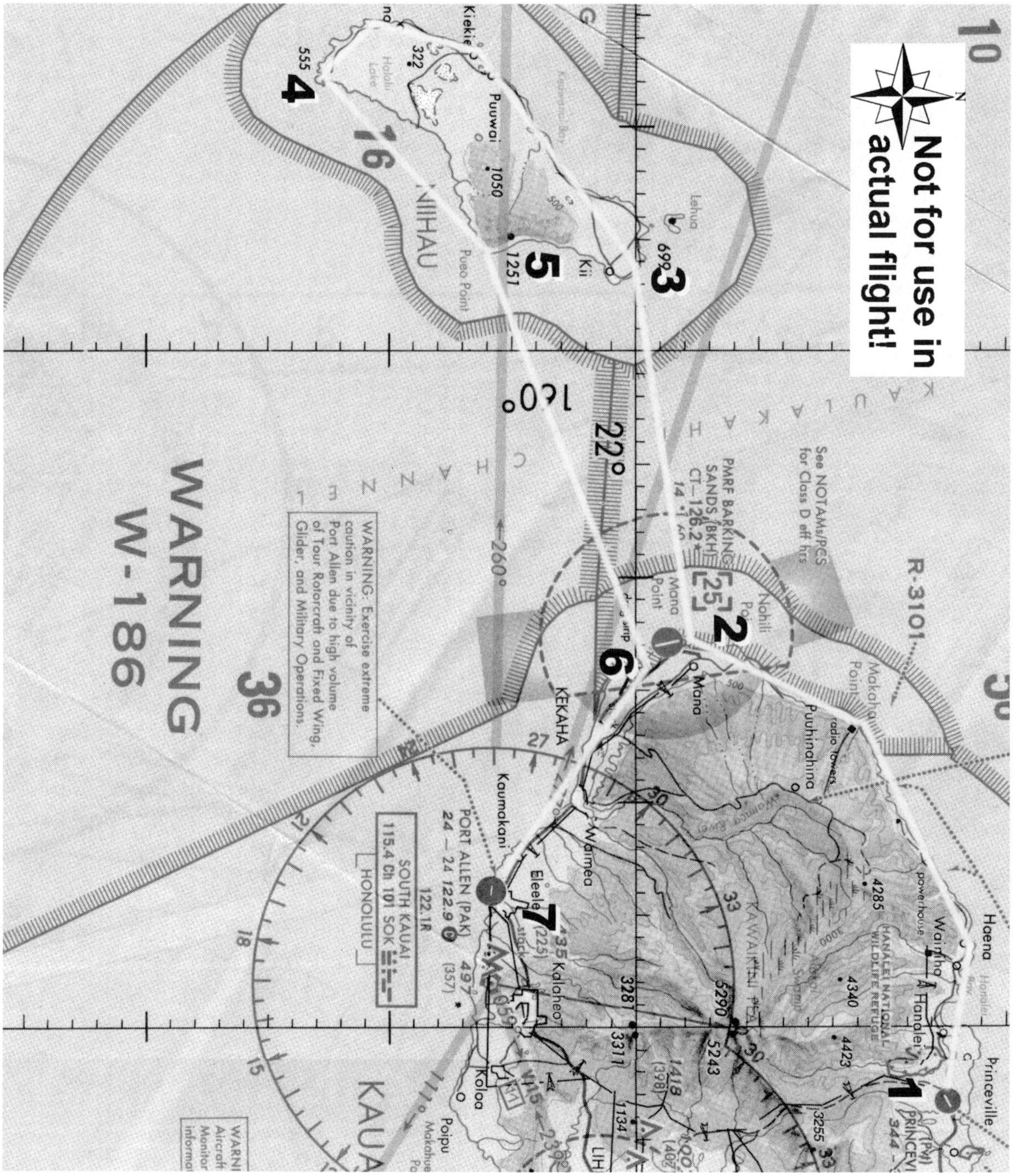
Not for use in actual flight!
1
2
3
4
5
6
7
WARNING W-186
WARNING: Exercise extreme caution in vicinity of Port Allen due to high volume of Tour Rotorcraft and Fixed Wing, Glider, and Military Operations.
R-3101
See NOTAMs/RCS for Class D eff hrs
PMRF BARKING SANDS (BKH)
NIIHAU
Lehua
Kii
Pueo Point
Puuwai
Kiekie
Mana Point
Nohili Point
Mana
KEKAHA
Kaumakani
Waimea
Eleele
Kalaheo
Koloa
Poipu
PORT ALLEN (PAK)
SOUTH KAUAI
115.4 Ch 101 SOK
HONOLULU
Puuhinahina
Makaha Point
Haena
Wainiha
Hanalei
Princeville
HANALEI NATIONAL WILDLIFE REFUGE
KAWAIKINI PEAK
KAUAI
KAULAKAHI
CHANNEL
22°
160°
260°

I've planned the flight for calm conditions, but that is not all that realistic—trade winds often blow 20 knots or more. You can dial in some wind if you want to increase the challenge.

The flight starts at Princeville with your plane positioned on Runway 23. The picture of the sectional for this area shows your route. After take-off, you'll proceed along the rugged north shore of the island, making your way around to Barking Sands airport on Mana Point, then across the Kaulakahi Channel to Niihau. There you'll flight out along the north shore, then back along the south side of the island, and then back across the channel. Then you can follow the Kaumaulii Highway (Route 30) along the south shore to Port Allen airport near Hanapepe.

Port Allen is on a point, and can be a little tough to spot on your first trip to the field. You can help yourself out with a radio beacon. Note that the South Kauai VOR is located a bit beyond Port Allen. The airport is located 4 nm from the VOR on the 256° radial, so you can tune a NAV radio to that station (115.4) and then watch the DME readout; if you get to within 4 miles of the VOR, the airport is somewhere close by.

DANGER, WILL ROBINSON!

The sectional also has a number of warnings that you must consider when planning this trip. First and foremost is the question of special use and restricted airspace. The "25" in the segmented square near Barking Sands indicates that the Class D airspace around that field has a ceiling of 2500 feet. You must be above that altitude when you pass within the dotted line around the airport, or else you need to be in radio contact with the control tower there.

You'll also notice a lot of parallel-hatch shadings on the sectional; these indicate Restricted and Warning areas which are reserved for military aerial operations. I'll assume that you're told that these areas are not "hot" (meaning that there are missions going on in them) when you check for your weather briefing, but I'll still plan to keep you out of the restricted area as much as possible. This means that you'll stay over the land as you approach Barking Sands from the northeast. (If you want to add a navigating challenge, adjust your flight so that you stay over Kauai until you are south of Barking Sands and clear of the R-1301 restricted space, and then plan your return across the channel so you remain clear of that space again.) Even though you've been told that there is no activity, don't count on it; plan on keeping your head on a swivel as you scan the skies for hot shot fighter aircraft.

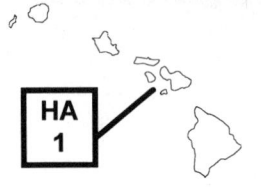

Other notes on the sectional (some of which do not show here) provide additional warnings for heavy "Tour Aircraft" traffic along the north shore and again around Port Allen. You'll do well to keep a sharp eye out for other aircraft all the way along your trip.

Finally, there's an unusual warning on the chart. The page here in this book was not big enough to include it, so here is what it says:

> "Electromagnetic radiation will continuously exist within a 2500' radius and 2500' above unified s-band antenna located at 22°07'N, 159°40'W near Kakee NASA Telemetry Station, Kaui.
> "Helicopters and slow speed aircraft flying within above airspace will be exposed to direct radiation which may produce harmful effects to personnel and equipment. Radiation is not visually apparent and must be presumed by all pilots to continuously exist."

That sounds like a good place to avoid. Fortunately, that location is easy to stay away from, since it is located up on the ridge, well away from the shoreline.

THE FLIGHT LOG

I've prepared a flight log that takes all these different factors into account. It lists your checkpoints, the distances, and an estimate of the amount of time it should take to complete the flight.

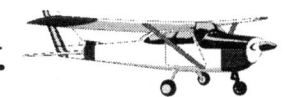

VFR Flight Log

Departure: Princeville (Private)
Destination: Port Allen (PAK)

FIXES	ROUTE MAG COURSE (1)	NAUT. MILES	ESTIMATED GROUND SPEED (KT)	TOTAL TIME	ACTUAL TIME
1. Depart Princeville southwest along coastline	260°		80 knots	1 (2)	
2. Cross Barking Sands (at above 2500 feet)	250°	19	80 / 130	12	
3. Landfall at Niihau Island	230°	34		19	
4. Southern tip of Niihau	10°	48		25.5	
5. Leave Niihau	70°	63		32.5	
6. Cross Barking Sands, follow road southeast	110°	78		39.5	
7. Arrive Port Allen airport		90		45 (3)	

(1) Headings are approximate, using pilotage for navigation
(2) Includes take-off and climb-out to 3,000 feet
(3) Plus 3-5 minutes to enter pattern and land

Princeville Airport (Private)
Coordinates: N22-12.55; W159-26.47
Elevation: 344 feet MSL
Runways: 5-23 3,500

Port Allen
Coordinates: N21-53.81; W159-36.20
Location: 4.2 nm from South Kauai VOR (SOK) 115.4, 256°
Elevation: 24 feet MSL
Pattern altitude: 800 MSL
Runways: 9-27 2,260x60
UNICOM/CTAF: 122.9
Notes: right traffic for Runway 9

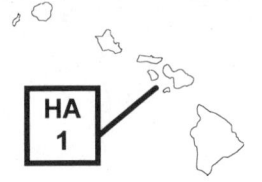

Note that the log shows an airspeed of "80 /130" knots for the second leg. You'll be departing Princeville about on your desired heading, so I have planned on a cruise climb at 80 knots until you reach your cruising altitude of 3,000 feet. This is high enough to put you above the helicopter traffic and the Barking Sands Class D airspace, but low enough to still enjoy the sights. At a cruise climb of 80 knots (about 500 feet per minute), that should take about six minutes after take-off. Then you can transition to a level cruise at 130 knots.

The only other altitude issue is coming back down. From your cruising altitude of 3,000 feet, you'll need to lose 2,200 before you enter the pattern at Port Allen. (Plan on making the landing in the same direction that you took off in Princeville, so plan on entering a left downwind leg for Runway 27 when you get to Port Allen.) At a typical 500 fpm descent rate, that means you must start down at least 4.5 minutes before you arrive at the pattern, and at 130 knots, this means starting down when you are at least 10 miles from the airport. The simple solution is to start your descent as soon as you reach Barking Sands—just make sure that you are over the highway before you get down below 2,500 feet so that you don't bust into the Class D airspace.

GETTING READY TO FLY

Princeville is on the World Airports... menu for the Hawaii add-on, but for the wrong runway. You can either use the menu and then back-taxi to the other end of the runway, or you can use the World Set Exact Location menu to place your airplane at the right spot. Here are the values to enter for the exact location:

North/South Lat.:	N 22 12 36.8
East/West Lon.:	W 159 26 28.8
Altitude (ft):	344
Heading (deg magnetic):	232

If you want to use the South Kauai VOR as a backup to find Port Allen, tune your NAV1 radio to 115.4, set the OBS to 76°, and make sure that the DME readout is set to show the distance (and not your speed).

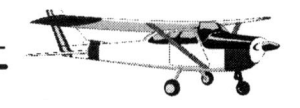

With this, you should be ready for your first flight around this Pacific paradise. Just remember not to get distracted by the beautiful surroundings, and keep your mind on your flying!

💾 Situation file: XC-HA1

Hawaii Flight 2

Triple Play

Three islands in one flight: that's your goal on this flight. You'll start on a private airport on the beautiful shoreline of Maui, cruise over to Lanai—one of the smallest inhabited islands in the chain—and then another short water crossing to your final destination on the north shore of Molokai.

Your landing will be at Kalaupapa National Historical Park. Among the sights there are the former leper colony, which a Belgian priest, Father Damien, helped develop in the last century. He worked among the lepers to build a hospital, farm, and other facilities. While you're there, you can also enjoy a hike on the trails in the park.

PLANNING THE ROUTE

As you can see in the section of the chart, there is a VOR beacon conveniently located on Lanai, so navigation will be simple. You can fly directly to Lanai on one radial, and then back out another to find Kalaupapa.

There are no airspace restrictions that you need to be concerned about for this trip; the dotted circles around the Kapalua and Lanai airports represent Class E airspace (which is printed in magenta on the real sectional chart, but you can't tell that from the black and white image shown here). You do not need to make any radio calls in this airspace under VFR conditions.

The only complications come from questions of altitude. The first one has to do with mountains in your path.

A direct line between Kapalua and Lanai airports takes you almost right over the 3,367 foot-high peak on the east side of Lanai. You could fly high enough to cross above it, but then you'd be faced with a slam dunk approach into the airport, about 2,000 feet below. A better idea might be to swing along the shore of the island to the south of the mountain, and get a clearer shot at the runway without having to act like a dive bomber.

There is also a sizable ridge—nearly 5,000 feet high—in the eastern half of Molokai which poses a similar problem. If you were high enough to clear the ridge, you'd then be faced with a dramatic descent down canyons to reach the sea-level airport. The lines with dots inside mark the national park boundaries, and indicate areas where pilots are requested not to fly lower than 2,000 feet AGL (above ground level) to reduce engine noises for those on the ground. So I've planned for you to take the long way around, swinging around the eastern end of the island to get to the airport.

The other altitude consideration is one that you must think about any time you fly over water—especially in a single-engine craft. What will you do in the unlikely event that the fan in the front stops turning? It's an extremely rare occurrence, but it's better to plan for the possibility and not have it happen, than the other way around.

By maintaining altitude in your water crossing and minimizing the distance over water, you can maximize your gliding distance and your chances of reaching dry land should you encounter engine troubles. Figure on about a mile per thousand feet of altitude (you can actually do better than that, and it's something worth practicing when you have a chance).

HA 2

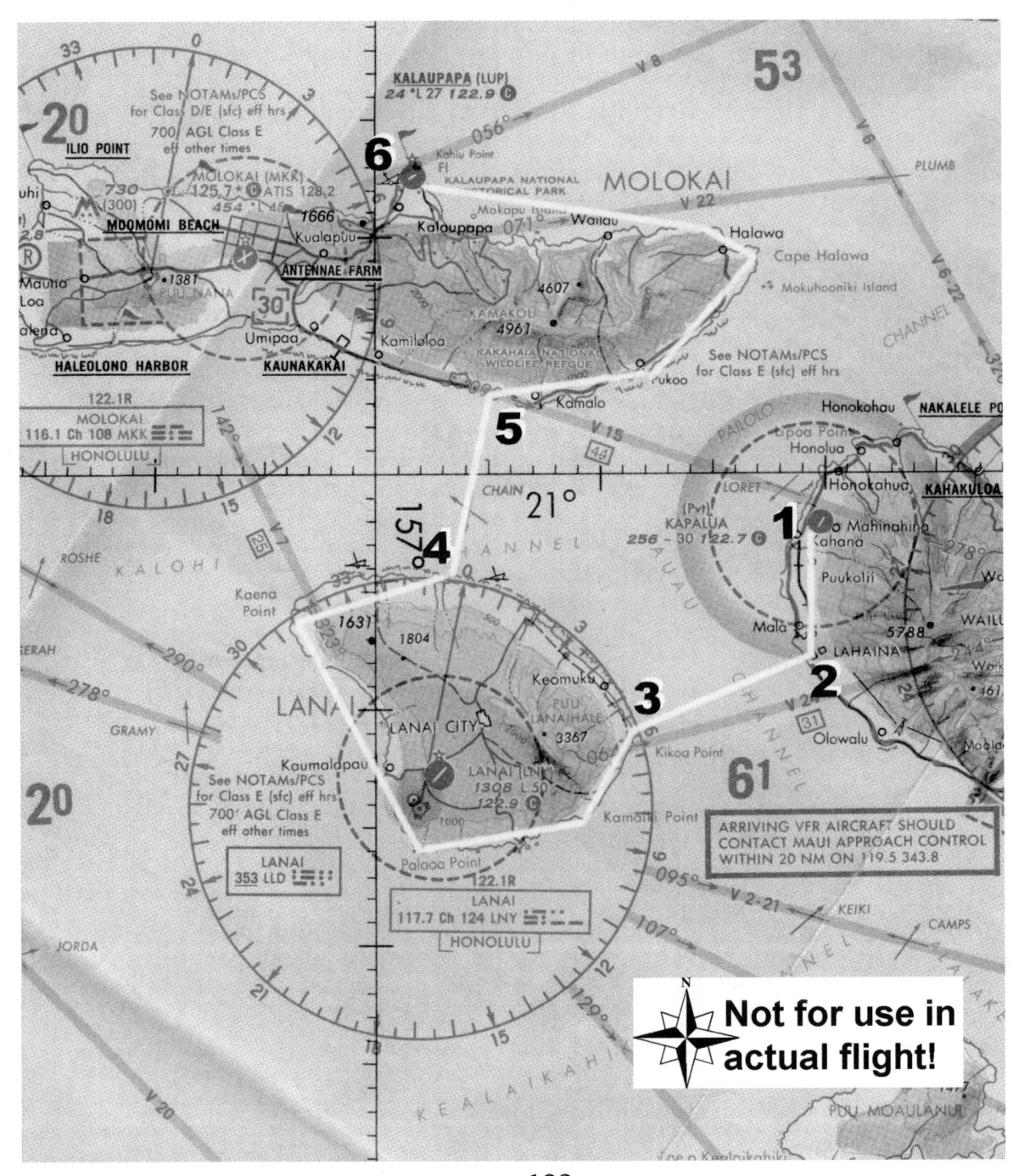

If you were to fly direct from Kapalua to Lanai, you'd travel nearly 10 nm over water. Instead, travel down the coast a bit to Lahaina, and your crossing will be only about 7 miles, which means that a 3,500 cruising altitude will put you within gliding distance of land for your entire crossing.

In a similar vein, you can follow the coast of Lanai after leaving the airport there, and then follow the 0° radial from the VOR to Molokai, for a crossing of about 7 miles which means that your 3,500 foot cruising altitude will work there as well. Once you're safely across the Kalohi Channel and over Molokai, you can drop down to about 2,000 feet for a good sight-seeing altitude.

The flight log for this flight is fairly simple. You'll fly down the coast of Maui until you intercept the 235° radial of the Lanai VOR, then head out across the Auau Channel. With a cruise climb of 80 knots from take-off, you will need to continue your climb for a few minutes after you make your turn at Lahaina, and then you can level off at 3,500 feet altitude and 130 knots cruise speed.

Once on the other side, follow the island coast to the south and continue around until you see the airport inland. I have not included the stop at Lanai airport on the log—if you feel like stopping off for lunch, go right ahead, and then pick up the flight after your break.

Then you'll retune the OBS on your NAV1 for the 0° radial, and follow the Lanai coast around to the northern side. When the needle centers, strike out across the Kalohi Channel for Molokai. Then turn right and follow the coast around until you reach the Kalaupapa airfield and the park. Plan on landing in the same direction as you took off, which means you'll want to use Runway 23. This runway has a right-hand traffic pattern, so fly out over the water to enter the pattern with a 45-degree entry onto a right downwind leg for your landing.

Remember to start your descent to the airport early enough so that you're at the 800 foot pattern altitude by the time you reach the field.

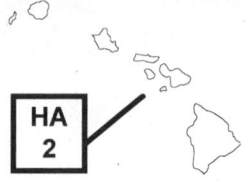

VFR Flight Log

Departure: Kapalua (Private)
Destination: Kalaupapa (LUP)

FIXES	ROUTE		ESTIMATED		ACTUAL
	MAG COURSE (1)	NAUT. MILES	GROUND SPEED (KT)	TOTAL TIME	TIME
1. Depart Kapalua southwest along coastline	180°		80 knots	1 (2)	
2. Leave Maui at Lahaina	235°	5		4.5	
3. Landfall at Lanai Island, follow coast southwest	varies°	12	80 / 130	10.5	
4. Leave Lanai	0°	35		21	
5. Landfall at Molokai	varies°	42		24	
6. Arrive Kalaupapa airport		67		37 (3)	

(1) Headings are approximate, using pilotage for navigation
(2) Includes take-off and climb-out to 3,500 feet
(3) Plus 3-5 minutes to enter pattern and land

Kapalua Airport (Private)
Coordinates: 20-57.95; 156-40.24
Elevation: 256 feet MSL
Runways: 2-20 3,000

Kalaupapa
Coordinates: 21-12.63; 156-58.51
Location: 11.6 nm from Molokai VOR (MKK) 116.1, 57°
Elevation: 26 feet MSL
Pattern altitude: 800 MSL
Runways: 5-23 2,700x50
UNICOM/CTAF: 122.9
Notes: right traffic for Runway 23

GETTING READ TO FLY

You can use the World Airports... menu command to place your airplane on Runway 20 at Kapalua on Maui. The only adjustment you will have to make to those settings is to make certain that your NAV1 radio is tuned to the Lanai VOR (117.7) and that the OBS is set to 235°.

That's all there is to it. Enjoy your lunch at Lanai, if you should decide to stop there, and have a great time touring the coasts of these three Hawaiian islands.

💾 Situation file: XC-HA2

Hawaii Flight 3

Vulcan Visit

Hawaii is famous for its sun, sand, and surf, but it's also well-known for its many volcanoes—many of which are still active. This flight gives you an up-close and personal look at the highest peak on Maui, plus lands you on the "Big Island" of Hawaii at Upolu Point, birthplace of King Kamehameha who ruled the chain of islands.

PLANNING A ROUTE

The section of the chart shows your route for this trip, which will combine some simple pilotage, some VOR navigation, and a long stretch of over-water flight.

The chart also shows a symbol that is a bit unusual. Notice the wedge-shaped symbols around the Haleakala volcano. These represent hang gliders, and are used to mark areas where hang glider activity is particularly heavy. With their steady winds and rugged topography, the Hawaiian mountains make particularly attractive places to jump into the sky with a large kite strapped to your back (if you are the type of person who finds that type of activity attractive). So be alert for hang gliders in your area as you fly near these regions.

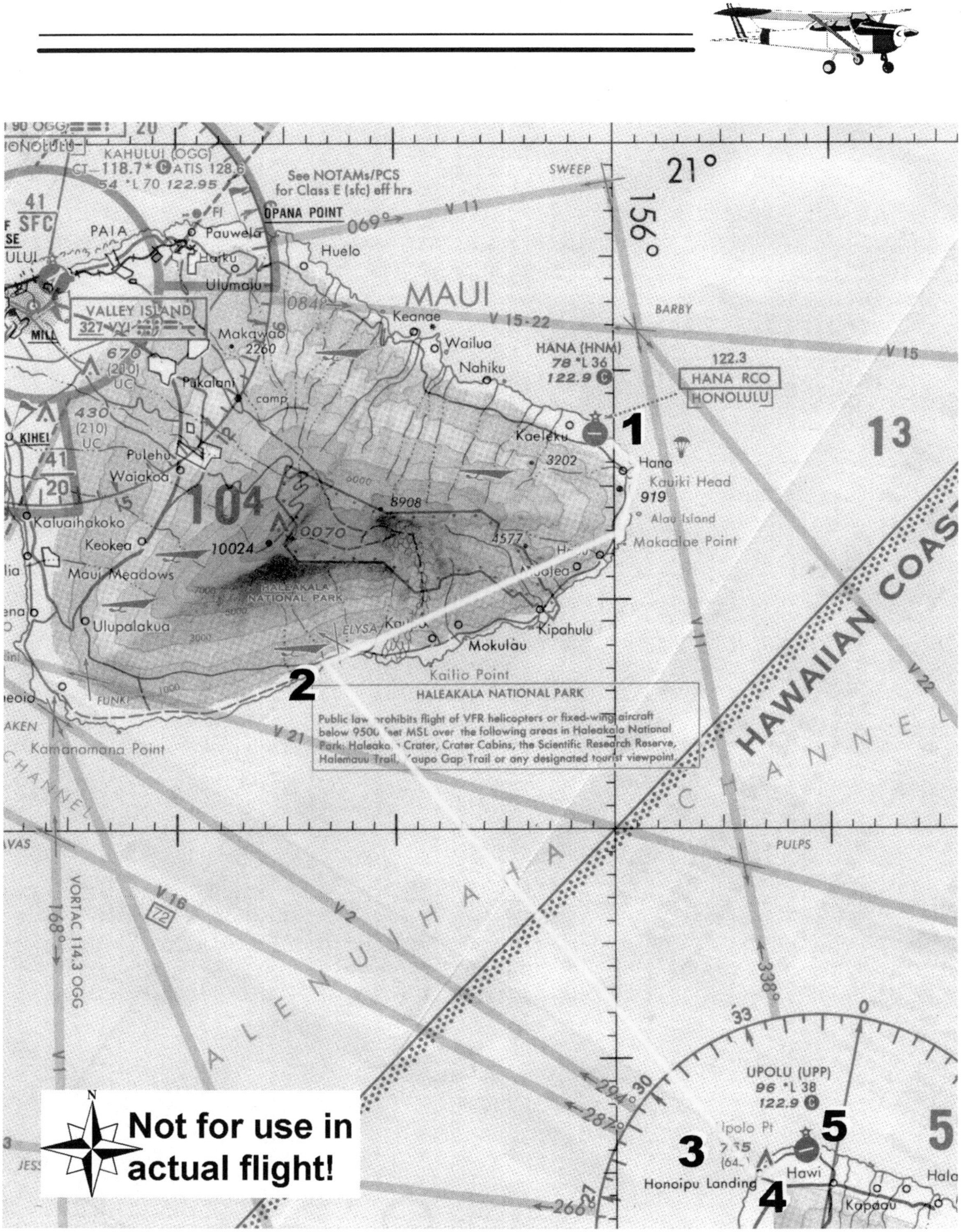
KAHULUI (OGG)
CT-118.7* ATIS 128.6
54 *L 70 122.95
See NOTAMs/PCS
for Class E (sfc) eff hrs
OPANA POINT
069°
V 11
SWEEP
21°
156°
PAIA
Pauwela
Haiku
Huelo
Ulumalu
MAUI
VALLEY ISLAND
327 VYI
Makawao
2260
Keanae
V 15-22
BARBY
Wailua
Nahiku
HANA (HNM)
78 *L 36
122.9
122.3
HANA RCO
HONOLULU
V 15
Pukalani
camp
Kaeleku
1
13
KIHEI
Pulehu
Waiakoa
3202
Hana
Kauiki Head
919
Alau Island
Makaalae Point
104
8908
10024
4577
Kaluaihakoko
Keokea
Maui Meadows
HALEAKALA NATIONAL PARK
HAWAIIAN COAST
Ulupalakua
Kipahulu
Mokulau
Kailio Point
2
HALEAKALA NATIONAL PARK
V 21
V 11
V 22
Kamanamana Point
CHANNEL
PULPS
VORTAC 114.3 OGG
168°
V 16
72
V 2
ALENUIHAHA
338°
33
0
30
UPOLU (UPP)
96 *L 38
122.9
5
294°
287°
Upolu Pt
3
Honoipu Landing
Hawi
4
Kapaau
266°
27
Not for use in actual flight!

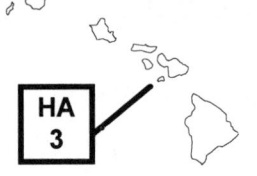

Your starting point is Hana Airport on the northeast corner of Maui, and you could simply plan a straight shot across the Alenuihaha Channel over to Hawaii, but that would give you about 30 nautical miles of over-water flight with no time to gain altitude before leaving land. Instead, I've planned your route so that you gain some gliding altitude before you go "feet wet" and have a chance to tour Haleakala a bit in the process.

You'll depart Hana and head west, climbing as you go. You'll circle the mountain counterclockwise as you climb, and then pick up the 128° radial for the Upolu VOR (112.3). You still will have a 30-mile crossing over the channel, but you will be able to climb to 7,500 feet (or higher, if you want) so that you will be able to remain within gliding distance of land for at least half of the flight.

There are a few special airspace considerations for the flight. There is a Class C area around Kahului Airport west of Hana. Two sectors stick out to 10 nm from the field, with ceilings of 4100 feet, but if you stay close to the mountain as you climb, you should remain well to the east of these areas.

You will find a dotted line inside the boundaries of the Haleakala National Park, which means that you are requested to remain at least 2,000 feet above the ground level. According to the chart, however, you must be at least at 9,500 MSL altitude over certain areas of the park, so to avoid these restrictions over the eastern side of the mountain, I have planned your route around the western side.

FLYING THE PLAN

The flight log for this trip is fairly simple. You will depart from Runway 26 at Hana Airport, and climb as you head west. Follow the contours of the volcano as you fly, keeping at least 500 feet above the ground level as you go. (1,000 feet is even better, since this gives you more time to make plans in the event that you have to make an emergency landing.)

VFR Flight Log

Departure: Hana Airport (HNM)
Destination: Upolu Airport (UPP)

Fixes	Route Mag Course (1)	Naut. Miles	Estimated Ground Speed (Kt)	Total Time	Actual Time
1. Depart Hana southwest	260°		80 knots	1	
2. Circle mountain, intercept 128° radial of Upolu VOR	128°	30	130	14.5	
3. Landfall at Hawaii	varies	62		29.5	
4. Circle to lose altitude at red and white tower	50°	62		39	
5. Arrive Upolu airport		64		40 (2)	

(1) Headings are approximate, using pilotage for navigation
(2) Plus 3-5 minutes to enter pattern and land

Hana Airport
Coordinates: 20-47.74; 156-00.87
Elevation: 78 feet MSL
Runways: 8-26 3,605x100
Note: right traffic Runway 26

Upolu
Coordinates: 20-15.92; 155-51.60
Elevation: 96 feet MSL
Pattern altitude: 800 MSL
Runways: 7-25 3,800x75
UNICOM/CTAF: 122.9
Notes: right traffic for Runway 25

After 15 minutes, you will have traveled about 20 miles and will be at 7,500 MSL altitude. This will be sufficient to let you level off to a 130-knot cruise speed and then follow the 7,000-foot contour of the volcano around to the southwest. Note that the peak of the volcano will still be 2,500 feet above to your left. Once you clear the ridge, turn to the southeast until you intercept the 128° radial of the Upolu VOR.

At 130 knots, it will take you just under 14 minutes to cross the channel. If you were to start a 500 fpm descent the moment you left Maui's shoreline, you'd be about at pattern altitude when you got to the other side, but you'd end up spending most of your flight out of gliding distance from land. As a result, it would be better to wait until you were within 7 miles of land before starting your descent. You can use the DME readout for the VOR to judge your distance; the VOR is about 3 miles inland, so start your descent when the DME indicates 10 nm.

Even if you slow way down during your descent, you will still have lots of excess altitude when you make landfall. Plan on making a number of slow 360-degree spiral turns once you reach land to shed this excess altitude, maintaining a comfortable 500 fpm descent rate.

You should make landfall aimed right at a tall red and white tower. Aim for this as you get down toward the pattern altitude of 800 feet, and then head east to the airport. Enter a right downwind leg (over the water) for a landing on Runway 25.

GETTING READY TO FLY

There is an entry for Hana Airport in the World Airports... menu for Hawaii, but it places you on Runway 8. You can either back-taxi to the other end of the runway, or use the following entries with the World Set Exact Location command to place you in position on Runway 26.

North/South Lat.:	N 20 47 41.7
East/West Lon.:	W 156 00 31.4
Altitude (ft):	80
Heading (deg magnetic):	255

Then tune your NAV1 radio to 112.3 for the Upolu VOR, and set the OBS to 128° so you can intercept that radial as you round the volcano.

- 140 -

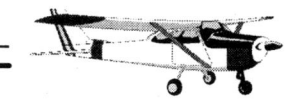

With that, you should be ready to rock and roll. Enjoy your flight, and be sure to say hello to King Kamehameha (or at least his statue) when you get to the Big Island.

⌑ Situation file: XC-HA3

Section B:
Las Vegas

Feeling lucky? Head on out to Las Vegas. For most people, Las Vegas conjures up images of slot machines, floor shows, and acres of neon lights. In fact, the city is a small oasis in the middle of a large desert. There's lots to see outside the city, which is just as well, since the McCarren International Class B airspace makes it impossible to cruise the Strip without permission from Air Traffic Control. So your three flights based on the Las Vegas scenery collection will take you to other parts of the region. With a little luck, you may even win a game of chance or two before you're finished.

Las Vegas Flight 1

Lake Cruise

Surrounded by desert, your first flight in the Las Vegas region is going to be spent largely over water. As improbable as this may seem, your route will take you along more than 30 miles of Lake Mead, a giant man-made lake on the border between Nevada and Arizona. You'll need sharp eyes to complete this flight successfully.

PLANNING A ROUTE

As shown in the section of the chart, your route starts at Perkins Field in Overton, at the north end of Lake Mead. You'll follow the western shoreline down past Echo Bay (where you can stop off at Echo Bay Airport for lunch at the Tail of the Whale restaurant if you can find the airport), then across the fork in the lake to the airport in Temple Bar, Arizona. It's a short flight, suitable for sight-seeing along the lake. Just keep in mind that the lower you fly, the harder it can be to spot your destination.

LV 1

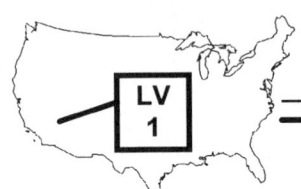

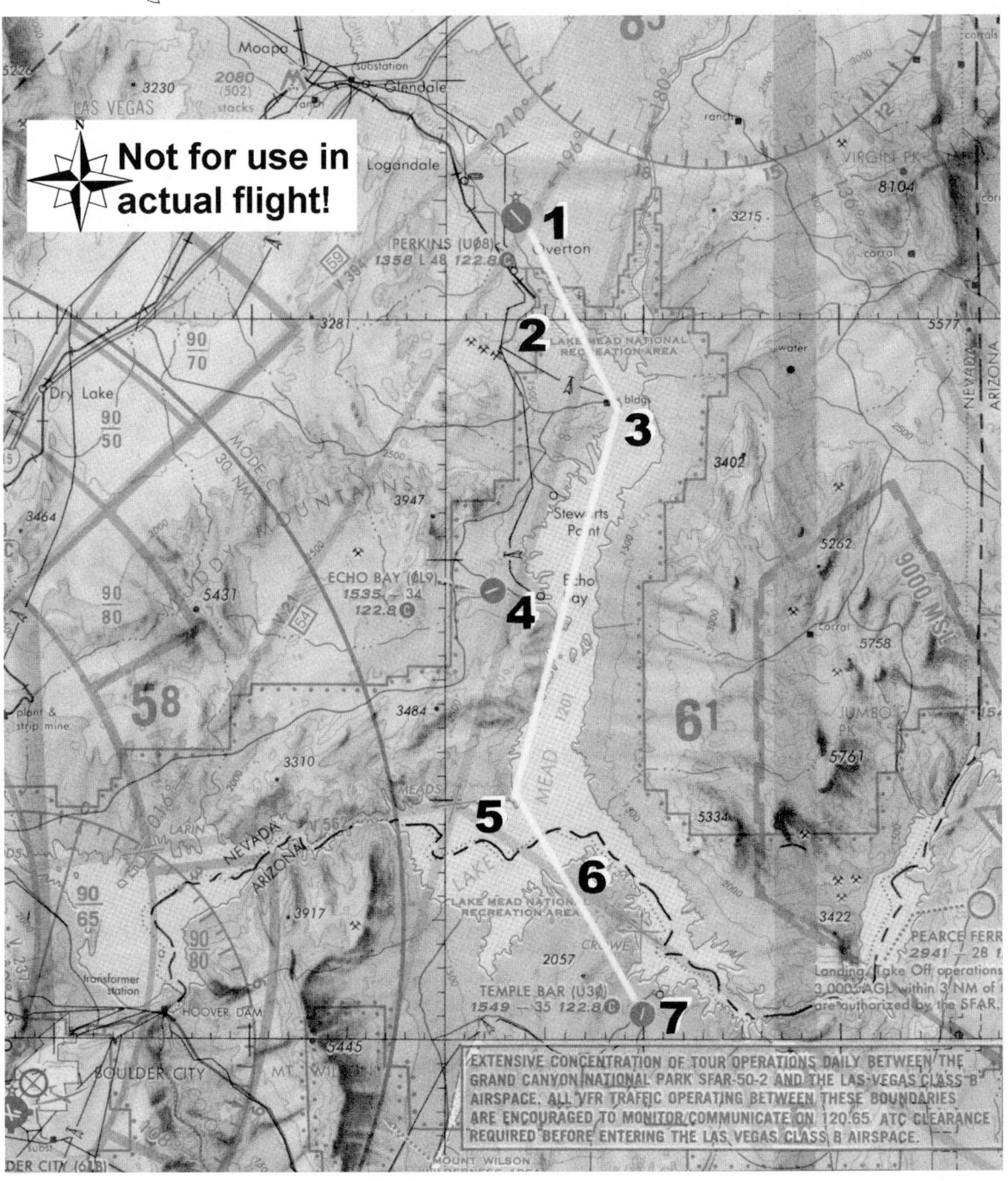

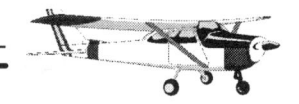

I've created a flight log for you that shows the waypoints that you can use to keep track of your progress. Departing from Runway 13 at Perkins Field, you'll be able to climb out toward Lake Mead. The entire area is a national recreation area, and the dots inside the boundary line indicate that aircraft are requested to fly at least 2,000 feet AGL over those areas. Since the lake's surface is at 1,200 feet, I've planned your route for 3,500 feet.

The route is fairly easy to follow. Just keep to the right-hand shoreline as you go. You'll turn the corner at Overton Beach, across from where the Virgin River joins the lake on its eastern shore.

A bit further down the lake, you'll see Jumbo Peak on the eastern shore, and Echo Bay below you on the western shore. If you're feeling like taking a break, head west and land for lunch at Echo Lake Airport (the Tail of the Whale restaurant is just three miles from the field). It can be a tough airport to spot, however, so check your landmarks carefully.

I've assumed that you'll continue on your way, however, without the break. Follow the western shore all the way down to the point where it turns right to the west towards Las Vegas; you'll turn left and head out across the lake for the southern shore. Halfway across, you'll leave Nevada and enter Arizona.

You'll cross over a large point of land, and then a bay on the other side. Your destination, Temple Bar Airport, is located on the other side of the bay, and in a mile or two from the shoreline.

In spite of the fact that you're flying over some pretty deserted territory, it is still difficult to spot the airports in this scenery. To prevent an unplanned trip to Phoenix, it's a good idea to build a fence in the sky to help you find the airport. In this case, you can use the VOR at Boulder City (BLD 116.7) to keep you from going past the airport. The airport is located on the 72° radial, 25.8 nm from the VOR. So if you tune your NAV1 radio to the beacon and then set the OBS to 252° (so that you get a TO reading on the OBI), you can watch the needle to help you find the airport. When the needle centers, you should be close to the airport.

LV 1

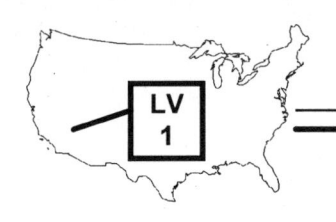

VFR Flight Log

Departure: Perkins Field (U08)
Destination: Temple Bar Airport (U30)

Fixes	Route Mag Course (1)	Naut. Miles	Estimated Ground Speed (Kt)	Total Time	Actual Time
1. Depart Perkins southeast	130°		80 knots	1	
2. Follow right shoreline	varies	6		5	
3. Turn at Overton Beach		9	130	6.5	
4. Pass Echo Bay		19		11	
5. Leave shore at point	130°	28		15	
6. Cross southern shoreline		32		17	
7. Arrive Temple Bar Airport		39		20 (2)	

(1) Headings are approximate, using pilotage for navigation
(2) Plus 3-5 minutes to enter pattern and land

Perkins Field
Coordinates: 36-34.08; 114-26.06
Elevation: 1358 feet MSL
Runways: 13-31 4,800x100
Note: right traffic Runway 31

Temple Bar Airport
Coordinates: 36-01.23; 114-20.11
Elevation: 1549 feet MSL
Pattern altitude: 2298 MSL
Runways: 18-36 3,500x50
UNICOM/CTAF: 122.8
Notes: right traffic for Runway 18; livestock in the vicinity

If the DME readout shows less than 25.8 miles when the needle centers, then the airport will be east of your position. If the readout shows a greater distance, then the airport is west of you. This extra help should make it easier to find the airport on the first try.

Flying at 3,500 feet, you'll have just a bit more than 1,000 feet of altitude to lose to get down to the pattern altitude at Temple Bar. At 500 fpm, you'll want to start your descent at least two minutes from the airport. According to the flight plan, starting your descent when you reach the southern shore of Lake Mead should work out fine.

Once you find the airport, plan on entering a right downwind leg for Runway 18. And don't forget the note in your flight log—you don't want to end up in an argument with a steer on short final, so keep a sharp lookout when you're landing.

GETTING READY TO FLY

This is an easy flight to prepare. Just pick the Perkins Field from the Las Vegas scenery list of airports in the World Airports menu. This will place you in position for takeoff on Runway 13. All you have to do is set your NAV1 radio to the Boulder City VOR (116.7) and set the OBS to the correct radial (252°).

With that, you're all ready to fly. Enjoy your over-water flight in the middle of a desert!

⌑ Situation file: XC-LV1

Las Vegas Flight 2

Making a Pass

The Las Vegas Strip is a world-famous attraction, and you can hardly plan a trip in this scenery without getting close enough to visit it. The problem is that the downtown airport—McCarren International—is surrounded by Class B airspace. While it's true that small general aviation aircraft are welcome there, you still must contact air traffic control for clearance into the airspace, which eliminates McCarren from our list of potential destinations.

Fortunately, Las Vegas has lots of small airports, some of which are quite close to the action. I've planned this trip to Henderson Sky Harbor Airport, which is less than 10 miles away from The Strip.

I've planned this trip for daylight, but you can increase the challenge and enjoy a view of the lighted city from a distance by flying at night.

- 149 -

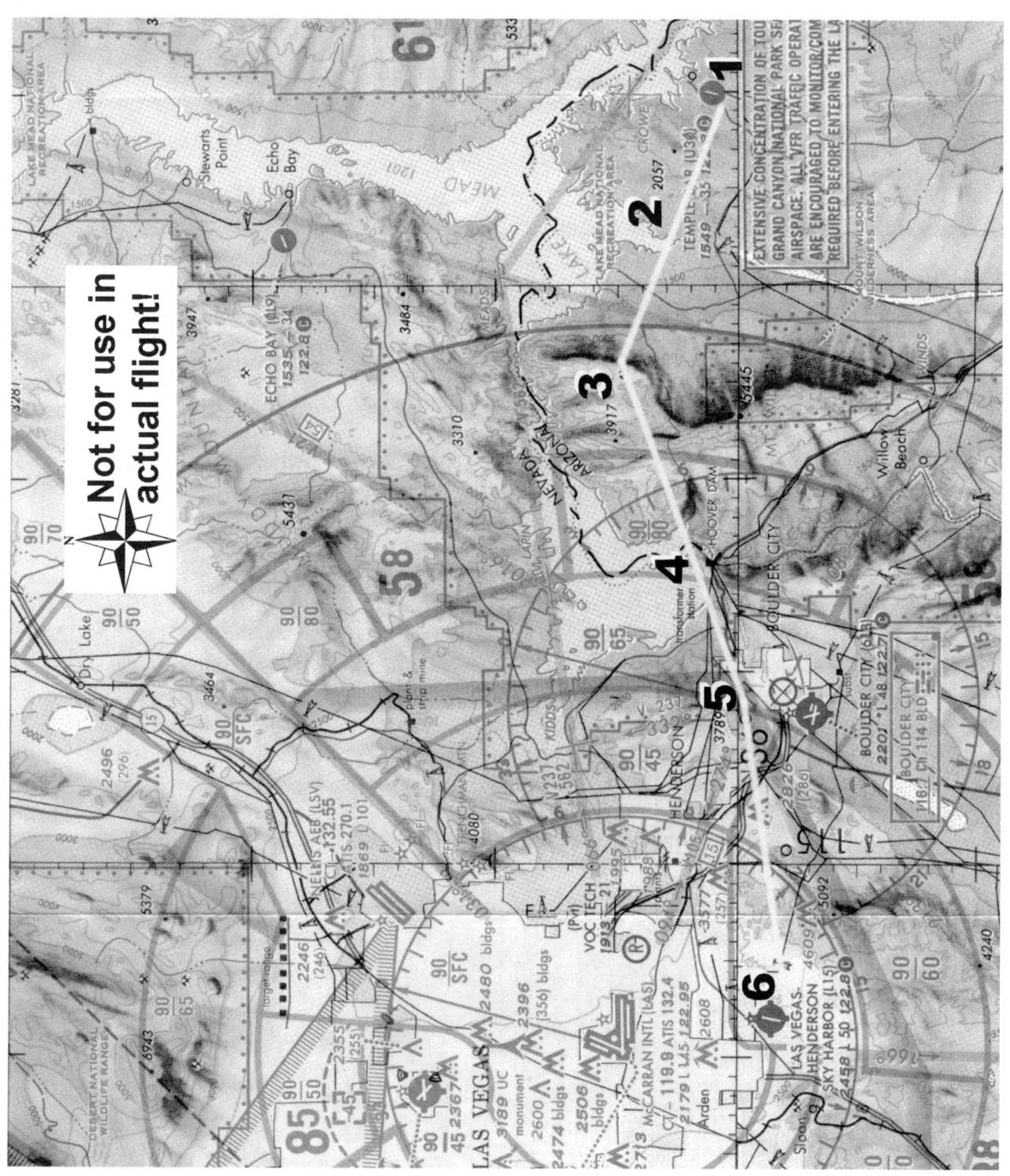

PLANNING A ROUTE

The flight begins in Temple Bar, where the last flight ended. A look at the section of the chart shows the route I have planned for you.

Notice that the trip could have been shorter if I had taken a straight line between the two airports. The problem with this route is that it would take you over the high point on the mountain ridge east of Boulder City. At 5,445 feet in elevation and surrounded by national recreation area, this bit of rock would mean that you'd have to climb to at least 7,500 feet for just a forty-mile flight.

A detour to the south of the ridge would let you fly a lot lower, as would a route that would take you back along the southern shore of Lake Mead. These both add a lot of extra distance to your route, however. Instead, I've chosen a path that goes through a notch in the ridge, called Indian Pass. (The pass is shown in greater detail on the Las Vegas Terminal Area Chart, which comes as part of the documentation for the scenery package.) The pass has a maximum elevation of just 3,268, which means that a cruising altitude of 5,500 feet will keep you above the recreation area, but you won't have to go too far out of your way or spend the whole trip climbing.

The flight plan that I have prepared for this trip shows you the key checkpoints and headings for the flight.

You'll take off from Runway 36 at Temple Bar, and climb as you head for the pass. You'll head about west until you intercept the 235° radial for the Boulder City VOR (116.7). Turn to follow the VOR, and it will take you right through the pass. Continue to track the VOR radial, past the Hoover Dam, until you reach the beacon.

Then reset your OBS to 250°, and follow that heading. Henderson Sky Harbor is 13 nm from the VOR.

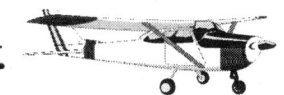

VFR Flight Log

Departure: Temple Bar Airport (U30)
Destination: Henderson Sky Harbor (L15)

Fixes	Route Mag Course	Naut. Miles	Estimated Ground Speed (Kt)	Total Time	Actual Time
1. Depart Temple Bar	270° (1)		80 knots	1	
2. Reach cruise altitude of 5,500 feet		6		5	
3. Intercept 235° radial BLD VOR	235°	9	130	6.5	
4. Pass Hoover Dam		19		11	
5. Cross BLD VOR	250°	28		15	
6. Arrive Henderson Sky Harbor Airport		39		20 (2)	

(1) Heading is approximate, using pilotage for navigation
(2) Plus 3-5 minutes to enter pattern and land

Temple Bar Airport
Coordinates: 36-01.23; 114-20.11
Elevation: 1549 feet MSL
Runways: 18-36 3,500x50
UNICOM/CTAF: 122.8
Notes: right traffic for Runway 18; livestock in the vicinity

Henderson Sky Harbor Airport
Coordinates: 35-58.58; 115-07.97
Elevation: 2458 feet MSL
Pattern altitude: 3200 MSL
Runways: 18-36 5,000x60
UNICOM/CTAF: 122.8
Note: right traffic Runway 18

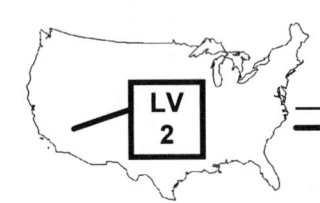

Your cruise altitude of 5,500 feet should be adequate for all of the en route portions of the trip. As shown on the chart, the floor of the Las Vegas Class B airspace is down to 5,000 feet by the time you reach Henderson Sky Harbor, but you will have started your descent to pattern altitude well before that, so you should have no problems with the special use airspace requirements.

Pattern altitude at the airport is 3,200 feet, so you'll have nearly 2,500 feet to lose from your cruising altitude. At a 500 fpm descent rate, you'll want to start at least five minutes before you arrive at the airport, which works out to about 11 miles at a speed of 130 knots. So plan to start your descent when you make your turn at the Boulder City VOR, and you should be at pattern altitude within a couple of miles of the airport.

When you get there, watch out for the heavy sight-seeing traffic bound for Las Vegas and the Grand Canyon, as well as airline service. You'll be landing on Runway 36, but keep in mind that the Class B airspace goes all the way down to the surface just about a mile north of the airport, so be careful not to bust the boundary if you have to go around on a landing attempt. It's a standard left traffic pattern for Runway 36, so plan on entering a left downwind leg as you approach the field.

GETTING READY TO FLY

Preparation is simple; pick Temple Bar from the Las Vegas list in the World Airports menu. The only other setting you have to make is to tune the NAV1 radio to the Boulder City VOR (116.7) and set the OBS for the 235° radial.

With that, you're ready to head to The Strip and try your luck. Just remember to keep some get-out-of-town cash safe in your shoe, so you can pay the FBO fee when you're ready to leave town.

💾 Situation file: XC-LV2

Las Vegas Flight 3

Leaving Las Vegas

Feeling lucky today? Fate has something in store for you today, but whether it is good luck, bad luck, or some combination of the two remains to be seen.

I have planned a trip where you won't reach the intended destination; there's a surprise or two waiting for you along the way. The trip is designed to take you from Las Vegas to Lake Tahoe, though you'll be making an unscheduled stop before you get there.

PLANNING A ROUTE

A look at the chart shows your route for this flight. You'll take off from Henderson Sky Harbor, and then follow US Route 95 northwest out of Las Vegas. Though the chart doesn't show the entire route, you can follow the road up through Tonopah and Hawthorne, Nevada, until you can pick up the Mustang VOR outside of Reno. From there, you can find your way west to Lake Tahoe and the Truckee-Tahoe Airport northwest of the lake.

LV
3

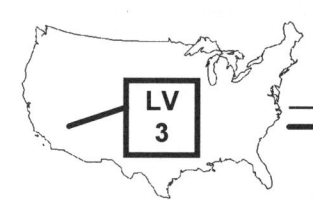

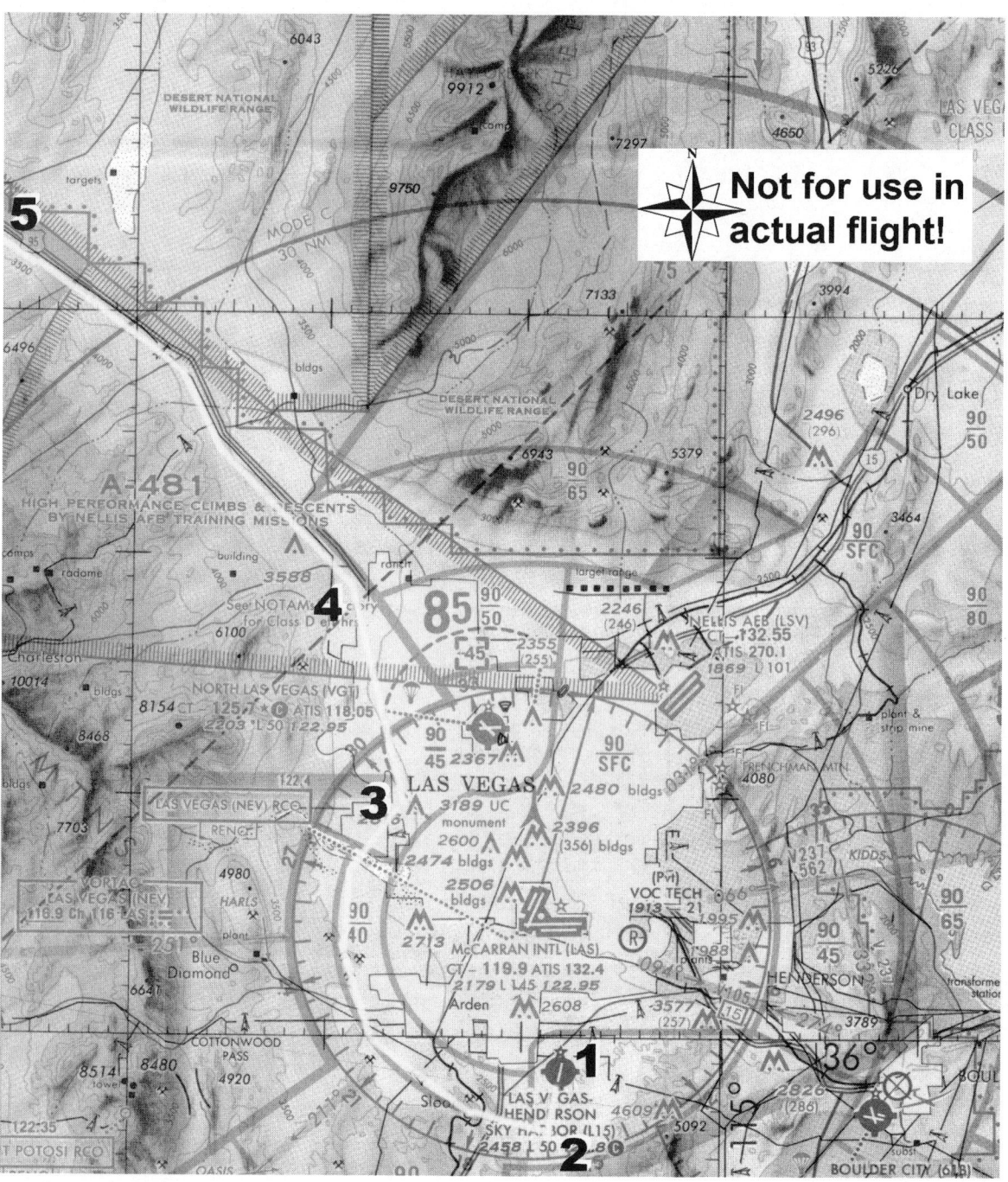

Not for use in actual flight!

- 154 -

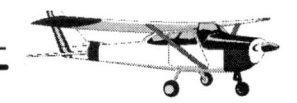

You can't just blast off from Henderson Sky Harbor, however, and go along your merry way; there's that big inverted wedding cake of Class B in your way. You'll have to find a way to circle it to the west before you pick up your heading out of town.

This flight is another example where flying in FS 5.1 scenery can be much more difficult than navigating in the real world. The real world has roads and buildings and other landmarks that make it much easier to know where you are; not all of these details are present in the Las Vegas scenery, so you'll have to resort to a mix of pilotage, radio navigation, and ded reckoning techniques to steer clear of the Class B airspace.

You'll depart on Runway 18 from Henderson Sky Harbor. An altitude of 3,500 feet will give you sufficient room above the ground, but will still keep you low and out of the way of the commercial airliner traffic headed in and out of McCarren International. This will also keep you below the 4,000 foot floor of the Class B space to the southwest of the airport.

The outside edge of the 4,000 foot area of the Class B space is 8 nm from McCarren, which is also where the Las Vegas VOR (NEV 116.9) is conveniently located. You can use the DME readout on your navigation radio to help you stay 8 nm away from the VOR, which will give you a two-mile cushion from the Class B space.

As you swing around Las Vegas, keeping your 8 nm distance from the VOR, you will eventually come to a radio tower that is northwest of the city. If you were to continue on your curved path, you would run the risk of busting the Class D space around North Las Vegas Airport. To avoid this, you'll change your heading to 345° (nearly true north) and take up a position parallel to Route 95. When the road turns northwest beyond North Las Vegas, you'll intercept it and can follow it out of town. At that point, you'll want to gain some altitude as the terrain rises; go on up to 4,500 feet to start.

LV
3

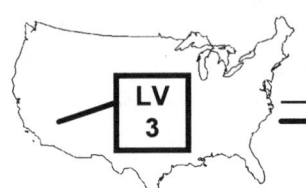

VFR Flight Log

Departure: Henderson Sky Harbor (L15)
Destination: Truckee-Tahoe (TRK)

FIXES	ROUTE		ESTIMATED		ACTUAL
	MAG COURSE (1)	NAUT. MILES	GROUND SPEED (KT)	TOTAL TIME	TIME
1. Depart Henderson Sky Harbor	180°		80 knots	1	
2. Reach cruise altitude of 3,500 feet, turn west, remain 8 nm from NEV VOR	varies	2.5	130	2	
3. Reach radio tower	345	22.5		11	
4. Intercept Route 95	varies	30		14.5	
5. At 37.5 nm from NEV, kill engine.		39		26 (2)	

(1) Headings are approximate, using pilotage for navigation
(2) Plus 3-5 minutes to land

Henderson Sky Harbor Airport
Coordinates: 35-58.58; 115-07.97
Elevation: 2458 feet MSL
Pattern altitude: 3200 MSL
Runways: 18-36 5,000x60
UNICOM/CTAF: 122.8
Note: right traffic Runway 18

Truckee-Tahoe Airport
Coordinates: 39-19.22; 120-08.40
Elevation: 5900 feet MSL
Pattern altitude: 6900 MSL
Runways: 1-19 4,650x75
UNICOM/CTAF: 122.8
Note: right traffic Runway 19

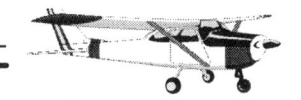

Spotting Route 95 is much more difficult in FS 5.1 than it would be in real life. Instead of showing up as a road, it looks more like a faded or flattened patch in the scenery. The fact that it is in a fairly straight line helps you find it, and you can also use the map view zoomed out a bit to help see the big picture. Even so, I get a feeling that I'm flying over a post-apocalyptic, Mad Max landscape, following a road that has long-since disappeared.

The flight log that I have prepared shows the flight plan to this point. If you want, you can work out the rest of the details for the route to Lake Tahoe.

As promised, however, you won't get there. When your DME readout shows 37.5 nm from the Las Vegas VOR, turn off your engine (use either mixture to full-lean cutoff, or switch off the magnetos by pressing M then the Minus key until the engine stops. You are now the pilot of a glider, and not a very good glider at that. Trim your airplane for the best glide speed—70 knots should work—and start figuring out where you're going to put it on the ground. The desert can be an unforgiving place to lose an engine in a single, but who knows? Maybe this will be your lucky day....

GETTING READY TO FLY

Henderson Sky Harbor Airport does have an entry on the World Airports list, but it is only for Runway 36. You can either use that choice to place your plane on the runway, then back taxi all the way to the other end, or you can enter the following values in the World Set Exact Location menu:

North/South Lat.:	N 35 58 58.4
East/West Lon.:	W 115 07 50.8
Altitude (ft):	2463
Heading (deg magnetic):	179

Then set your NAV1 radio to the Las Vegas VOR (116.9). You don't have to be concerned about the OBS setting, because you're only interested in the DME readout.

- 157 -

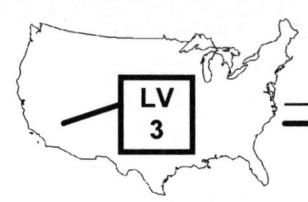

With that, you're ready to roll. Just make sure that you stay clear of the special use airspace, watch for traffic, find that elusive Route 95, and don't forget to kill your engine at 37.5 nm from the VOR. Let's hope that Fortune smiles on you....

🖫 Situation file: XC-LV3

Section C:
New York A

New York, New York! The default scenery for this part of the country includes Manhattan and some of the familiar sights in that area, but it also stretches to cover large portions of the New York Sectional chart—all the way out to Martha's Vineyard off Cape Cod and up to Boston. The add-on scenery from Microsoft fills in some of the details in the greater metropolitan New York area. In addition to the three major area airports—Kennedy, La Guardia, and Newark—there are many smaller fields with plenty of general aviation activity. For these three flights, you'll stay clear of the more crowded skies over Manhattan, and instead will take a circle route to some of the less-famous airports in New York and New Jersey.

New York A
Flight 1

On the Beach

On aviation charts, built-up areas are represented by solid yellow fills. I've always figured that this choice was made because all the lights at night make city areas glow yellow at night.

The New York Terminal Area Chart is largely covered with light blue for the water and bright yellow for New York City and surrounding areas. Long Island is part of that area; a long, broad yellow finger pointing eastward from Manhattan. Not until you get out near the eastern tip do you reach areas where the suburban sprawl finally surrenders to the remaining potato farms and other rural land uses, and the yellow ink is replaced with the pale green of low-lying land. Your flight will take you around the busiest, most densely-populated portions of New York City, from Republic Airport on Long Island, to Linden Airport under the shadow of Newark International. And you'll be able to make the flight without contacting Air Traffic Control.

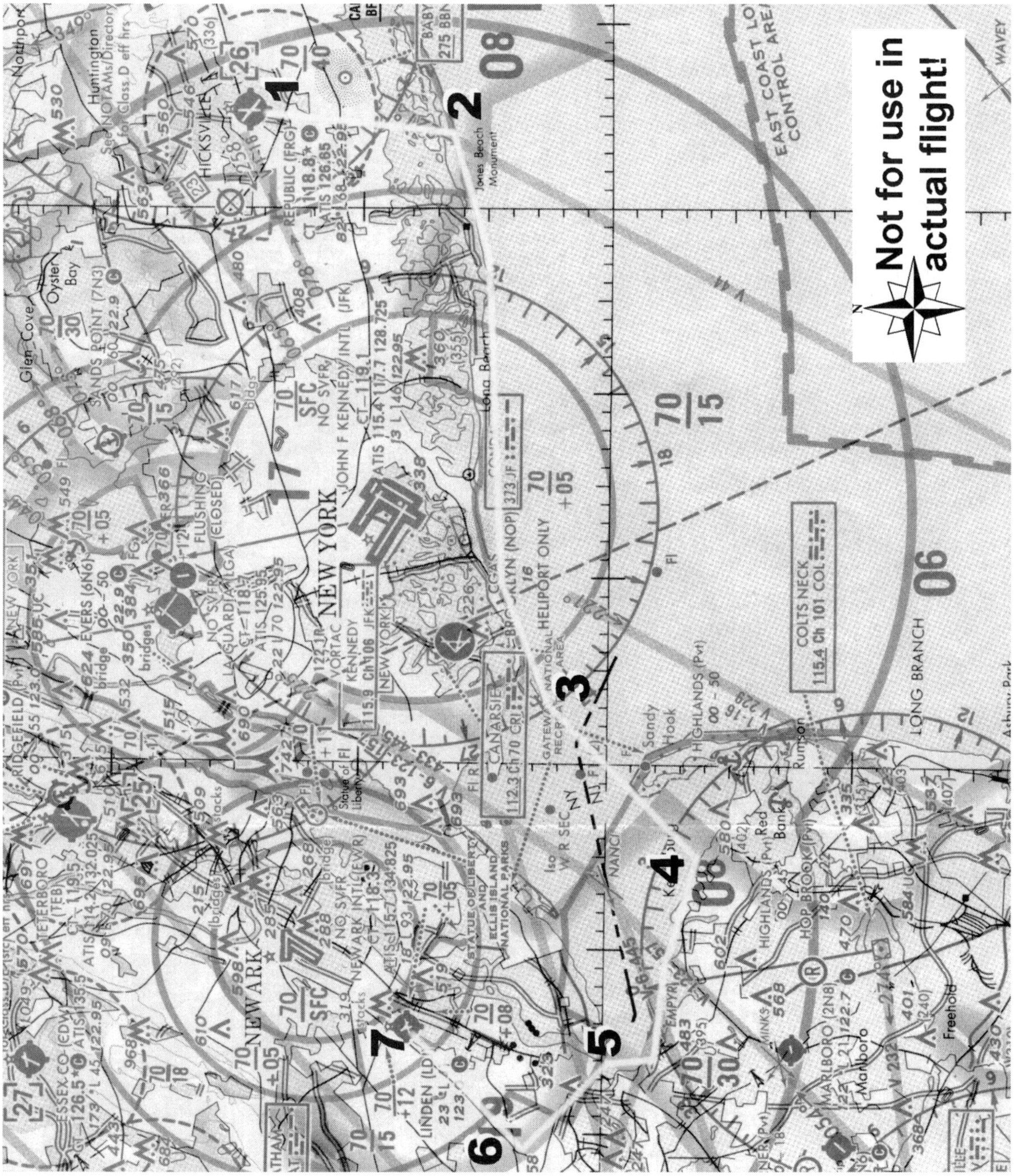
Not for use in
actual flight!
1
2
3
4
5
6
7
NEW YORK
NEWARK
EAST COAST
CONTROL AREA
LONG BRANCH
Jones Beach
Monument
COLTS NECK
115.4 Ch 101 COL
HICKSVILLE
Huntington
Northport
Glen Cove
Oyster
Bay
Sandy
Hook
Freehold
Marlboro
Rumson
Red
Bank
Statue of
Liberty
NATIONAL
HELIPORT ONLY
WAVEY

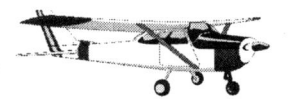

PLANNING A ROUTE

The section of the chart shows the route for the flight; for a better look at the area, you might want to use the New York Terminal Area Chart which shows more detail. There is a complex of intertwining Class B airspace sections over all three of the major New York airports, making VFR navigation a bit trickier than in most other parts of the country.

The portion of the Class B space that has the most impact on this trip is the section surrounding Kennedy Airport on the south side of Long Island. Some sections have boundaries that follow the coastline, and it is possible to fly just off-shore and remain under the Class B floor. Right next to Kennedy, the floor comes down to 500 feet, which means you will need to get down on the deck at 400 feet (to give yourself a little room at the top) but you'll have to be sharp about holding your altitude.

Once you get past Kennedy, you can climb to 800 feet and head 240° to cut across the mouth of the Hudson River to Sandy Hook, which is a spit of land that runs north and south. Sandy Hook is also a national recreation area, which means that you are requested to stay at least 2,000 feet above it when flying over it. The Class B airspace floor is only at 1,500 feet just to the east of it, however, so you won't be able to climb over it. As a result, you can stay just to the west of it.

Once you make landfall at New Jersey, you can follow the coast around to Perth Amboy. There is a swampy area at the west end of Raritan Bay, where you head northwest until you intercept the 45° radial of the Teterboro VOR (TEB 108.40). You can then follow this radial, which will keep you safely to the west of landing and departing traffic at Newark International.

Linden Airport is about 16 nm from the Teterboro VOR, so you can use your DME readout to warn you as you get closer to the airport. You can't go very far beyond it without busting the Class B airspace around Newark, so be careful. Once you reach the airport, enter a left downwind leg for Runway 27, and you'll be all set to land.

VFR Flight Log

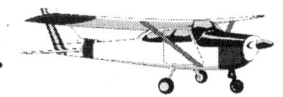

Departure: Republic Airport (FRG)
Destination: Linden Airport (LDJ)

Fixes	Route Mag Course (1)	Naut. Miles	Estimated Ground Speed (Kt)	Total Time	Actual Time
1. Depart Republic, right turn, depart to the south	190°		80 / 130 knots	1	
2. Cross Tobay Beach, follow shore to the west	varies	8	130	5	
3. Cross tip of Rockaway Beach	240°	32		16	
4. Cross New Jersey shore	varies	42		20.5	
5. At swamp, head northwest	315°	52		25	
6. Intercept 45° TEB radial	45°	55		26.5	
7. Arrive at Linden		64		31 (2)	

(1) Headings are approximate, using pilotage for navigation
(2) Plus 3-5 minutes to land

Republic Airport
Coordinates: 40-43.73; 073-24.80
Elevation: 81 feet MSL
Pattern altitude: 1100 MSL
Runways: 1-19 5,516x150, 14-32 6,827x150
Control Tower/CTAF: 118.8 (Tower open 7 am to 11 pm)
Note: right traffic Runways 1 and 32

Linden Airport
Coordinates: 40-37.07; 074-14.67
Elevation: 23 feet MSL
Pattern altitude: 800 MSL
Runways: 14-32 2,494x75, 9-27 4,137x100
UNICOM/CTAF: 123.0

I've created a flight log with key checkpoints and headings. One major problem with the flight as planned is that you will spend a lot of time over water at very low altitudes. For the portion along Long Island, you will be able to set down on the beach in case of trouble, but the densely-packed buildings in Jersey would make it a big challenge to find a safe place for an emergency landing. So keep your life vest handy over the water, and think kind thoughts about your engine once you get over the city.

GETTING READY TO FLY

You can get ready to fly by choosing the Farmington Republic entry from the World Airports menu under the "USA - New York Addon" list. This will place you in position for takeoff on Runway 1 at Republic.

Republic does have a Control Tower, from which you must get clearance before you depart. You can pretend to make contact with the tower, or you can pretend that you received a clearance by telephone before you left (and are using light gun signals), or you can set your clock back to 6:30 am. The tower doesn't open until 7:00 am, so you can depart without any clearance at all before that hour.

You'll also want to tune your NAV1 radio to the Teterboro VOR (108.40), and set the OBS to 45° so you can intercept that radial when you get to the Jersey side.

Other than that, all you have to do is watch your altitude and be careful about staying out of the Class B airspace. Be sure to take a few moments to enjoy the beach and the approach to New York Harbor; at 400 feet, you're going to get a close-up view!

🖫 Situation file: XC-NYA1

New York A
Flight 2

I Follow Roads

Los Angeles may have the reputation of "Freeway Capital of the World", but metropolitan New York is a prime contender for the title. There are enough highways, freeways, beltways, parkways, turnpikes, and other fancy-named rush-hour parking lots to confuse even the native drivers.

Not only does flying let you rise above the mundane frustrations of bumper-to-bumper transportation, it also lets you take advantage of those concrete ribbons to help you find your way. Granted, the roads are not labeled so you can identify them from 2,000 feet up (and they're rarely identified by name or number on charts, either) but they still can be useful for navigation.

Unfortunately, not all the roads are shown in the New York add-on scenery, so you'll have to add some ded reckoning and radio navigation to the mix in order to make it from Linden Airport to Lincoln Park.

NYA
2

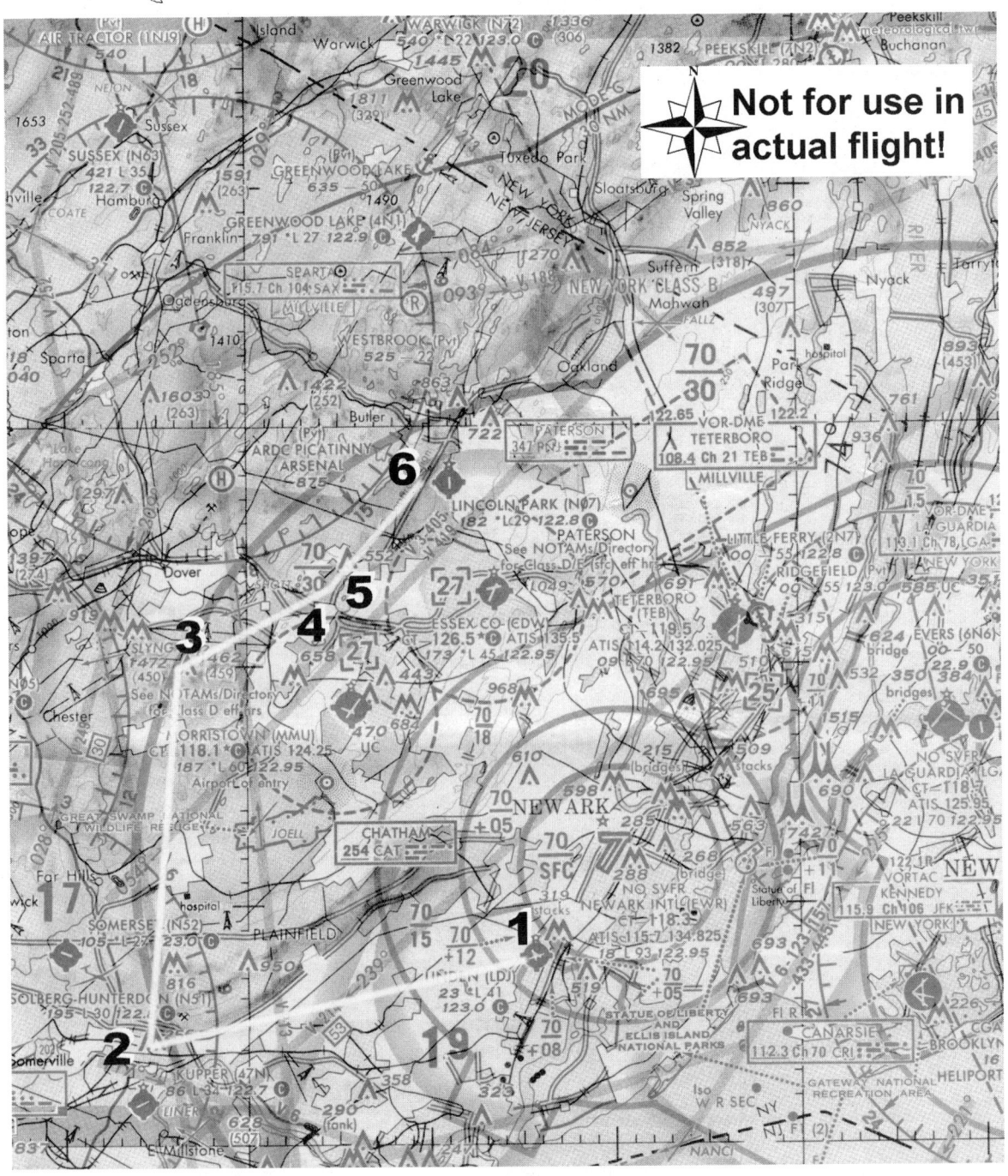

Not for use in actual flight!

PLANNING A ROUTE

It would be great if you could simply head off in a straight line from Linden to Lincoln, but the FAA regulations don't make that easy. In addition to the complex Class B airspace that blankets the area, you also have other special use airspace to consider.

The section of the chart shows the route I have chosen for your flight. Notice the dotted circles around the Morristown and Essex airports; these represent Class D airspace, and the "27" notations within the broken squares indicates that the airspace extends up to an altitude of 2,700 feet. The floor of the Class B airspace in this area extends down to 3,000 feet, which offers only a thin layer for passage where you don't have to talk to an air traffic controller.

Notice also that Lincoln lies just to the north of the Essex Class D airspace. To fly over Essex at 2,800 feet would mean that you'd have to spiral down over Lincoln in order to land.

An easier path is to simply sidestep all these restrictions, and go around them to the west. As a result, I have figured out a route that takes you west from Linden, then you turn roughly north until you can turn again to the northeast to find your destination.

The flight log shows the different checkpoints along your route. The first leg starts with a straight-out departure from Runway 27 at Linden. If you head about west, you will see the ridge northwest of Plainfield, and will find that you're traveling between Route 22 to your right and I-287 to your left. Your route should take you right over their intersection (where they abruptly end in the scenery, but they do continue on in real life). Soon after, you will intercept the 15° radial of the Sparta VOR (SAX 115.7). You can follow this, and it will keep you safely to the west of the Morristown Class D airspace.

Once you get within 14 nm of the Sparta VOR (use your DME readout to track the distance), you can turn northeast toward Lincoln.

VFR Flight Log

Departure: Linden Airport (LDJ)
Destination: Lincoln Park Airport (N07)

Fixes	Route		Estimated		Actual
	Mag Course (1)	Naut. Miles	Ground Speed (Kt)	Total Time	Time
1. Depart Linden, head west toward ridge	270°		80 / 130 knots	1	
2. Intercept Sparta VOR 15° radial	15°	13	130	7	
3. 14 miles from Sparta VOR	50°	29		14.5	
4. Cross I-80	varies	34		16.5	
5. Intercept and follow I-287	varies	39		19	
6. Arrive at Lincoln Park		45		22 (2)	

(1) Headings are approximate, using pilotage for navigation
(2) Plus 3-5 minutes to land

Linden Airport
Coordinates: 40-37.07; 074-14.67
Elevation: 23 feet MSL
Pattern altitude: 800 MSL
Runways: 14-32 2,494x75, 9-27 4,137x100
UNICOM/CTAF: 123.0

Lincoln Park Airport
Coordinates: 40-56.85, 074-18.87
Elevation: 181 feet MSL
Pattern altitude: 1180 MSL
Runways: 1-19 2,942x40
UNICOM/CTAF: 118.8
Note: right traffic Runway 1

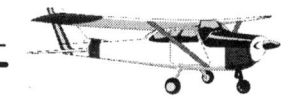

You'll fly over Route 46, and then I-80, at which point you will be able to see I-287 heading off to the northeast. You must stay west of the intersection of I-80 and I-287 in order to stay clear of the Morrisville Class D airspace. Fly over to I-287 and you'll be able to follow it to Butler; Lincoln Park will be just southeast of the town, waiting for your arrival. Enter a left downwind leg and land on Runway 19.

HOW HIGH TO FLY?

The Class B airspace puts some limits on how high you can fly. Right after you depart Linden, the floor of the space is at 1,200 feet, then 1,500 feet. When you reach your turning point to follow the Sparta VOR radial, it is at 3,000 feet. As a result, you should climb to an initial altitude of 800 feet for the first leg—this doesn't give you much time to react in the event of a mechanical problem, but it gives you plenty of cushion below the Class B airspace.

You'd need more than a cushion, however, to complete this flight at an 800 foot altitude. The ridge north of Basking Ridge along your route has a high point of 870 feet, and your route takes you within a couple of miles of this point. To be safe, climb to 2,000 feet after you make your turn toward the VOR, and you'll have plenty of air above and below you at that altitude.

The next question is when to start your descent. At a planned speed of 130 knots and a cruising altitude of 2,000 feet, you'll need to lose less than 1,000 feet to get down to the pattern altitude of 1,180 feet at Lincoln Park. That will take less than two minutes at a 500 fpm descent, which translates to just over four miles. This means that you should start your descent just before you reach I-287 north of I-80, and you should be at pattern altitude by the time you reach the airport.

GETTING READY TO FLY

There is an entry on the World Airports menu for Linden, but it places you in the takeoff position for Runway 9, and this flight is planned for Runway 27. You can either use the Airports menu to go to Runway 9 and then taxi to the other end, or you can enter the following items in the World Set Exact Location window:

North/South Lat.:   N 40 37 04.0

East/West Lon.:	W 074 14 18.3
Altitude (ft):	29
Heading (deg magnetic):	272

Then, tune your NAV1 radio to the Sparta VOR (115.7) and set the OBS to 15°.

With that, you should be all set to fly. You'll get a good view of some of the major roads in northern New Jersey, and with a little imagination, you can just see all the cars stuck in traffic jams down there as you soar over them in your plane.

🖫 Situation file: XC-NYA2

New York A
Flight 3

Dawn Patrol

Big airports have control towers, and little airplanes have to talk to the tower before landing. Not all towers are open around the clock, however, which makes it possible for you to sneak into a big airport without talking to anyone at all.

Westchester Airport in White Plains may not be as large or as busy as Kennedy or Newark, but it still qualifies as a big airport. It has scheduled commercial flights, and along with its large general aviation activity, the air and the ground can get pretty crowded at times. The tower is only open from 6:00 am to 10:00 pm, however, which means that an early morning flight will let you arrive (or depart) without being required to talk to air traffic controllers. In this flight, you'll race the dawn from Lincoln Park to Westchester, with only the anglers along the Hudson and the early-morning commuters on the Tappan Zee Bridge on hand to witness your trip.

NYA
3

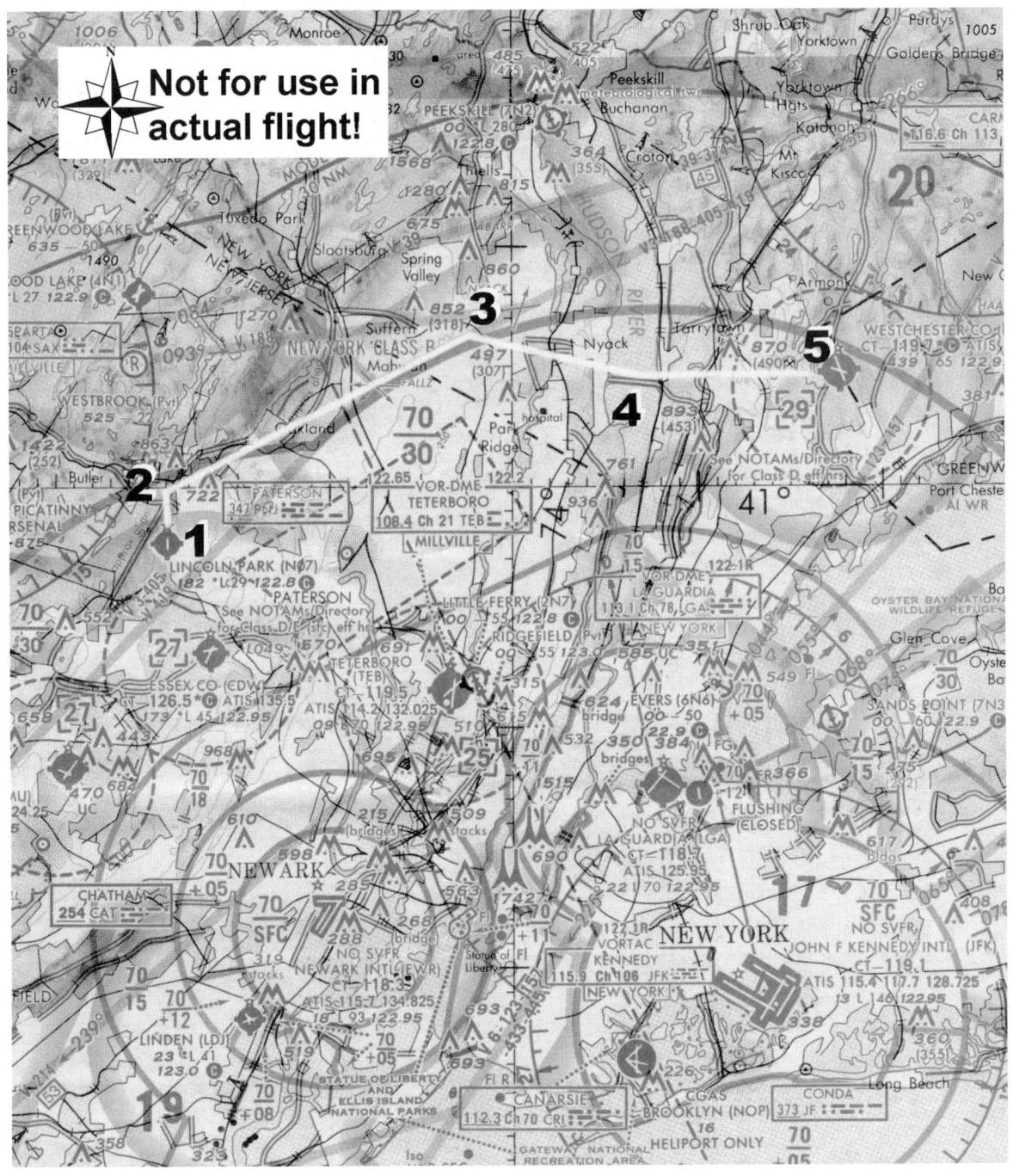

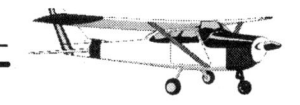

PLANNING A ROUTE

The section of the chart shows your route, which is fairly simple. You'll depart from Runway 1 at Lincoln Park, and climb out straight ahead until you reach a cruising altitude of 1,500 feet. Aside from the Class B airspace above you that starts at 3,000 feet, there is no special use airspace that you have to worry about. (The rectangular area to the northeast of Essex County Airport is printed in magenta, not blue, on the chart, which means that it is Class E airspace and only affects flights in instrument conditions. You don't have to be concerned about it during VFR conditions.)

When you intercept the 75° radial for the Carmel VOR (CMK, 116.60), you'll turn and follow it. After six to eight minutes on this heading, you probably will be able to spot the Tappan Zee Bridge crossing the Hudson river; it should be a bit to the right of your course. Given the time of day—you'll be flying in the dark—all you'll see is a mass of orange street lights.

Head for the bridge, and when you reach it, you will spot the lights of Westchester Airport, which should be on your nose or slightly to the left. While an airport as large as Westchester does stand out dramatically in the dark in real life, it is still much easier to spot when flying FS5.1.

If you have trouble finding the airport, it is helpful to know that it is 14 nm from the Carmel VOR on the 216° radial. If you get lost, just dial that heading into the OBS on your NAV1 radio, and fly until the needle centers. Then fly either toward or away from the VOR depending on whether your DME readout is greater than 14 (fly *toward* the VOR) or less than 14 (fly *away* from the beacon). When the DME reads 14, you should be right over the field.

Assuming that you do find the field on the first try, you'll want to be sure to be on the ground before the tower opens for business. We'll assume that there are no other aircraft in the pattern, so you can make a straight-in approach for a landing on Runway 11.

VFR Flight Log

Departure: Lincoln Park Airport (N07)
Destination: Westchester County Airport (HPN)

FIXES	ROUTE MAG COURSE (1)	NAUT. MILES	ESTIMATED GROUND SPEED (KT)	TOTAL TIME	ACTUAL TIME
1. Depart Lincoln, climb on runway heading	10°		80 knots	1	
2. Intercept Carmel VOR 75° radial	75°	2	80	3	
3. Turn towards Tappan Zee Bridge	varies	18	130	11	
4. At bridge, turn toward Westchester airport		23		13.5	
5. Arrive at Westchester		31		17 (2)	

(1) Headings are approximate, using pilotage for navigation
(2) Plus 1-3 minutes to land

Lincoln Park Airport
Coordinates: 40-56.85, 074-18.87
Elevation: 181 feet MSL
Pattern altitude: 1180 MSL
Runways: 1-19 2,942x40
UNICOM/CTAF: 118.8
Note: right traffic Runway 1

Westchester County Airport
Coordinates: 041-04.0; 073-42.5
Location: 14 nm from Carmel VOR (CMK) 116.6, 216°
Elevation: 439 feet MSL
Pattern altitude: 1499 MSL
Runways: 11-29 4,451 x 150; 16-34 6,548 x 150
Tower/CTAF: 119.7

GETTING READY TO FLY

Setting up at Lincoln Park is easy; select the airport from the World Airports menu, on the "USA - New York Addon" list. This will place you right on Runway 1, ready for takeoff.

There's one more setting to change, however. Choose the World Set Time and Season menu command, and then Set Exact Time. Set the time to 05 hours and 30 minutes. Then choose OK to return to the program. According to the flight plan that I have worked out for you, that should give you at least 10 minutes to spare in order to get on the ground at Westchester before the tower opens for business. You should be able to make that with no trouble, so long as you don't lose *too* much time getting lost en route.

And once you're on the ground at Westchester, take a few minutes to sit in your plane on the ramp and watch the dawn break in the sky—it's a beautiful sight.

💾 Situation file: XC-NYA3

Section D: Caribbean

Ahhh, the Caribbean! Miles and miles of crystal waters, dotted with some of the most beautiful island beaches in all the world. Parts of it are so close that you can visit on a short jump from the Florida coast, but the chain of islands (and the Microsoft scenery collection) stretches all the way down to the top of the South American continent.

There are two simple truths about flying in the Caribbean; some of the distances are great, and every flight involves some over-water travel. Combine these two factors, and you can have some long legs without much to look at along the way. You can hurry progress along with the use of the autopilot and Rate of Simulation features in FS5.1, but for the real experience, hand fly these legs in real-time. The extra effort will make you appreciate your beach time all the more when you reach your destination.

Caribbean Flight 1

Keys to the Bahamas

Follow the Florida Keys northeast then cross the Gulf Stream, and you'll find the Bimini Islands—gateway to the Caribbean. Many pilots use Bimini as their first stop on the way to other islands in the Bahamas, because it is just about a 50-mile hop from the Florida coast, and is a good way to get your feet wet (or keep them dry, as the case may be) for a long over-water crossing.

This flight uses a combination of pilotage and radio navigation procedures, and the most difficult parts of the trip will be having the patience to hold your course and the confidence to trust your navigation when you're trying to spot a small island in the middle of a large ocean. Just remember that there's a beautiful beach and a tall, cold rum drink (or other beverage of personal preference) waiting for you at the end of your flight.

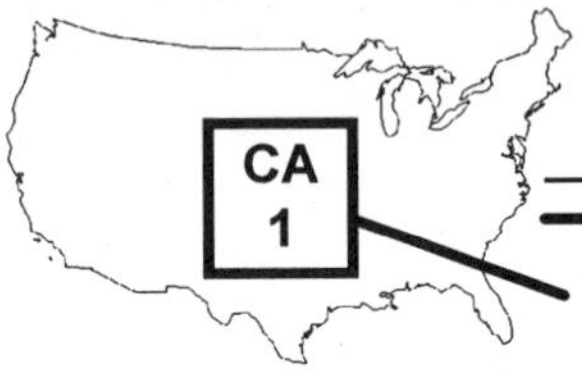
CA
1

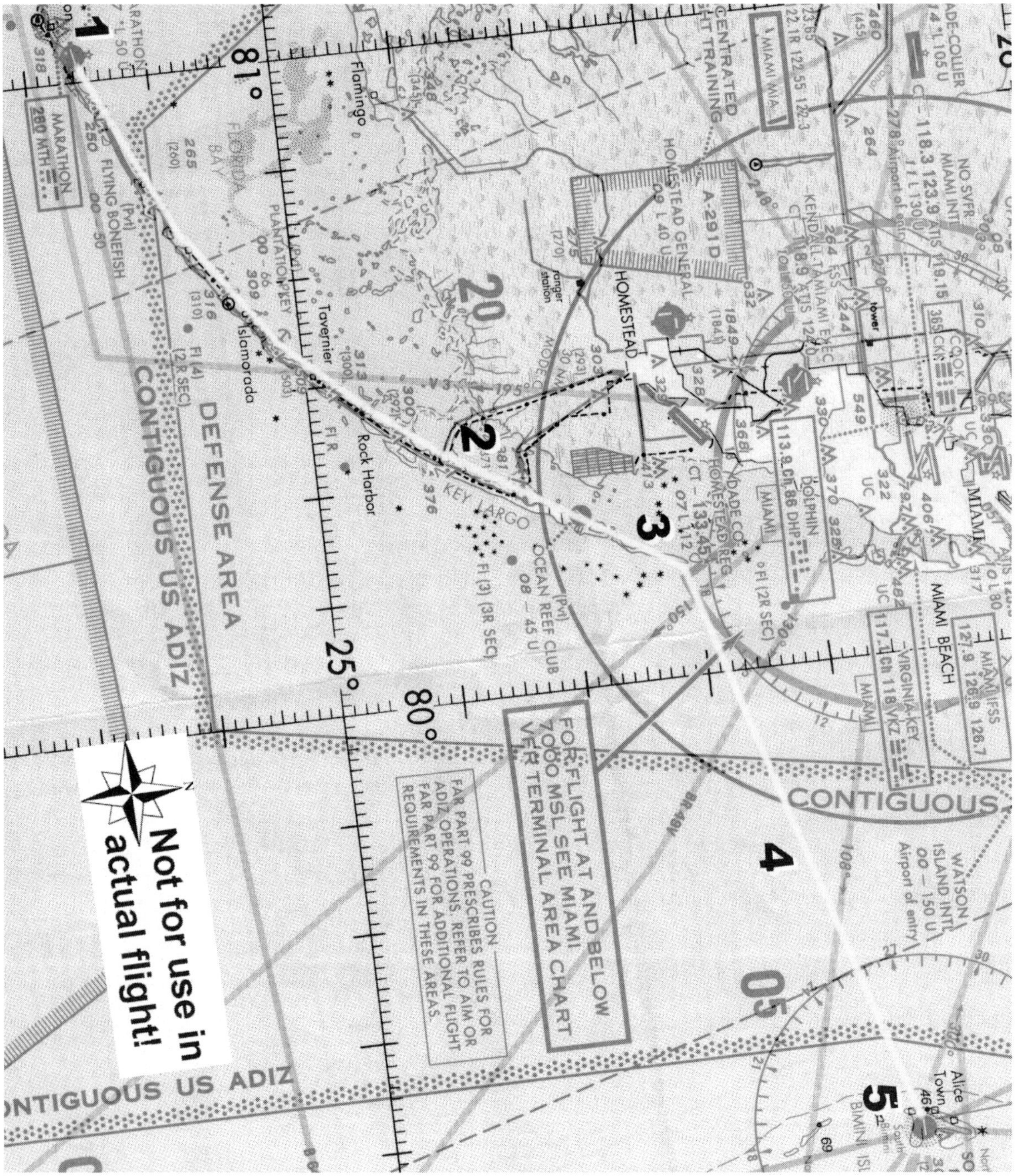
Not for use in actual flight!
FOR FLIGHT AT AND BELOW 7000 MSL SEE MIAMI VFR TERMINAL AREA CHART
CAUTION
FAR PART 99 PRESCRIBES RULES FOR ADIZ OPERATIONS. REFER TO AIM OR FAR PART 99 FOR ADDITIONAL FLIGHT REQUIREMENTS IN THESE AREAS.
CONTIGUOUS US ADIZ
DEFENSE AREA
CONTIGUOUS
81°
80°
25°
1
2
3
4
5
MARATHON
280 MTH
FLYING BONEFISH
Flamingo
FLORIDA BAY
PLANTATION KEY
Islamorada
Tavernier
Rock Harbor
KEY LARGO
OCEAN REEF CLUB
HOMESTEAD
HOMESTEAD GENERAL
A-291D
KENDALL-TAMIAMI EXEC
DADE-COLLIER
DOLPHIN
113.9 Ch 86 DHP
MIAMI
MIAMI BEACH
VIRGINIA KEY
117.1 Ch 118 VKZ
MIAMI FSS
WATSON ISLAND INTL
Airport of entry
Alice Town
BIMINI
20
05

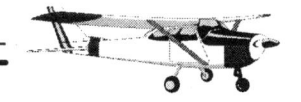

PLANNING A ROUTE

This is an international flight, and as a result, there are a number of requirements that I won't bother simulating here—especially since most of them can be handled on the ground. To make this flight in real life, you'd have to file a flight plan before leaving the United States, and you'd have to have paperwork in order for both Bahamian and US Customs officials. There are also requirements for details such as the size of the numbers on the side of your aircraft, life-saving equipment such as rafts and flotation devices, and other details that you'd have to attend to before departure.

Also, while I have planned all Cross Country flights so that you are not required to communicate with Air Traffic Control facilities, I personally recommend that pilots take advantage of ATC services whenever possible for all flights. This is especially true for a long over-water flight such as this one. If you're getting traffic advisories from Miami Center as you fly over the ocean, it means that you'll already be in communication with them in the unlikely event that you encounter mechanical problems. This in turn means that it will take that much less time for help to arrive if you are forced to turn your Cessna into a seaplane.

So keep in mind that this flight and the others in this section are simplified a little more than the flights that remain within the boundaries of the United States.

You'll start your flight from Marathon Airport, halfway down the Florida Keys. You'll depart Runway 7 straight out, and follow Route 1 as you cruise-climb to your crossing altitude.

The only special use airspace that you need to consider is the Class B airspace that sits over Miami. There's a piece that juts out over Elliott Key in Biscayne Bay, but it only extends up to 7,000 feet. Since you'll want plenty of altitude for your crossing, you'll be higher than that when you leave Florida behind.

CA 1

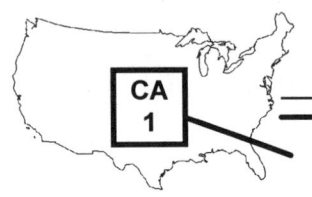

VFR Flight Log KMTH ✓

Departure: Marathon Airport (MTH)
Destination: South Bimini Airport (MYBS)

FIXES	ROUTE		ESTIMATED		ACTUAL
	MAG COURSE (1)	NAUT. MILES	GROUND SPEED (KT)	TOTAL TIME	TIME
1. Depart Marathon	varies		80 knots	1	
2. Cruise climb to 9,500 feet		25	130	20	
3. Intercept Bimini VOR 78° radial	78°	60		36	
4. At 24 nm from Bimini, slow and start descent		86	80	48	
5. Arrive at Bimini		110		66 (2)	

(1) Some headings are approximate, using pilotage for navigation
(2) Plus 1-3 minutes to land

Marathon Airport
Coordinates: 24-43.57, 081-03.08
Elevation: 7 feet MSL
Pattern altitude: 1000 MSL
Runways: 7-25 5,008x100
UNICOM/CTAF: 118.8

South Bimini Airport
Coordinates: 025-41; 079-16
Elevation: 10 feet MSL
Runways: 9-27 5000

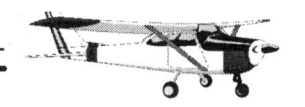

How high *should* you fly? The VFR guideline for travel in the eastern half of the compass headings is to fly at odd thousands plus 500 feet. To stay above the Class B airspace, your choices would include 7,500, 9,500, and 11,500 feet. To maximize gliding distance, you'll want to go as high as practical. There's another limit to consider at the top, however—and that's oxygen.

The air gets thinner as you go up, which reduces the amount of pressure of the air in your lungs. This in turn reduces your lungs' ability to absorb the oxygen and pass it along to your blood; too little oxygen leads to a condition called *hypoxia*, which can impair your thinking and perception. The FAA regulations require that aircraft crews use supplemental oxygen when the aircraft cabin pressure is at an altitude of 12,500 feet to 14,000 feet for more than 30 minutes. The Aeronautical Information Manual (AIM) is only advice—not regulations—but it recommends that "for optimum performance, pilots are encouraged to use supplemental oxygen above 10,000 feet during the day". (At night, the effects of reduced oxygen are more pronounced, especially in terms of vision, and the AIM recommends supplemental oxygen for flights above *5,000* feet.)

Based on all the AIM's advice, I've planned your flight for a cruising altitude of 9,500 feet. This strikes a compromise between maximizing gliding distance while minimizing the effects of hypoxia (also you stand a better chance of spotting that island in the ocean).

At a 500 fpm cruise climb as you leave Marathon, you'll take 19 minutes of climbing to reach this altitude. At 80 knots, you'll cover 25 nm in this time, which should bring you to Plantation Key—about halfway from Marathon to Key Largo. From there, you can transition to a straight and level cruise at 130 knots.

Remember that the thinner air at this altitude will also affect the performance of your aircraft's engine. For best performance (and lowest fuel consumption), you'll want to lean the engine using the mixture control. Don't forget to enrich the mixture to full rich again before you land at the end of the trip. (For more information on how to use the engine mixture control, see Appendix C.)

Key Largo is the last large island at the northeast end of the Keys, followed by the thin, sandy Old Rhodes Elliott Keys. As you near the end of Elliott Key, you will intercept the 78° radial for the Bimini VOR

(ZBV, 116.7). Yes, there's a VOR right off the end of the airport on South Bimini Island, so you can track your way straight to the field.

When the needle centers for this radial, turn your back on Florida and head out over the water. It's a 50 mile stretch, which will take just 23 minutes to cross at 130 knots, so you won't be out of sight of land for very long, if at all. Still, straining to find the island may cause you some anxious moments.

In the real world, you'll often find clouds building over the Bahama Islands, making it easier to spot them, though it is not uncommon to mistake the shadow under a cloud for land. The water color changes from dark blue to light blue or green around the islands, so watch for these shade changes to help spot land.

You'll have a lot of altitude to lose as you near Bimini, but you won't want to descend so fast that you can't reach land if something goes wrong. As a result, I have planned for you to slow to 80 knots when you're still 24 nm out, and then start a 500 fpm descent from that point. It will add about seven minutes to your crossing time, but it would work out about the same if you were to spiral down over the island once you got there.

As you approach your destination, you'll see that there are two islands. The airport is on the southern one, to your right. Fly toward the red and white radio tower on the western shore, and you'll see the airport directly beyond it. Go ahead and make a straight in approach for Runway 9.

GETTING READY TO FLY

To start, you can use the World Airports menu, and pick the "CBN - USA - Florida" list to find the Marathon Runway 7 option. Then tune your NAV1 radio to the Bimini VOR (116.70) and set the OBS to the 78° radial. At this point, you will be more than 110 nm from the VOR, and you won't be able to pick up the signal. As you travel up the Keys, the needle will come alive, and you can then verify that you have the correct VOR tuned in (see Appendix C).

You're ready to rock and roll. It will be a little tricky to see where you're going as you climb out from Marathon, but you can lower the nose from time to time as you go along to make sure that you're still on course.

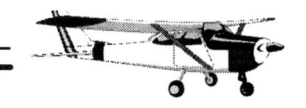

And if you start to wonder whether the Bimini Islands will ever show up on the horizon, just remember that you've got a tropical paradise waiting for you at the end of your flight where you'll be able to relax in the sun.

🖫 Situation file: XC-CA1

Caribbean Flight 2

From Paradise to the Stars

The Bahamas are a study in contrasts. From the crowded Freeport nightclubs to the isolated beaches of the out islands, from the high-rise tourist resorts in Nassau to the thatched hide-aways, there's a setting for just about every taste and temperament.

This flight takes you from one extreme to another. You'll depart from Paradise Island in Nassau, with its groomed golf courses and sparkling condos, and then fly down to Stella Maris, a simple resort on Long Island, east of Georgetown on Great Exuma Island. With its own airstrip, it is a favorite spot for divers and pilots who are looking for a low-key spot for rest and recreation.

- 185 -

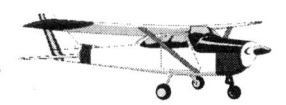

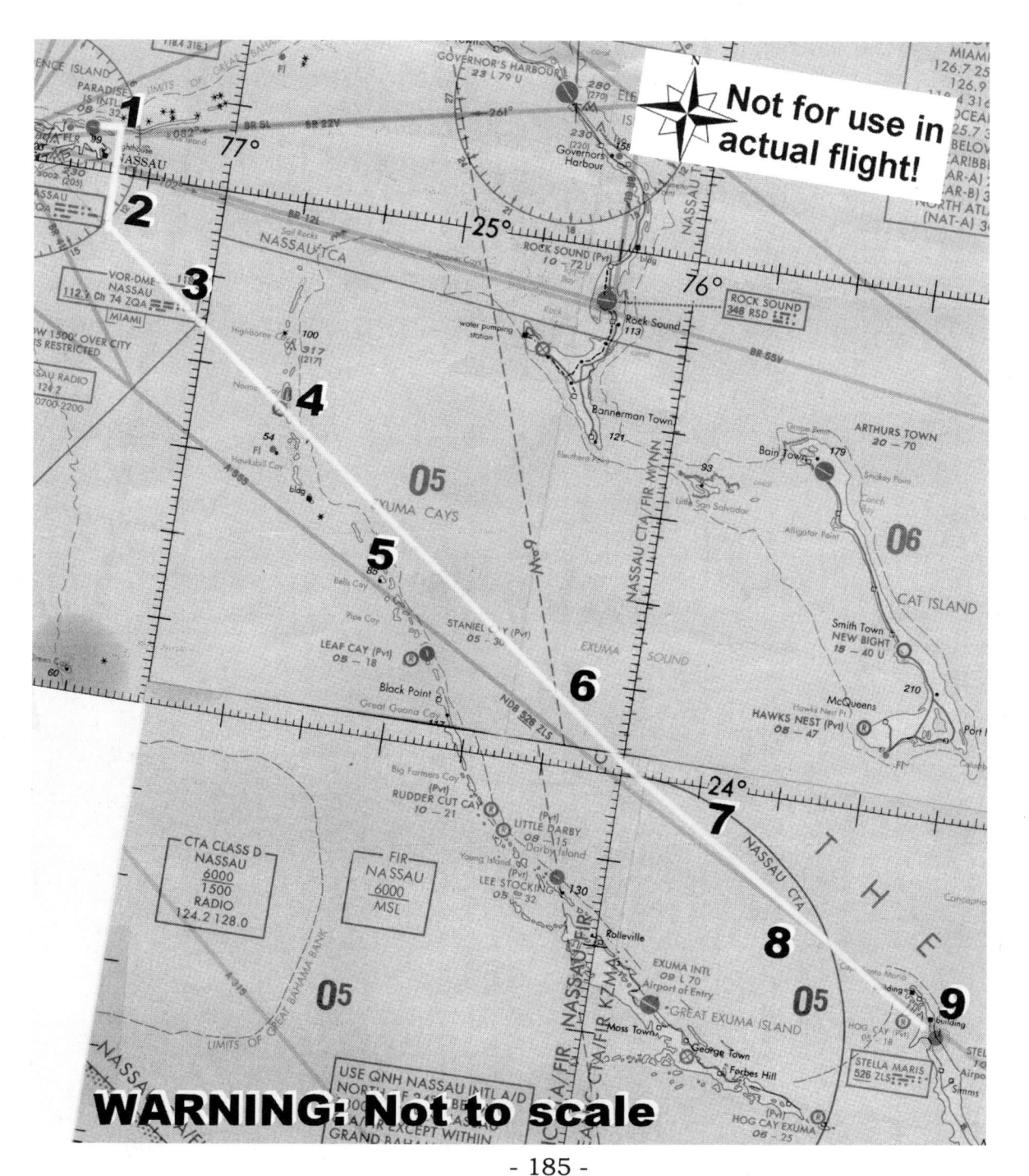

PLANNING THE FLIGHT

It's a long flight, and there is only an NDB at Stella Maris to guide your arrival (when it's working). You could follow the chain of islands leading to Great Exuma and then make the hop over to Long Island, but for this trip, I've planned a route for you to fly direct. You'll use VOR beacons to the side of your course to track your progress.

You'll depart from Runway 9 at Paradise Island, and then turn south as you climb out. Continue south until you intercept the 132° radial from the Nassau VOR (ZQA, 112.70) which should be at about 16 nm from the VOR as shown on your NAV1 DME readout. This should put you on the 71° radial for the Eleuthera VOR (ZGV, 112.50) at a distance of 54.7 miles, which you can check using your NAV2 radio OBI and DME readouts.

Turn to follow the outbound radial, and continue to climb. You'll probably be at about 6,000 feet by this point, and will want to climb for another 7 minutes or so to reach your cruising altitude of 9,500 feet.

When you reach this altitude, you should be about 25 nm from the Nassau VOR and about 51 nm from the Eleuthera VOR on the 62° radial; level out and trim for a 130 knot cruising speed. At this point, check your time. The checkpoints—shown on the flight log that I have created for the flight—are now spaced every 10 minutes for the next 40 minutes. You will use your NAV radios to check your position, though you may also want to keep track of the islands that you'll be able to see along your route.

After 10 minutes, Nassau will be 46 nm behind you, and Eleuthera will be 48.5 nautical miles away on the 38° radial. If the distance to Eleuthera is greater than that when you cross the 38° radial, it means you are to the right of your desired course. If the distance is less, then you are to the left.

VFR Flight Log MYNN
Departure: Paradise Island Airport MYLS
Destination: Stella Maris Airport

FIXES	ROUTE MAG COURSE	NAUT. MILES	ESTIMATED GROUND SPEED (KT)	TOTAL TIME	ACTUAL TIME
1. Depart Paradise, climb to 1,000 feet before turn south	180°		80 knots	3	
2. Intercept Nassau VOR 132° radial	132°	14		14	
3. Reach crusing altitude		23	130	21	
4. Nassau: 132° at 46 nm, Eleuthera: 38° at 48 nm		45		31	
5. Nassau: 132° at 68 nm, Eleuthera: 15° at 55 nm		67		41	
6. Eleuthera: 356° at 72 nm, Mosstown: 116° at 37 nm		89		51	
7. Mosstown: 198° at 22 nm		111		61	
8. At 24 nm from Stella Maris, slow and start descent		123	80	70	
9. Arrive at Stella Maris		147		88 (1)	

(1) Plus 1-3 minutes to land
Paradise Airport
Coordinates: 25-04, 077-20
Elevation: 4 feet MSL
Runways: 9-27 3,190
UNICOM/CTAF: 118.8
Stella Maris Airport
Coordinates: 025-03; 073-17
Elevation: 10 feet MSL
Runways: 13-31 4,300

- 187 -

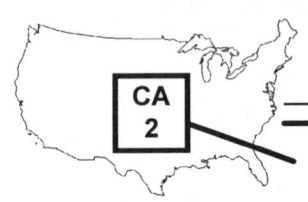

After 20 minutes, Nassau will be 68 nm away, and Eleuthera will be about 55 nm away on the 15° radial. Sometime during the next 10 minutes, you'll lose the Nassau VOR signal; the flag on the OBI dial will switch to OFF. At this point, tune the NAV1 radio to the Mosstown VOR on Great Exuma Island (ZEM, 112.2) and set the OBS for the 166° radial.

At 30 minutes since starting your cruise flight, Eleuthera should be 72 nm away on the 356° radial, and Mosstown 37 nm on the 166° radial. In the next few minutes, you'll lose the Eleuthera signal. Switch your navigation panel to show the ADF instead of the OBI for NAV2 (see Appendix C for details on the ADF), and tune it to the Stella Maris beacon frequency of 526. If the beacon is in service, you should see the ADF needle pointing straight ahead.

After 40 minutes from the start of cruise, Mosstown should be 22 nm away on the 198° radial, and the ADF needle for Stella Maris should be pointing straight ahead. At this point, you may be able to see your destination.

When Mosstown is 21 nm away on the 237° radial, you will be about 24 nm from your destination. Slow down to 80 knots and start a 500 fpm descent. You should be in perfect position to make a straight-in approach and landing on Runway 13 at Stella Maris. Give a call to the hotel and they'll send a car for you, and there will be a tall, cool drink waiting for you when you reach the reception desk.

GETTING READY TO FLY

You can either use the World Airports menu to select Paradise Runway 27 from the "CBN - Bahamas" list and then taxi to the other end of the runway, or you can enter the following into the World Set Exact Location window:

North/South Lat.:	N 25 04 40.8
East/West Lon.:	W 077 18 02.3
Altitude (ft):	7
Heading (deg magnetic):	90

Next, set your navigation radios. Tune NAV1 to 112.7 for the Nassau VOR, and set the OBS to 132°. Tune the NAV2 radio to 112.5

for the Eleuthera VOR, and set its OBS to your first cross-check radial: 71°.

With that, you should be ready to take off. In spite of the long flight, you will never be out of sight of land, and the VORs will make it easy to track your way right down the chain of islands to your secluded destination. Have a great time in the islands, and don't miss snorkling on the reef off the beach on Santa Maria Bay, at the northwest corner of the island.

🖫 Situation file: XC-CA2

Caribbean Flight 3

Flight to Visit the King

Off the eastern tip of Puerto Rico lie the chain of emerald jewels known as the Virgin Islands. The first in the chain is Saint Thomas—one of the United States islands—which is served by Cyril E. King Airport.

For this flight, you'll travel along the rugged and beautiful southern coast of Puerto Rico, cross the Pasaje to Vieques and the Virgin Passage, and find your island in the sun.

PLANNING A ROUTE

Your point of departure will be Ponce Airport, in the middle of Puerto Rico's southern coast. You can then use pilotage to follow the coastline around to the east.

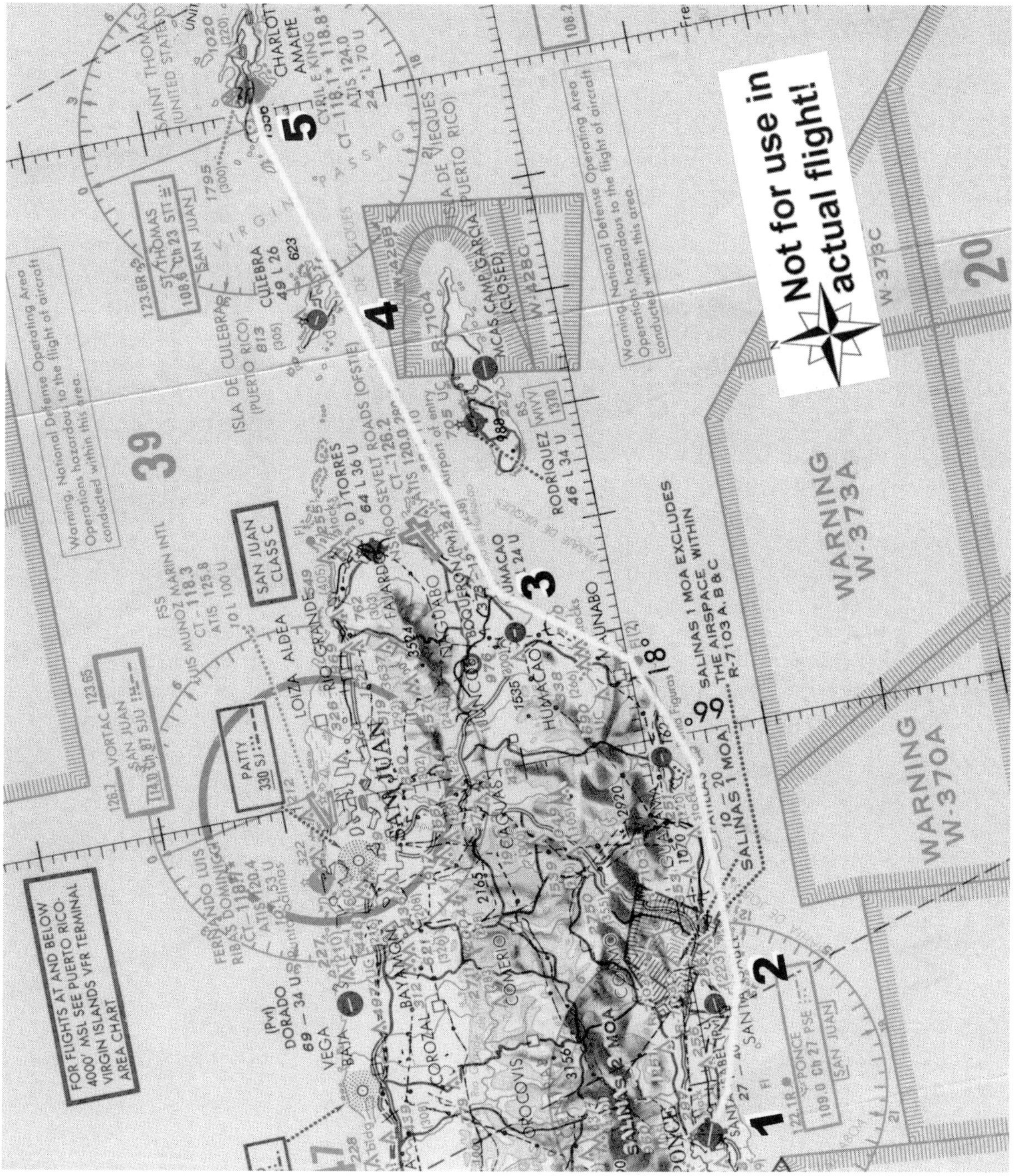
Not for use in actual flight!
1
2
3
4
5
WARNING W-373A
WARNING W-370A
W-373C
39
20
SAN JUAN
SAN JUAN CLASS C
FOR FLIGHTS AT AND BELOW 4000' MSL SEE PUERTO RICO-VIRGIN ISLANDS VFR TERMINAL AREA CHART
SALINAS 1 MOA EXCLUDES THE AIRSPACE WITHIN R-7103 A, B & C
ISLA DE CULEBRA (PUERTO RICO)
SAINT THOMAS (UNITED STATES)
CHARLOTTE AMALIE
PONCE
HUMACAO
FAJARDO
MCAS CAMP GARCIA (CLOSED)

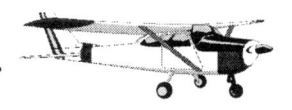

CA 3

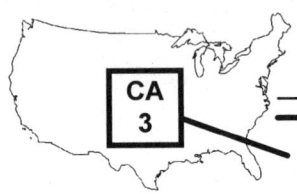

Saint Thomas has a VOR located near the western tip of the island, making it easy to find. The only tricky parts about planning this trip are the restricted airspaces used for military operations. There is one area just northeast of Santa Isabel on the south side of Puerto Rico, and another surrounding the eastern half of Isla de Vieques. On the section of the chart, I've plotted a course that keeps you clear of both areas.

You'll take off from Runway 30 at Ponce, and then make a standard left turn and head to the south shore. You'll then follow the shoreline (which will keep you out of the Salinas MOA (Military Operations Area). As you round the southeast corner of the island, the Saint Thomas VOR (STT, 108.60) will come alive. Just before you reach the Roosevelt Roads airfield on the eastern tip of Puerto Rico, you'll intercept the 85° radial to Saint Thomas. You can now follow this over a sequence of small islands to your destination, while remaining safely to the north of the R-1704 restricted airspace over Isla de Vieques.

Once you reach Saint Thomas, you'll want to aim to the right towards the harbor. You should soon see the airport emerge from the scenery, and you can make a straight-in approach to land on Runway 10.

You may notice that there is a "CT-118.1* 118.8*" notation on the chart under the name of the Cyril E. King airport; this indicates that the airport has a control tower. Now, you can either pretend that you have contacted the tower and received permission to land, or you can plan your flight to be completed before the tower opens for business. Its hours of operation are 7:00 am to 10:30 pm, so an early morning flight will not only be beautiful, but will also let you complete your trip without talking to any Air Traffic Control facility.

VFR Flight Log

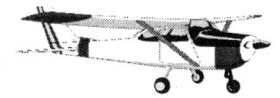

Departure: Ponce Mercedita Airport (PSE)
Destination: Cyril E. King Airport (STT)

TJPS
TIST

Fixes	Route Mag Course	Naut. Miles	Estimated Ground Speed (Kt)	Total Time	Actual Time
1. Depart Ponce, head south and follow coastline	varies		80 knots	1	
2. Reach crusing altitude		13.5	130	11	
3. Intercept Saint Thomas VOR 85° radial		60		33	
4. Start descent		96		49	
5. Arrive at Saint Thomas		118		59 (1)	

(1) Plus 1-3 minutes to land

Ponce Mercedita Airport
Coordinates: 018-00.50; 066-33.78
Elevation: 29 feet MSL
Runways: 12-30 6,904x150
Pattern Altitude: 800
UNICOM/CTAF: 122.7

Cyril E. King Airport
Coordinates: 025-03; 073-17
Elevation: 15 feet MSL
Runways: 10-28 7,000x150
Pattern Altitude: 600
Tower/CTAF: 118.8

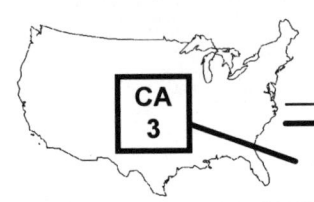

HOW HIGH TO FLY?

As with the other Caribbean flights, this trip involves a fair amount of over-water travel. The difference for this trip, however, is that you will never be out of sight of land. There is even a convenient emergency landing site halfway to your destination: Culebra Airport.

As a result, you don't need to gain as much altitude as you have in other flights. According to the VFR guidelines of odd thousands plus 500 feet for headings in the eastern half of the compass rose, you could choose 3,500, 5,500, or 7,500. I picked 5,500 because this will give you a good view without having to climb too far up, and you will be able to keep the land in sight along your route.

As a result, you'll need to continue your takeoff climb for about 13 minutes (assuming a standard 500 fpm cruise climb rate) before leveling off for a 130 knot level cruise speed. At the other end, you will need to lose nearly 5,000 feet to get to pattern altitude, which will take about 10 minutes at 500 fpm, which uses up about 22 miles at 130 knots. This works out to starting your descent just before you get to Isla de Culebra.

GETTING READY TO FLY

It is easy to set up this flight. You can choose "Ponce - Mercedita" from the CBN-Puerto Rico list in the World Airports menu. This will place you on Runway 30, ready for takeoff.

Next, tune your NAV1 radio to 108.60 for the Saint Thomas VOR; you won't be able to verify this setting until the signal comes alive later in your flight. Set the OBS to the 85° radial.

If you want to get in ahead of the control tower, you'll have to take off before dawn. Choose the World Set Time and Weather command, and set the exact time to 5:50 am. This will make it tight getting in before the 7:00 am deadline, but if you fly efficiently, you can make it. This also means that you must start your trip in the dark, but you can follow the lights of the roads along the coast; keep them to your left, and you can follow the coastline until the sky gets lighter.

💾 Situation file: XC-CA3

Section E: Japan

Japan is an island nation rich in culture and history—a perfect place for sight-seeing and travel. The Japan scenery collection for FS5.1 provides an incredible range of places to fly and see. In the real world, general aviation is far more limited in Japan than we are used to here in the United States; civilian recreational flight is more expensive and more closely-regulated than it is in this country. Rather than try to adhere to Japan's regulations, I have planned the following three flights as if they were to be flown under United States rules and procedures.

Japan Flight 1

Mt. Fuji Fly-By

One landmark stands out as a unique part of the Japanese landscape: Mt. Fuji. This sacred and beautiful mountain is located on the main island of Honshu, near the southern shore at the middle of the island.

Japan is a country of varied terrain, with rugged mountains, long river valleys, and smooth coastal plains. This flight starts on one of the small islands near Tokyo—Oshima—and takes you past Mt. Fuji and on to Matsumoto in the middle of Honshu. And to make your trip even more beautiful, you'll get to see a new day dawn as you fly by Mt. Fuji.

PLANNING A ROUTE

This flight can be completed using nothing more than basic pilotage skills, though you'll use the VOR beacon at Matsumoto as a backup. Your route is shown on the section of the Operational Navigation Chart (ONC), which provides coverage for areas that are not covered by World Aeronautical Charts (WACs) or sectional charts. ONC charts use the same scale as WAC charts.

Not for use in actual flight!

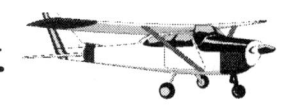

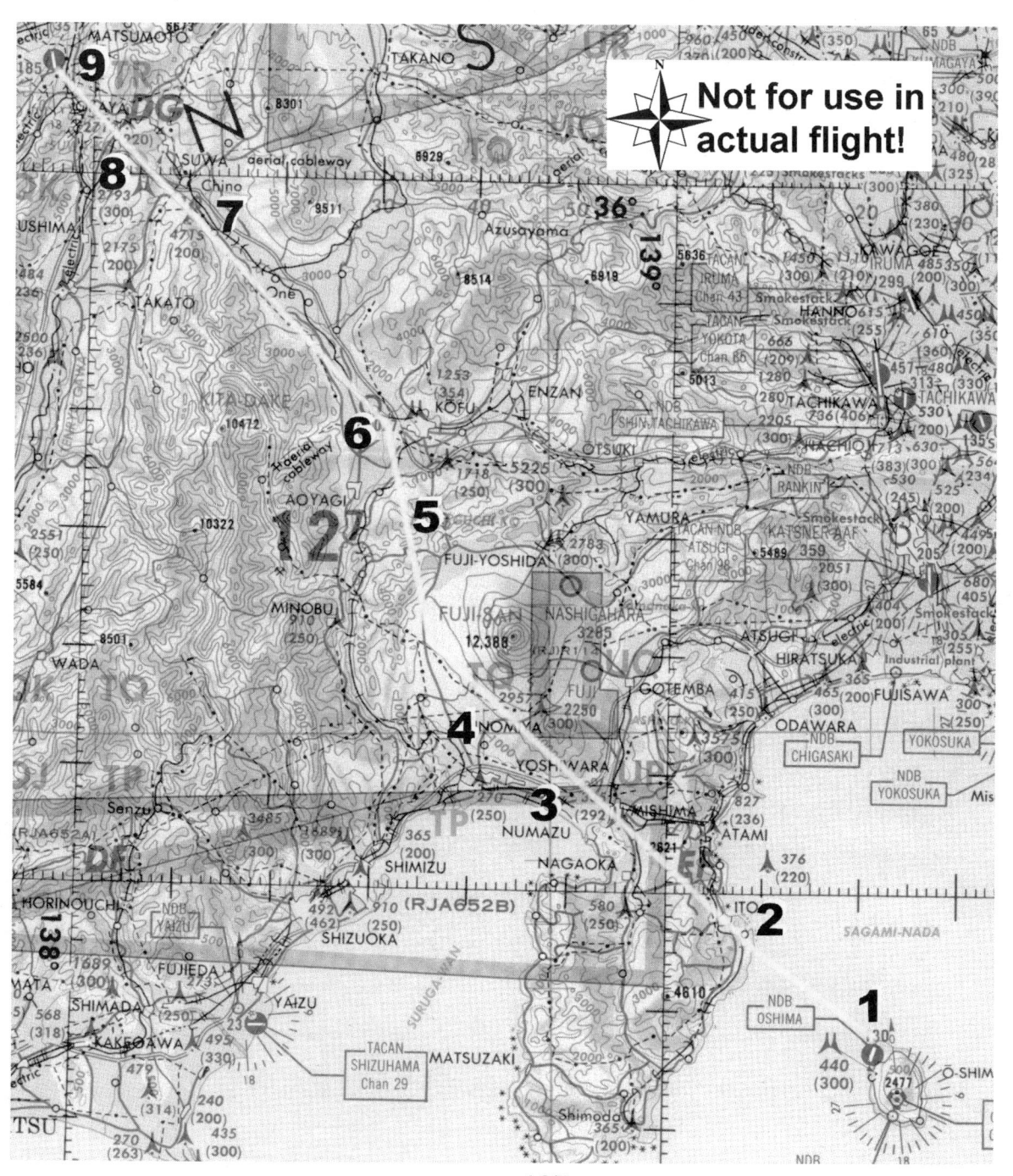

JA 1

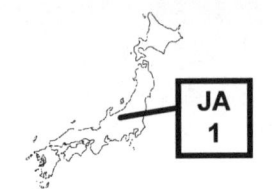

You'll start from Runway 3 at Oshima Airport, and then turn to the northwest as you climb out. The peak of Mt. Fuji is above 12,000 feet, so it doesn't make sense to try to climb high enough to fly over the summit. Instead, I've planned your cruise altitude at 7,500 feet which is high enough to give you time to find a place to land even when traveling through the mountains, but not so high that you'll need oxygen. This means that you'll have about 15 minutes of climbing after take-off, assuming a 500 fpm cruise climb at about 80 knots.

You won't see Mt. Fuji right away, so just head for the mountainous peninsula and Ito. As you get closer to land, Mt. Fuji will appear; adjust your course (if necessary) so that you are headed to the left of the peak.

As you climb, you'll be able to see the lights of Fujisawa and Yokohama off your right wingtip, across the bay. You'll also be able to see Numazu and Yoshiwara at the head of the peninsula once you get past the first mountains.

As you fly over the southern edge of Mt. Fuji, you'll find a valley headed north, with a road running down the middle. Follow this valley, and you'll pass a large lake near Kofu. The valley then takes a turn to the left, and you can follow a pair of roads up this valley.

There aren't many checkpoints along this leg, until you reach Suwa and its large lake. Follow the valley as it bends to the right beyond the lake, and Matsumoto will be waiting about a dozen miles ahead, just beyond the built-up areas and to the left of the two roads that are headed north.

The airport at Matsumoto is at 2,185 feet, so planning on a standard pattern altitude of 1,000 AGL (above ground level), you'll need to lose about 4,500 feet before you get to the airport. At 500 fpm, that will take nine minutes, and at a 130-knot cruise speed, that means you must start your descent about 20 miles out. So plan on starting your descent about 10 miles before you reach the lake at Suwa. When you arrive at the airport, you can make a straight-in approach to land on Runway 36.

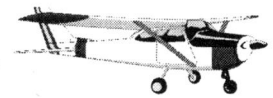

VFR Flight Log

Departure: Oshima
Destination: Matsumoto

	ROUTE		ESTIMATED		ACTUAL
FIXES	MAG COURSE (1)	NAUT. MILES	GROUND SPEED (KT)	TOTAL TIME	TIME
1. Depart Oshima, head northwest	320°		80 knots	1	
2. Reach land near Ito		14		11.5	
3. Pass over Numazu		30	80/130	20.5	
4. Mt. Fuji off right wing	350°	46		28	
5. Lake south of Kofu		57		33	
6. Follow valley to the left	315°	70		39	
7. Start descent		90			
8. Cross lake at Suwa		100		49	
9. Arrive at Matsumoto		110		59 (2)	

(1) Navigate by pilotage; all headings are approximate
(2) Plus 1-3 minutes to land

Oshima Airport
Coordinates: N034 46-34; E139 21-46
Elevation: 128 feet MSL
Runways: 3-21

Matsumoto Airport
Coordinates: N036 10-02; E137 55-027
Elevation: 2,155 feet MSL
Runways: 18-36

A LOOK AT THE LOG

I have prepared a flight log for your trip. The checkpoints are easy to find, and they are fairly far apart, so you will have plenty of time to enjoy the sights along the way.

Each checkpoint has the distance and estimated time shown, as well as approximate headings. Your actual heading will depend on where you make your turns along the route; follow the instructions and keep track of your position on the chart, and you should make it to your destination without any problems.

As I mentioned at the start of this flight, you will have a radio navigation backup for this flight. There is a VOR at Matsumoto (at least, there is in the FS5.1 add-on scenery), which you can tune in to give yourself an idea of where you are; if you get lost, you can always tune the OBS until the needle centers, then follow that heading to the airport.

The other advantage of tuning in the VOR is that it can tell you when you are 20 miles out—using the DME readout—so that you can judge when to start your descent to Matsumoto.

PREPARING TO FLY

There is an entry on the World Airports menu for Oshima Airport, and it will place you on Runway 3, ready for take-off. Tune your NAV1 radio to the Matsumoto VOR frequency: 117.60. Don't be concerned that the OBI dial shows an "OFF" reading; you're more than 100 miles from the beacon, and you can't get the signal that far away. The needle and DME readouts will come alive before you reach Mt. Fuji.

The only other setting that you need to make is to use the World Set Time and Season command to pick Dawn for the Time of Day. This will let you enjoy the full majesty of Mt. Fuji as a new day starts.

Enjoy your flight.

Situation file: XC-JA1

Japan Flight 2

Peace Pilgrimage

"Hiroshima." It is more than the name of a city; it's a symbol of the horrors of war, known throughout the world. And it's the home of a shrine dedicated to peace, a monument to those who died and a tangible hope that atomic weapons are never used again.

This trip takes you on a flight from Okayama, along the inland sea around the island of Shikoku, to Hiroshimanishi Airport in Hiroshima.

PLANNING A ROUTE

The Japanese scenery for FS5.1 is so rich that this is another flight that can be completed entirely using pilotage techniques, relying on visual references. You'll start from Runway 7 at Okayama, and then turn south to follow the shoreline.

The inland sea area is full of islands; if you're careful, you can use individual islands as checkpoints along your route, but they form a maze of channels and correctly distinguishing one from another can be difficult. As a result, I have planned your route to take a broader view of the landscape, as shown on the section of the chart.

JA 2

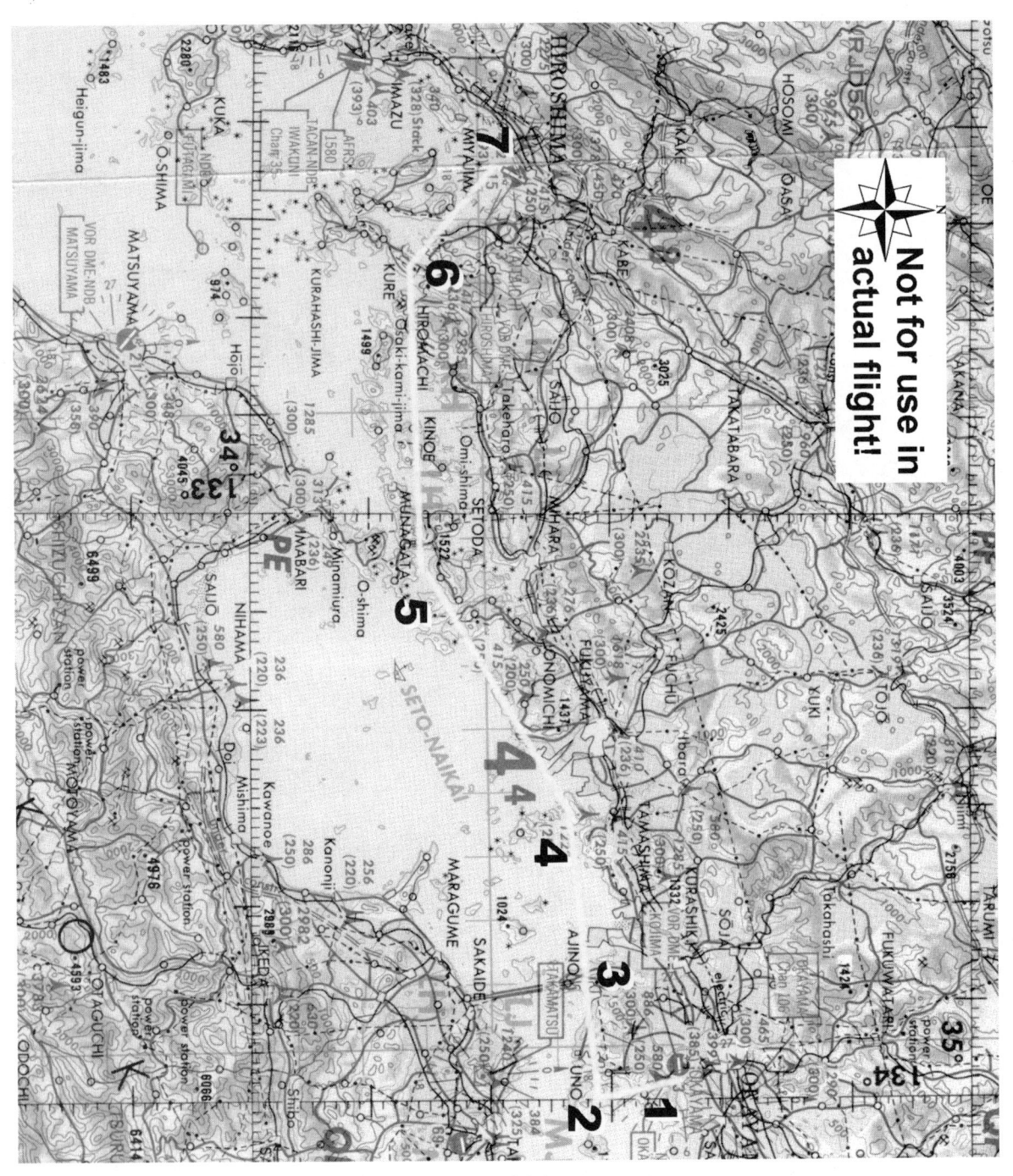

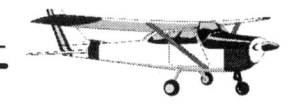

After leaving Okayama, you'll make the turn to the west at the end of the peninsula near Uno. Shortly after making this turn, you'll see the impressive bridge joining Ajino on Honshu (the "mainland" of Japan) and Sakaide on Shikoku.

From this point, you'll simply follow the coastline westward. You'll next encounter a small clump of islands west of Tamashima—about 15 nm west of the bridge, and then a larger mass of islands around Setoda, about 15 nm beyond that.

Once you're past this second set of islands, the shoreline turns almost due north at the city of Kure, and that leads you straight to Hiroshima.

Hiroshimanishi Airport can be difficult to spot. It is located toward the western side of the harbor area, and runs almost at right angles to the shoreline. The problem is that there numerous rivers and inlets in the area, and it can be difficult to spot the correct spit of land where the airport is located.

To help you out, there is a VOR on the field (109.85). Dial this into your NAV1 radio, and you'll be able use the OBI needle to lead you straight to the field.

Since you'll be close to land the entire flight, and since there is no terrain along the route that poses any particular hazard, I have planned the flight at a low cruising altitude of 2,500 feet, suitable for sight-seeing. This can make it a little more difficult to pick out your checkpoints, but if you get confused, just climb to gain altitude and a better perspective. You'll need to descend to 1,000 feet to enter the pattern when you reach the airport; plan on entering a left downwind leg for a landing on Runway 4 when you arrive.

I have also created a flight log for this trip, showing your checkpoints along the route. The distances between checkpoints is a bit longer than you might want, but there is little chance of you're becoming lost when following a shoreline; the biggest danger from the widely-spaced points is that you might become bored or impatient for the next point to arrive.

JA 2

VFR Flight Log

Departure: Okayama Airport
Destination: Hiroshimanishi Airport

FIXES	ROUTE MAG COURSE (1)	NAUT. MILES	ESTIMATED GROUND SPEED (KT)	TOTAL TIME	ACTUAL TIME
1. Depart Okayama, head south and follow coastline	180°		80 knots	1	
2. Reach crusing altitude, turn west over Uno	270°	8	130	6	
3. Cross Ajino-Sakadei bridge		16		9.5	
4. Reach small islands beyond Tamashima		31		16.5	
5. Reach larger islands near Setoda		46		23.5	
6. Turn northwest at Kure		81		39.5	
7. Arrive at Hiroshimanishi		91		44 (2)	

(1) Navigate using pilotage; all headings are approximate
(2) Plus 1-3 minutes to land

Okayama Airport
Coordinates: N034 44-52; E133 50-44
Elevation: 791 feet MSL
Runways: 7-25

Hiroshimanishi Airport
Coordinates: N034 21-32; E132 24-49
Elevation: 13 feet MSL
Runways: 4-22

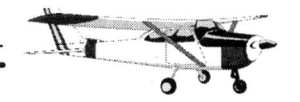

PREPARING TO FLY

Flight preparation is simple for this flight. There is an entry on the World Airports menu under the Japan Add-On for Okayama Airport, which will put you on Runway 7, ready for take-off.

All you need to do is tune your NAV1 radio to 109.85, for the Kanon VOR at Hiroshimanishi Airport. You might want to tune the OBS to a heading of 315°, because that will be the approximate heading to the airport when you round the point at Kure. Having the approximate heading set will make it easier to make a quick adjustment to the OBS if you decide you need the radio's help in locating the airport.

There's a lot of beautiful scenery to enjoy along this flight, and for a treat, try flying it at dusk, and watch the cities along your route light up as night falls.

💾 Situation file: XC-JA2

Japan Flight 3

Concrete Compass

During the "Golden Age" of aviation in the United States, there were few aeronautical charts, and even fewer navigational aids. Barnstorming pilots would find their way from town to town using whatever they could, including road maps. One of the best navigation aids of all, however, was what the early pilots called "the iron compass": the steel rails of the railroads that connected many towns throughout the country.

On this flight, you'll follow a "concrete compass" instead. If you're good at judging your airspeed and altitude simply by the sound of the engine and the view out the window, you'll be able to complete this flight without looking at any of your panel gauges. So hit the W key (for the full-screen view) and take off for a scenic flight the old-fashioned way.

PICKING A ROUTE

Your flight will take you nearly to the southern tip of Honshu, the main island of Japan. You'll depart from Nyutabaru Aero, on the eastern shore, and fly down to Kanoya on Kagoshima Bay.

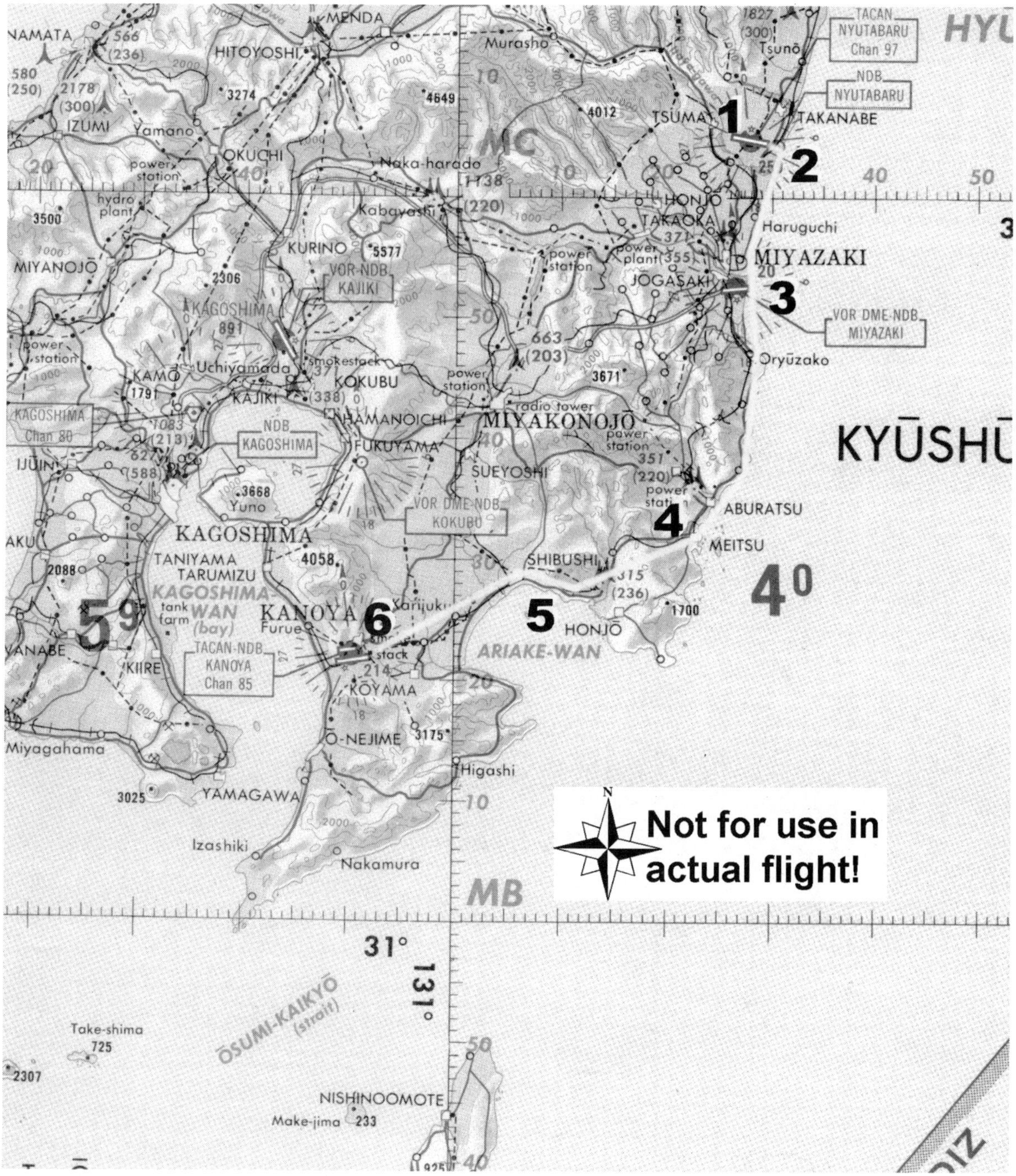

MENDA
NAMATA
HITOYOSHI
Murasho
TACAN NYUTABARU Chan 97
NDB NYUTABARU
Tsuno
TSUMA
TAKANABE
IZUMI
Yamano
OKUCHI
power station
Naka-harado
hydro plant
Kabayashi
HONJO
TAKAOKA
Haruguchi
MIYAZAKI
KURINO
VOR-NDB KAJIKI
MIYANOJO
power station
power plant
JOGASAKI
KAGOSHIMA
VOR DME-NDB MIYAZAKI
Oryuzako
KAMO
Uchiyamada
smokestack
KOKUBU
power station
KAJIKI
radio tower
KAGOSHIMA Chan 80
HAMANOICHI
MIYAKONOJO
power station
NDB KAGOSHIMA
FUKUYAMA
SUEYOSHI
KYŪSHŪ
IJUIN
Yuno
VOR DME-NDB KOKUBU
ABURATSU
KAGOSHIMA
MEITSU
TANIYAMA
TARUMIZU
SHIBUSHI
KAGOSHIMA-WAN (bay)
tank farm
KANOYA
Furue
Karijuku
HONJO
ARIAKE-WAN
TACAN-NDB KANOYA Chan 85
KIIRE
stack
KOYAMA
O-NEJIME
Miyagahama
Higashi
YAMAGAWA
Izashiki
Nakamura
MB
MC
31°
131°
OSUMI-KAIKYO (strait)
Take-shima
NISHINOOMOTE
Make-jima
ADIZ
1
2
3
4
5
6
Not for use in actual flight!

JA 3

Your sole navigation aid for the trip will be a coastal highway. The section of the ONC chart shows the road and your route. You'll take off from Runway 28 at Nyutabaru, and then make a left 180° turn to head east toward the coast. You'll see a pair of roads running north and south; follow the one closest to the ocean.

The road passes through Miyazaki, and then to the west of the airport located just south of the city. One of the safest ways to transit an airport's airspace is to fly well above pattern altitude, and right across the center of the field; this way, you are least likely to conflict with an aircraft approaching for a landing or climbing out on take-off. So plan to veer a bit to the left so you can cross over the middle of the runway.

The road then skirts a series of mountains that come right down to the water's edge. It then turns to the west, around Ariake Bay and through the town of Shibushi. Finally, it cuts across the plain separating Kanoya from Airake Bay, and leads you straight to the airport. When you see the airport, assume that the tower has cleared you for a direct approach and landing on Runway 26 Right—this is the shorter of the two runways, but it's long enough for the Cessna.

I have prepared a flight log for this flight, and it shows all the checkpoints and distances between them. You should also follow along on the chart to keep track of your progress; situational awareness is an important element in navigating solely by ground references.

The remaining question is how high you should fly for this trip. There are no over-water legs, so gliding distance to reach land is not a factor. We'll assume that you'll be able to make an emergency landing on the highway if you can't find any other suitable spot to set down. Also, there is no high terrain that you must cross, so there is no reason to fly high.

VFR Flight Log

Departure: Nyutabaru Aero
Destination: Kanoya Airport

	ROUTE		ESTIMATED		ACTUAL
FIXES	MAG COURSE (1)	NAUT. MILES	GROUND SPEED (KT)	TOTAL TIME	TIME
1. Depart Nyutabaru, head east to coastal road	varies		80 knots	3 (2)	
2. Follow road south	180°	5	130	6.5	
3. Pass Miyazaki Airport		17		12	
4. Road heads inland at Meitsu	240°	41		23	
5. Pass Shibushi on Ariake Bay		57		30.5	
6. Arrive at Kanoya		73		38 (3)	

(1) All headings are approximate; use pilotage for navigation
(2) Includes time to climb and turn to heading
(3) Plus 1-3 minutes to land

Nyutabaru Aero
Coordinates: N032 04-29; E131 28-12
Elevation: 262 feet MSL
Runways: 10-28

Kanoya Airport
Coordinates: N031 24-45; E130 49-54
Elevation: 217 feet MSL
Runways: 8R-26L; 8L-26R

The main factor is being able to see the road in order to follow it. The textures used for the Japan scenery in FS 5.1 are incredibly rich, and it can be difficult to spot the roads and other features if you're too high. As a result, I have planned this flight for a low 2,500 foot cruising altitude.

PREPARING TO FLY

There is an entry in the World Airports menu for Nyutabaru Aero that will put you on Runway 28, ready for take off. There's nothing else that you need to set.

If you want to increase the challenge factor for the flight, dial in some haze. About 10 miles of visibility (use the World Weather Visibility option) will make it difficult to see too far ahead, and will force you to keep a sharp watch for your road so that you stay on course.

⌷ Situation file: XC-JA3

Appendix A

Situation Files and the Disk

What's on the disk? It's simple—the disk included with this book includes 30 situation files, one for each of the Cross Country flights.

How do you use these files? That's just about as easy. First, you have to copy the files from the disk into your PILOTS directory for FS 5.1 on your hard disk. Once you have done this, they will become available on the Options Situation menu.

All the situation descriptions start with "XC" for "Cross Country", which means that they will appear at the bottom of the list of situations in the FS 5.1 program. The situation names correspond to each flight, which match the codes used on the headings of each flight. For example, the first flight in this book is in the Chicago area, and as the first flight in that area, the code for the flight is "CH1". The situation file for this flight is named XC-CH1.STN, and the title starts with "XC-CH1-..." The code for each flight is shown with the disk symbol at the end of each chapter.

To make use of these situations, start FS 5.1 as you would normally. You can use the default configuration for your startup setting, or you can choose to use a different situation file as your startup. A custom situation file lets you configure the program the way you want; I use one that uses the Cessna, but sets the engine to fixed pitch, turns on the mixture control, turns off coordinated flight, and sets the scenery complexity to the maximum level. Your startup situation can pick a different aircraft, or some other customization feature; use this feature to customize the program to match your preferences.

After the program has loaded, you can then use the Options Situation menu to load the Cross Country situation for the flight you want to take. You could also follow the directions in each chapter to set up for the flight yourself, but the situation file gives you the advantage of being able to restart without having to enter those settings all over again. (The reason that I wrote all the instructions in each chapter—even though I provide the situation files—is so that you can still fly these trips even if you should lose the disk.)

The situation files make it easy to position your aircraft, ready to start each flight. If you want to add some more realism to your flights, don't be in too much of a rush to take off—the next appendix has a number of suggestions on how you can make your experience seem even more real.

Appendix B

As Real As It Gets

Microsoft Flight Simulator may well be the best-selling computer game of all time, in spite of the fact that there is no way to keep score or win, aside from not crashing. One reason behind its success is its realism—from the navigation radio beacons to the accurate scenery to the complex weather feature to the detailed cockpit panels, it goes a long way toward convincing you that you're actually flying in a real airplane.

Now, I'll concede that not many people are going to be fooled into thinking that they are really in a plane when flying FS 5.1, but the realism is sufficient to help you "suspend disbelief", as the saying goes, and convince yourself that the experience is real.

If you're one of the millions who enjoy flying FS 5.1—whether or not you have ever flown a real plane—there are a number of ways that you can enhance the realism of the experience. Some of these additions cost money, while you can implement others for free. I divide these changes into three categories, and I present them more or less in increasing order of cost: procedures, environment, and controls.

REALISTIC PROCEDURES

"Kick the tires and light the fires." It sounds great, but it's a derisive summary of the preflight procedures used by too many pilots in the real world. Safe pilots carefully follow an extensive preflight ritual before they even get into their aircraft. They also use checklists for almost every aspect of flying, from starting the engines to shutting down on the ramp at the end of the flight.

Unfortunately, FS 5.1 (and its earlier versions) do little to encourage sim pilots to follow standard procedures; you load the program to find yourself sitting at the end of the Meigs runway with full gas tanks, the engine idling, and the parking brakes engaged. Pop the brakes, ram the throttle forward, and you're flying.

At the default settings, nothing ever goes wrong with the FS 5.1 airplanes—you don't even run out of fuel. But just because nothing can go wrong doesn't mean that you shouldn't practice safe flying procedures. It only adds a minute or two to each flight, and can make you feel much more in touch with your aircraft and more immersed in the flying experience.

The typical aircraft owner's manual includes checklists for a number of procedures, including preflight, take-off, cruise, landing, shut-down, and various emergencies. Many of these steps cannot be executed with FS 5.1; there's no way to check the oil level in the engine, or drain the fuel sumps to check for water in the fuel lines. There are many steps that you can follow, however.

I have created some procedure checklists for you that work well for the default Cessna 182 when flown in fixed-pitch mode, which I have included in this appendix. You might want to make photocopies of these lists so that you can keep them handy when you fly. (If you use them on every flight, as you should, its better to wear out the copies than the originals in the book.)

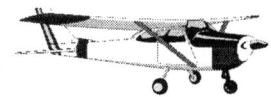

Procedure Checklists

PREFLIGHT INSPECTION
1. Empennage: Control Surfaces — **CHECK** freedom of movement and security.
2. Right Wing Trailing Edge: Aileron — **CHECK** freedom of movement and security.
3. Right Wing: Main Tire — **CHECK** for proper inflation.
4. Nose: Propeller and Spinner — **CHECK** for nicks and security.
5. Nose: Nose Wheel Strut and Tire — **CHECK** for proper inflation.
6. Left Wing: Main Tire — **CHECK** for proper inflation.
7. Left Wing Trailing Edge: Aileron — **CHECK** freedom of movement and security.

BEFORE STARTING ENGINE
1. Preflight Inspection — **COMPLETE**.
2. Passenger Briefing — **COMPLETE**.
3. Brakes — **TEST** and **SET**.

STARTING ENGINE
1. Carburetor Heat — **OFF**.
2. Mixture — **FULL RICH**.
3. Propellor Area — **CLEAR**.
4. Magnetos — **START**. (Automatically goes to **BOTH** after engine starts.)
5. Throttle — **ADJUST** for 1000 RPM or less.
6. Oil Pressure — **CHECK**.
7. Navigation Lights and Flashing Beacon — **ON** as required.

If you want more detailed checklists, or a checklists for another aircraft, try your local airport to see if you can purchase a copy of the aircraft owner's manual for the type of airplane you want. You can also look in aviation publications such as *Trade-A-Plane* for sources for manuals and other references.

PERFORMING THE PRE-FLIGHT

Here's how to execute the standard walk-around and run-up before you take-off to fly. Follow along with the checklists.

Start by turning off the engine (if it's on) by pressing the M key and then the minus key until the magneto switch is in the Off position. Then walk around the entire plane. Use the Spotter Plane view, placed at the same elevation as the plane, and position the view (or use the zoom feature) so that the aircraft fills the screen. Look over the plane from all eight angles (I find that pressing the Scroll Lock and then the numeric keypad keys works best for this.) You're looking for any damage or wear and tear; "hangar rash" is a not-uncommon malady caused by close contact with the wingtips of other aircraft or the walls of hangars. On a real plane, you'd use this walk-around to also visually inspect fuel and oil levels, drain the sumps, check the tires, make sure all the control surfaces are attached properly, and more.

Next, it's time to get back in the cockpit and prepare to start the engine. I'll assume that you're using the keyboard for the engine controls; a control panel makes these steps more realistic, but I'll get to panels later in this chapter. Make sure that the Carburetor Heat is off (H key), and that the mixture is full rich (Ctrl-Shift-NumPad9, enabled in the Sim Realism and Reliability menu). Check to make sure that there are no other aircraft, vehicles, people, or other obstructions near the propeller. Turn the Magnetos to Start (M key then the Plus key as needed), and the engine should start. (The Magneto switch will also drop back to the Both setting.) Check your Oil Pressure gauge to make sure that there is some oil pressure — below the green is okay when idling on the ground. Then make sure that your strobes are on (O key).

If you're not already on the runway, taxi to the threshold before the runway to perform your run-up tests on the Before Takeoff checklist. Set the parking brakes (Ctrl-Period). Then look out the side and back views as you move the elevator, aileron, and rudder controls. Make sure that all the control surfaces are moving in response to your controls, and that they are not obstructed. Also make sure that they are moving in the correct direction — there are accidents each year where a plane's controls have been rigged wrong, so that their control cables are reversed. The time to identify this problem is on the ground, before you've started your takeoff roll.

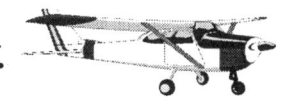

Check your panel gauges, including compass, directional gyro, altimeter, and attitude indicator. Make sure that you have fuel in your tanks, and that the mixture is set to full rich. Adjust the elevator trim for takeoff (one notch above neutral).

Now advance the throttle to about 1700 rpm. (You *did* set the parking brakes, right?) Aircraft engines are designed with a redundant ignition system; there are two spark plugs with separate sources of ignition spark for each cylinder. If you turn off the spark to one set of plugs, the engine power will drop a little, but not a lot. Turn the Magneto to the Left setting (M key then press the Minus key once) and the RPM readout for the engine should drop by less than 150. Press the Plus key to switch back to Both, then the Minus key twice to set it to Right. The drop should be about the same as for the Left magneto setting. Put it back to Both, and then press the H key to turn on the carburetor heat; the RPM should only drop about 50, but this indicates that the carb heat is indeed working.

Return the throttle to idle, then set your radios. Check that your wing flaps are in the desired position (which in most cases will be all the way retracted), release the brakes, and you're ready to go flying.

Procedure Checklists

BEFORE TAKEOFF
1. Parking Brake — **SET**.
2. Flight Controls — **FREE** and **CORRECT**.
3. Flight Instruments — **CHECK** and **SET**.
4. Fuel Quantity — **CHECK**.
5. Mixture — **RICH** (below 3000 feet MSL).
6. Elevator Trim — **SET** for takeoff.
7. Throttle — **1700 RPM**
    a. Magnetos — **CHECK** (RPM drop should not exceed 125 RPM on each magneto or 50 RPM differential between magnetos).
    b. Carburetor Heat — **CHECK** (for RPM drop when turned on).
8. Throttle — **1000 RPM** or less.
9. Radios and Avionics — **SET**.
10. Wing Flaps — **SET** for takeoff.
11. Brakes — **RELEASE**.

SECURING AIRPLANE
1. Carburetor Heat — **OFF**.
2. Wing Flaps — **UP**.
3. Parking Brake — **SET**.
4. Mixture — **FULL LEAN** (IDLE CUT-OFF).
5. Magnetos — **OFF**.

END OF THE FLIGHT

When you land, there's not much to do after you taxi to the ramp, but there is a checklist for shutting down the plane that you should follow. Make sure that the carb heat is off and that your flaps are up, then set the parking brakes. Now, you can turn off the engine by turning the magnetos to the Off setting, but this will leave fuel in the cylinders and could cause problems for you the next time you want to start the engine. Instead, use the mixture control; pull it all the way down (Ctrl-Shift-NumPad3 as needed) to put the control in the full-lean position. This cuts off the fuel flow to the engine and it stops. Then you can turn off the magnetos and go home.

REALISTIC ENVIRONMENT

Most sim pilots dream of taking a ride in a real, full-motion simulator. I'm one of the fortunate ones who has had the chance to enjoy this experience—thanks to MicroWINGS and SimuFlight in Dallas, Texas—when I flew a simulator that modeled a Hawker twin-engine business jet.

The flight was fantastic, but I discovered that while the motion aspect of the simulator did enhance the realism, it probably wasn't all that essential to the overall experience.

Perhaps that sounds incredible, but stop and think a minute; have you ever attended an IMAX movie? The seats don't move, yet the audience sways back and forth as the image shows a rollercoaster ride or a view from a helicopter or whatever. It really feels like you're moving, even though you're not. There have been times that I have felt so disoriented that I've nearly fallen out of my (motionless) chair.

How does the IMAX experience provide such a visceral sensation of motion, even though the audience is stationary? I learned the answer to this from Tom Kopke, an FS fan who also happens to be an engineer who works on the development of future flight simulators for the aerospace industry. He talks about "immersion", which refers to the pilot's psychological acceptance of a simulated experience as real. While motion can help achieve immersion, it's not necessary. Instead, if you load up the other senses—sight and sound—then your brain will "fill in the blanks" and invent the sensation of motion to go along with what you're seeing and hearing. It's the loud soundtrack and the screen that fills your field of vision that makes the IMAX experience so effective.

There are a number of ways you can enrich your flight sim environment to increase your immersion in the experience. Some involve sound, while others involve sight.

THE SOUND MACHINE

Good sound starts with a good sound card in your computer. The industry standard is the Creative Labs SoundBlaster card, and while there are lots of "SoundBlaster-compatible" cards on the market, I can't find a compelling reason not to get the real thing. If you already have another brand of sound card and it is working okay, there's no reason to change, but if you're shopping for a new card, I recommend you stick with a Creative Labs product.

The next step is to get a good pair of speakers. Now, it's true that most sound cards include an on-board amplifier that can drive a pair of speakers, but these have very little power and are only suitable for driving the smallest, most-efficient (and generally least-expensive and lowest-quality) speakers. For best sound quality, you'll want to get self-powered speakers, which means that they have their own amplification built into the speakers themselves. Some of the best speakers on the market are those from Altec Lansing; they cost more than most other speakers, but they are worth it in terms of quality.

To get the throbbing feel of a hefty Continental or Lycoming engine spinning the prop out in front of you, you need more than just a pair of desktop stereo speakers; you gotta have a sub-woofer. This is a non-directional speaker that provides just the very low-frequency sounds, and adding one adds immensely to the simulation experience. Again, Altec Lansing makes some of the best sub-woofer units, and you can get them in bundles with the stereo speakers.

To further add to the realism, consider a surround-sound speaker system. There are some that use sound phase-shifting to manipulate the signal, and others use multiple speakers spread around your room. My favorite, however, are the self-powered tower speakers from Altec Lansing (yup, you guessed it!) which provide Dolby Surround-Sound decoding with left, right, center, and surround channels. Even though there is no Dolby encoding in the FS5.1 sound effects, the surround effects of these towers (plus the bundled sub-woofer) go a long way toward wrapping you in sound.

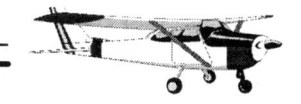

Now, if you already have a good stereo sound system installed in the same place as your flight sim computer, you're all set. Just run the line-out output from your sound card to an auxiliary input on your stereo amplifier and you're in business.

If you have a separate amplifier—such as a stereo system—or are willing to add one—such as an inexpensive single-channel amplifier that you can get at Radio Shack—then there is one more piece of sound equipment that you should consider: the Thunderseat. This is a hollow, molded-plastic seat that looks like it might have been taken off a dune buggy, and it's mounted on a wooden platform. Inside the platform, there's a huge sub-woofer mounted to the bottom of the seat, and the hollow cavity inside the seat becomes a resonance chamber. The Thunderseat requires an external amplifier, but it greatly adds to the realism of simulated flight; you can actually feel the engine noise in your body.

There's more to listen to when flying a real airplane than just engine, gear, and flap noises. You can add a lot of realism with Air Traffic Control (ATC) radio transmissions. There are two ways to do this. One way is to add Microsoft Flight Simulator Flight Shop to your FS5.1 installation. Among other features, this allows you to create interactive adventure flights that will give you clearances and instructions from controllers using digitized voice files as you fly along. None of the flights in this book are designed to use ATC instructions, however, so this is not so important for these trips.

The other way to add realistic sounds—especially if you live within 25 or 30 miles of a major airport—is to get a digital aviation-band radio scanner; Radio Shack has models that cost about $100. Set this up to play in the background as you fly, and you'll find it provides an ideal distraction as you try to navigate yet still pay attention to the radio calls for the real aircraft. Many of these scanners have an audio output; connect this to your sound card's input (or your stereo's, if you're using one) so that the radio sounds are also amplified and come through the same speakers.

THE EYES HAVE IT

Your computer's visual configuration can also play a role in helping you achieve immersion in your simulated environment. You want to load up your visual senses, and there are a number of ways to do this.

The easiest of all is to simply turn off the room lights. Without your desktop clutter and to-do list posted on a bulletin board distracting your vision, it's easier to imagine that you're in a real airplane, even if you're flying in the daylight.

Filling your field of vision also helps, so get the largest monitor you can afford. This can become expensive, certainly, but even stepping up to a 17-inch monitor from a 15-inch model can make a remarkable difference.

You can also improve your out-the-window display by building a "collimated display". Collimated means that the light rays are made parallel, and by placing a magnifying lens in front of your screen, the light rays are redirected so that they are traveling more or less perpendicularly to the monitor's surface. This in turn moves the apparent focal point further out toward infinity, making the out-the-window view look more distant and realistic. As an added benefit, the image is larger as well.

The result is amazing; your eyes are tricked into thinking that the image is more distant than it really is. The illusion is reinforced by the fact that the image shifts a lot when you only move your head a little.

These plans are based on ideas presented by my friends and flight sim fans, Tom Kopke and Rick Lee. The design calls for a Fresnel lens, named for a 19th century French physicist who invented optical systems for lighthouses, and which is a relatively flat lens with many concentric ridges. Plastic Fresnel lenses are used for everything from book magnifiers to solar heaters to overhead projectors. They are lightweight, relatively inexpensive, and are fairly easy to cut to size.

You'll need a lens with a diameter at least as large as your monitor's diagonal dimension. You can find lenses for sale at science supply and surplus stores, but keep in mind that the quantity and quality may vary over time. You can also get a pretty serviceable lens from an overhead projector, if you can find one that is slated for disposal. You should plan on spending between $10 and $50 for a lens, depending on size and quality.

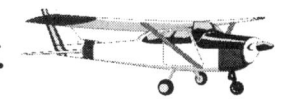

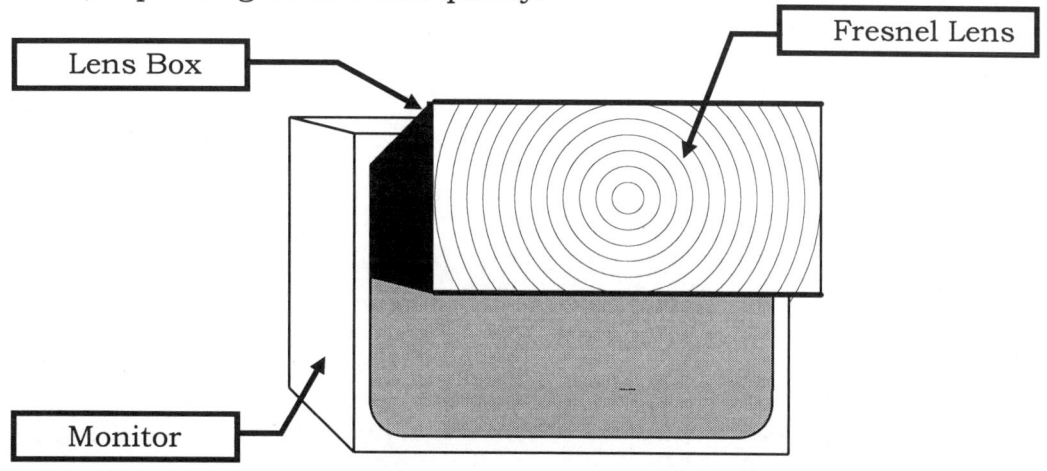

Diagram of Fresnel Lens mounted on Monitor

Before you cut your lens to size, cover your work surface with a soft cloth to prevent scratching. Use a utility knife to score the surface; a metal ruler helps keep your knife on track, and one with a cork backing won't scratch the delicate surface of the lens. Most lenses are one-sided—the ridges were formed only on one side—and it was much easier to work with the smooth side than the ridged side. After you have created a solid score in the lens, break it by putting the scored side down and bending up. Needle-nosed pliers are handy to trim off any extra that doesn't break cleanly, and then you can dress the edges with a file.

Cut your lens so that it is as wide as your monitor and at least 3/4 as tall as it is wide, keeping the middle circle of the lens centered on the middle of your screen.

The next step is to figure out how far to mount the lens from your screen, since this will determine how deep to make the sides of the mounting box. Fire up FS5.1 and experiment. I have found that about half the focal length works well; a lens with an 11.5 inch focal length should be mounted about six inches from the screen. Build an open box with curved edges on one side to match the surface of your screen, and the other side flat to hold the lens. 3/16th inch thick foam core presentation board makes an excellent construction material, and is available for about $3.50 at office and art supply stores. It's easiest to build the box if you start with a strip as wide as the distance you want between the screen and the lens.

If you build with the foam core board, you can use pins to hold the boards together when testing their fit. Paint the inside of the box before you put the box together permanently; use chrome paint for the top and sides, and flat black for the bottom to simulate the cowling. For the final assembly, use a hot melt glue gun to assemble the box, then mask the front and back openings and paint the outside with flat black paint. Then glue the lens onto the front of the box; if you are using a one-sided lens, make sure that the ridges are facing you and the smooth side is toward the monitor.

Put Velcro hooks on the top of your monitor and on the sides of the box, using strips of Velcro loop material to hold the box in place. This creates an unobtrusive mounting arrangement that is easy to attach when you want to go flying.

REALISTIC CONTROLS

Aside from sight and sound, the most important sense in flying is tactile. Now, I'm the first to admit that I have flown just a small handful of the hundreds of different types of aircraft that are out there in the real world, but I can tell you that I have never seen one where you fly the plane using a computer keyboard!

So the first extra that you should buy for your FS5.1 installation is an appropriate control. For most Cessnas and other general aviation aircraft, you'll want to get a yoke. There are lots on the market, but the most popular, inexpensive model is the Virtual Pilot Pro from CH Products. This includes a yoke and throttle control, plus a wheel that you can use for elevator trim. It also has buttons and "coolie hat" switches that you can use to control the landing gear, flaps, and out-the-window views. In short, you can do most of your flying without touching the keyboard.

Aerobatic and homebuilt aircraft cockpits are more often fitted with a flightstick instead of a yoke, in which case a joystick is a more appropriate control. There are lots of excellent products that are studded with features, but I'd have to pick the Microsoft SideWinder

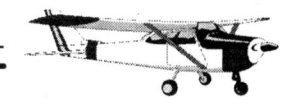

3D Pro over the rest of the field (in part because I'm already looking ahead to FS6, which is expected to run under Windows 95, and the SideWinder has some distinct advantages in that environment).

Next, you'll need a pair of rudder pedals. Most users never turn off the Coordinated Flight option on the Sim menu, and they're cheating themselves out of much of the fun in flying FS 5.1—especially when it comes to landing. In order to land in a crosswind, you need to be able to lower the upwind wing (as if turning) while adding opposite rudder (to keep going straight down the runway). It's a wonderful trick to learn, but you need rudder pedals to make it work. Rudder pedals also make it possible to perform a "slip", in which you hold the controls in much the same position as the crosswind landing, but even more so; this maneuver causes you to lose altitude rapidly without increasing your forward airspeed. It is my favorite trick for salvaging a lousy approach where I end up way too high on final. Thrustmaster makes a popular set of rudders with a wider stance, and CH Products make a set with a narrower track which is closer to the spacing in a typical single-engine airplane.

If you want to go whole hog, there are expensive control panels and other add-ons that provide yoke, throttle quadrant (with mixture and prop control), magneto switch, gear lever, and more. There are even some new radio stacks available that let you tune your NAV radios and adjust the OBS settings, and see the frequency readouts right on the stack (in addition to the on-screen panel display). Some of the companies making these products include NT Systems, Flight Link, and Thunderseat. You can spend from $1,000 to $3,000 on one of these systems, but you'll end up with a control panel that can control every aspect of the FS5.1 aircraft—you'll only need to touch the keyboard to start and end the program.

For the ultimate in realistic controls, you can build your own cockpit. I have seen enclosures with full panels, dual flight controls, separate displays for the panel and out-the-window view, and even projection video for the out-the-window view. If you're looking for something a bit unusual to build in your basement or family room (or even a large closet, as at least one person did), here's the perfect flight sim project.

Appendix C
Flight Simulator 5.1 Techniques

This book does not cover the basics. I assume that you already know how to fly FS5.1, and the basics of navigation and maneuvers such as take-offs and landings.

If you are not comfortable with these skills yet, there are some excellent books on the market that can be your own private flight instructor. One of my favorites for this purpose is "Adventures in Flight Simulator" by Timothy Trimble, published by Microsoft Press (1994, ISBN 1-55615-582-4). Not only does it cover all the basics and then some, it is also probably one of the most beautifully-designed flight sim book I have ever seen.

However, there are a few features that I refer to in the course of some of the Cross Country flights that are beyond the basics. Here are some quick instructions on how to use them.

MIXTURE CONTROL

For the Mixture Control to work, you must first enable it on the Sim Realism and Reliability window.

To adjust the mixture, pull back on the red handle (or Ctrl-Shift-F2) until the exhaust gas temperature (EGT) hits a peak, then push the handle back forward (Ctrl-Shift-F3) again until the EGT drops a notch or two. You should adjust the mixture every 1,000 feet or so as you climb in order to maintain best power and maximum fuel economy.

Remember to put the control back to fully-rich during your descent before you enter the pattern; as you descend, the mixture could become too lean, causing the engine to lose power or possibly stop altogether.

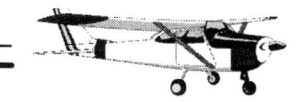

MAGNETOS

In order to use the Magneto switch, you have to enable the feature on the Sim Realism and Reliability window.

Once activated, you can press the M key followed by the + (plus sign) key to turn the key to the right, and the - (minus sign) key to turn it to the left. When you turn the key to Start, it will switch back to Both after the engine starts.

NAV RADIOS

You can tune the NAV radios in a number of ways, including the Nav/Com Navigation Radios window, or by pressing the N key followed by the 1 key for NAV1 or the 2 key for NAV2, followed by the plus or minus sign to change the tuning. To change the decimal portion of the frequency, press the N key twice in rapid succession. Personally, I find it easiest to use the mouse; point at the frequency display, and click to the left to decrease the setting, and to the right to increase it. The portion of the frequency that is being adjusted will be highlighted in yellow.

The OBS (Omni-Bearing Selector) lets you adjust the radial for the VOR you have tuned on that NAV radio, which controls the needle on the OBI (Omni-Bearing Indicator) gauge. If you adjust the radial setting so that the OBI needle is centered and the heading flag reads "TO" (as opposed to "FROM" or "OFF"), then you can fly that heading directly to the VOR (assuming that there is no wind pushing you off course).

The OBS can be adjusted by the keyboard or the Navigation Radios window, but again, I prefer to use the mouse. Click on the left or right side of the knob at the lower left of the gauge to increase or decrease the radial setting. You can also click to the right or the left of the radial readout itself as well.

ADF: AUTOMATIC DIRECTION FINDER

This is an older radio navigation technology, and it uses non-directional beacons, or NDBs. All you get is an arrow that points toward the radio station. (In the real world, you can also pick up broadcast radio on your ADF receiver, making it a handy way to follow your favorite ball club while in the air.)

On the standard Cessna panel, the ADF display takes the place of the NAV2 OBI gauge. In order to use the ADF, you must use the Nav/Com ADF window, where you can tune the radio and enable its display.

There are certainly lots of other powerful and realistic features contained in FS5.1, but if you can master these, you will be able to complete all the flights in this book.

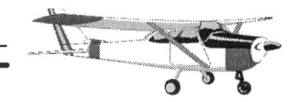

Production Notes:

This book is the product of desktop publishing. The layout and typesetting were all done using Microsoft Word 6 for Windows on a 90 Hz Pentium system with 24 MB of memory. In spite of the complex formatting (including the various graphics in the different headers), the program never got bogged down, even when the manuscript was assembled into a single, large file.

The text is set in Bookman Old Style (11 points) as a TrueType font, and was output using a Hewlett-Packard LaserJet 5P at 600 dpi resolution with enhanced resolution enabled for smoother characters.

Not all was done directly on the computer. As Daniel Will-Harris said in one of his books, nobody gives out medals for doing it all by computer. While the photographs and charts started as digital images, they were converted to film by a pre-production service and stripped in by traditional methods. Most of the photographs came from CD-ROM sources, and the remaining photos and the charts were scanned using an HP ScanJet 4c color scanner.

Comments and Orders

We want to hear from you. If you have any questions or comments, if you want to order additional copies of "Cross Country", or if you'd like to receive news about other Desktop Wings books and products for flight simulation, we want to know.

For your convenience, we've included this page (both sides) so you can use it, or make a copy of it. Your comments make a difference, so please let us know.

❑ I have a comment about "Cross Country":

_____
_____
_____
_____
_____

❑ I'd like to see a Desktop Wings book about:

_____
_____
_____
_____
_____

❑ Please let me know about new products:

❑ Please send me ____ (quantity) copies of "Cross Country".
    ❑ I have enclosed a check for $19.95 plus $4.95 shipping and handling for each copy.
    (PA residents please add 6% sales tax.)
    ❑ Please charge my credit card:
        ❑ American Express ❑ VISA ❑ MasterCard

Account: _____ Expiration: _____

Name: _____

Street: _____

City, State, ZIP: _____

Phone number: _____

Fax number: _____

Electronic mail address: _____

Send to:
    Desktop Wings, Inc.
    161 N. Main Street
    Dublin, PA 18917

Or fax to:
    215-453-0286

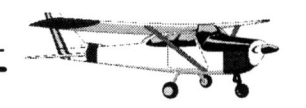

Free Flight Lesson!

Send today for your FREE issue of Full Throttle!

If you liked the flights you found in this book, then take advantage of all the full-throttle excitement Microsoft® Flight Simulator™ offers with a **FREE ISSUE** of *Full Throttle!* Published by The Cobb Group, the world's leading publisher of software-specific journals, *Full Throttle* offers insights, tips, and techniques that help you get off the ground fast.

Whether you're using Flight Simulator for pilot training or for fast-paced entertainment, *Full Throttle* will heighten your flying experience.

With *Full Throttle*, you'll receive step-by-step instructions for flight simulation such as:

- Making safe landings in various weather and visibility conditions
- Navigating with FS5's radio navigation beacons
- Learning to pilot all the exciting planes
- Choosing the best add-on scenery packages, joysticks, and flight yokes
- Understanding the cockpit and flight controls
- Mapping out a real-world flight and navigating through the flight plan
- Understanding the Visual Approach Slope Indicator and using it to guide your landings

Plus, *Full Throttle* shows you real-world flight procedures, provides practical solutions, and helps you uncover all the secrets that Microsoft built into Flight Simulator. Act today, and find out how real it can be!

Don't Rely On a Wing and A Prayer...
Mail the coupon below, Fax it to us at (502) 491-8050, or call Toll-Free (800) 223-8720, and get your FREE ISSUE!

Free Flight Lesson!

Yes! Rush my **FREE ISSUE** of *Full Throttle*. I understand I will be billed for a one-year subscription. If I like the **free issue**, I'll pay your bill for $39 and receive 6 issues in all. If I decide not to subscribe, I'll return the bill marked CANCEL. The **free issue** is mine to keep.

Name _____

Company _____

Address _____

City _____ State _____ Zip _____

Country (if outside the U.S.) _____ Phone (____) _____

Payment Method: ☐ Check enclosed   ☐ Bill me later
☐ VISA®   ☐ MasterCard®   ☐ American Express®   ☐ Discover®

Account Number _____ Expiration Date _____

Signature _____

THE COBB GROUP. P.O. Box 35160, Louisville, Kentucky 40232-9719

Outside the U.S., please add $20   2076   VTER

Full Throttle
The Microsoft Flight Simulator Pilot's Journal

- Using FS5's flight log
- We review BAO's Tower
- FAA exam prep software
- A handy flight term glossary

- "Cross Country" flies to Lake Tahoe
- Learn to fly the traffic pattern
- The latest industry news
- Reader mail

Free Flight Lesson!

Get off the ground fast with a FREE ISSUE!
Act now!

Get a New Perspective on Your Aircraft
Articles show specific illustrations that take you through each step.

By default, your point of view is from the cockpit looking over the nose of your plane.

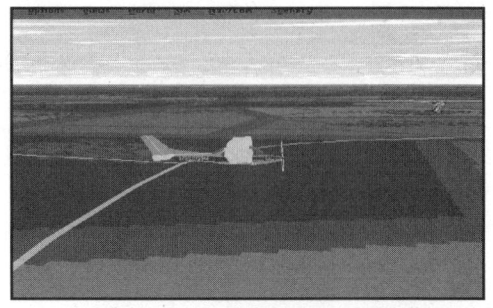

By default, the spot plane view shows the starboard side of your aircraft.

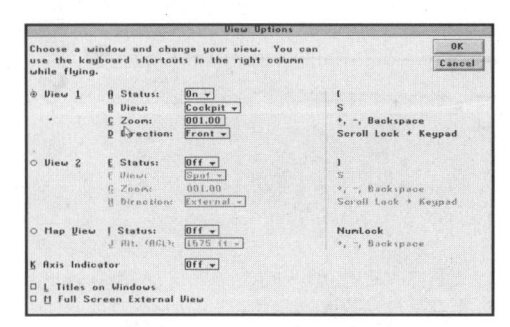

You can change your point of view by choosing an option from this dialog box.

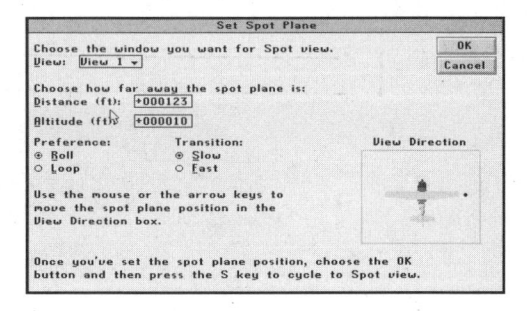

You adjust the position of your spot plane in this dialog box.

Microsoft is a registered trademark of Microsoft. Flight Simulator is a trademark of Bruce Artwick Organization, Ltd.